Best of
COOKING
For All Occasions

Best of
COOKING
For All Occasions

Delicious Recipes for All Occasions

Every recipe in *The Best of Cooking* is illustrated with a color photograph! So you can see at a glance what sort of dish you are dealing with, be it a soup, starter, salad or vegetable, fish, meat, poultry or game dish. Casseroles, pastry dishes from traditional recipes, fruit, ice cream or delicate mousse desserts make up hundreds of possible meals.

We have followed the established traditional elements and make changes only when improvements were necessary. So you will still find favorite recipes from both international and regional cuisines. In addition, though, you will now also find tips on using whole-grain products, wild herbs, exotic fruits and new vegetables. In general these recipes use fresh produce where available. We have aimed at achieving the best flavor without combining too many ingredients in any one recipe. When frozen foods can replace seasonal foods or are of better quality, we do not hesitate to recommend them. Canned foods, on the other hand, are only included if their quality is not adversely affected by canning.

—Christian Teubner and Annette Wolter

ANOTHER BEST-SELLING VOLUME FROM HPBooks®

Publisher	Rick Bailey
Executive Editor	Randy Summerlin
Editorial Director	Elaine R. Woodard
Editor	Rebecca La Brum
Art Director	Don Burton
Book Design & Assembly	Leslie Sinclair
Production Coordinator	Cindy Coatsworth
Typography	Michelle Carter
Director of Manufacturing	Anthony B. Narducci
Photography	Christian Teubner and Pete A. Eising

Published by HPBooks
A division of HPBooks, Inc.
P.O. Box 5367, Tucson, AZ 85703 (602) 888-2150
ISBN 0-89586-243-3   Library of Congress Catalog Card Number 86-81047
© 1986 HPBooks, Inc. Printed in the U.S.A.
1st Printing

Originally published as The Best of Today's Cooking
© 1986 Hamyln Publishing Group
© 1985 Gräfe und Unzer GmbH

Cover Photo: Veal Roast with Herbs, page 65

Contents

Stuffed Celery

8 celery stalks
1 ripe avocado
2 tablespoons lime or
  lemon juice
1 (8-oz.) pkg. cream cheese,
  room temperature
1 tablespoon brandy
Salt and freshly ground white
  pepper to taste

Trim leafy tops and ends from celery stalks, then cut each stalk in 4-inch lengths. Set aside. Halve and pit avocado; scoop flesh into a bowl and add lime or lemon juice, cream cheese and brandy. Beat until smooth. Season with salt and white pepper. Spoon avocado mixture into a pastry bag fitted with a fluted tip; pipe into celery stalks. Or spoon mixture into celery stalks and press down with spoon handle. Arrange celery on a plate; cover and refrigerate until ready to serve. Makes 4 servings.

Artichokes Vinaigrette

4 medium artichokes

Vinaigrette:
2 tablespoons white-wine vinegar
1/4 cup dry white wine
1 teaspoon sugar
Salt and pepper to taste
1 teaspoon Dijon-style mustard
3 hard-cooked egg yolks
1/4 cup olive oil
1 small onion, finely chopped
1/2 garlic clove, finely chopped
1 tablespoon chopped
  fresh tarragon
2 teaspoons dried leaf chervil

Cut stem and top 1 inch of leaves from each artichoke. Then snip off any remaining thorny leaf tips. In a large saucepan, bring about 2-1/2 quarts lightly salted water to a boil. Add artichokes, reduce heat, cover and simmer briskly 40 minutes or until leaves pull easily from artichokes. Meanwhile, prepare vinaigrette.
To make vinaigrette, in a small bowl, beat together vinegar, wine, sugar, salt, pepper and mustard. In another bowl, mash egg yolks with a fork; stir in oil. Then beat egg-yolk mixture into vinegar mixture. Stir in onion, garlic, tarragon and chervil.
To serve, drain cooked artichokes. Place each on a warm plate; accompany with vinaigrette. To eat, pluck off leaves 1 at a time, dip in vinaigrette and squeeze tender flesh from base of leaf by pulling leaf between your teeth. When you reach center of artichoke, remove small leaves and choke. Eat artichoke heart covered with vinaigrette. Makes 4 servings.

Tomato-Topped Belgian Endive

2 large, firm tomatoes
1 large seedless mandarin orange
** or 1 small navel orange**
3 tablespoons lemon juice
1 teaspoon maple syrup
3 tablespoons vegetable oil

Salt and freshly ground pepper
** to taste**
5 pimento-stuffed green olives,
** sliced**
2 heads Belgian endive

Peel tomatoes; cut in quarters, seed and dice. Set aside. Remove peel and all white membrane from mandarin orange or navel orange. Separate orange into segments; if using a navel orange, cut segments in half crosswise. Set aside. In a bowl, stir together 2-1/2 tablespoons lemon juice, maple syrup, oil, salt and pepper; stir in tomatoes, orange segments and olives. Cover and let stand 10 minutes. Meanwhile, remove any damaged outer leaves from each head of endive; trim root end. With a sharp knife, cut a small wedge out of root end; discard. Cut endive heads in half lengthwise and sprinkle evenly with remaining 1/2 tablespoon lemon juice.

To serve, place 1 endive half on each individual plate; top with tomato mixture. Makes 4 servings.

Stuffed Tomatoes

4 medium tomatoes
1 (6-1/2-oz.) can tuna
1 small garlic clove,
** finely chopped**
1 tablespoon chopped parsley
Salt and freshly ground white
** pepper to taste**

1/2 teaspoon paprika
1 tablespoon white-wine vinegar
1 (about 8-oz.) can whole-kernel
** corn, drained**
1 tablespoon chopped mixed
** fresh herbs**

Cut a 1/4-inch slice from top of each tomato. Discard cut-off slices or reserve for other uses. Carefully remove centers of tomatoes with a small pointed spoon; discard seeds and dice flesh. Set flesh aside. Invert tomatoes on paper towels to drain. Drain tuna, reserving 1 tablespoon of the oil. Flake tuna. In a bowl, beat together reserved tuna oil, garlic, parsley, salt, white pepper, paprika and vinegar. Stir in tuna, corn and diced tomatoes.

To serve, fill hollowed tomatoes with tuna mixture; sprinkle with mixed herbs. Makes 4 servings.

Cook's tip

If you wish, replace the tuna with cooked chicken, beef, or pickled tongue and add 1 to 2 tablespoons whipping cream to the mixture.

Cod in Scallop Shells

3 whole cloves	1/4 cup whipping cream
2 onions	1 tablespoon chopped fresh dill
1-1/4 lbs. cod fillets	1/4 cup freshly grated
1/4 lb. small fresh mushrooms	Parmesan cheese
2 tablespoons butter or	4 pimento-stuffed green olives,
margarine	sliced
2 tomatoes, peeled, diced	4 small dill sprigs
2/3 cup dry white wine	
Salt and freshly ground	
white pepper to taste	

In a large saucepan, bring about 2 quarts lightly salted water to a boil. Stick cloves into 1 onion. Add clove-studded onion and fish to boiling salted water. Reduce heat, cover and simmer 10 minutes or until fish flakes readily when prodded. Lift fish from pan. Cool, then flake into small pieces, discarding skin and any bones. Set aside. Preheat oven to 425F (220C). Finely chop remaining onion. Cut larger mushrooms in half; leave smaller ones whole. Melt butter or margarine in a medium skillet; add chopped onion and cook, stirring, until soft. Add tomatoes and mushrooms and cook a few minutes longer. Stir in wine. Cook, stirring occasionally, until almost all liquid has evaporated. Stir in fish; season with salt and white pepper. Stir in cream and chopped dill. Spoon mixture into 4 scallop shells or ramekins, sprinkle with cheese and bake until cheese begins to brown.
To serve, garnish with olives and dill sprigs. Makes 4 servings.

Mussels au Gratin

About 1 lb. mussels	Pinch of dried leaf thyme
2 tablespoons vegetable oil	1/8 teaspoon sugar
1 onion, finely chopped	1 cup water
1 garlic clove, finely chopped	1 tablespoon chopped parsley
2/3 cup dry white wine	1/4 cup shredded Cheddar cheese
2 tablespoons tomato paste	(1 oz.)
Salt, freshly ground white	2 tablespoons butter or
pepper and red (cayenne)	margarine
pepper to taste	

Scrub mussels with a brush to remove sand from shells; rinse well. Remove beards. Discard any mussels that remain open. Place mussels in a large kettle. Add water; cover and cook over medium heat until shells open, 7 to 10 minutes. Cool, then discard any unopened shells. Remove mussels from remaining shells; set aside. Preheat oven to 400F (205C). Heat oil in a medium skillet. Add onion and garlic; cook, stirring, until onion is soft. Stir in wine, tomato paste, salt, white pepper, red pepper and thyme. Reduce heat to low and simmer 10 minutes, stirring occasionally. Stir in sugar. Spoon sauce into 2 individual baking dishes; top evenly with mussels. Sprinkle parsley and cheese over mussels; dot with butter or margarine. Bake until cheese begins to melt and mussels are heated through. Makes 2 servings.

Shrimp Cocktail

**1 lb. cooked, shelled,
  deveined large shrimp**
1 tablespoon olive oil
1 teaspoon lemon juice
1 small head chicory
1/4 small honeydew melon
**1/2 green bell pepper, seeded,
  cut in thin strips**
**1/2 red bell pepper, seeded,
  finely diced**
**4 very thin lemon slices,
  if desired**

Cocktail Dressing:
1/4 cup whipping cream
1/2 teaspoon lemon juice
Few drops of hot-pepper sauce
6 tablespoons dry sherry
Salt to taste

Place shrimp in a bowl; sprinkle with oil and 1 teaspoon lemon juice. Cover and let stand at room temperature about 30 minutes. Separate chicory leaves; use inner leaves for cocktail and reserve outer leaves for other uses, if desired. Wash inner leaves in cold water, shake dry and chop. Line 4 cocktail glasses with chopped chicory. Remove seeds from melon; scoop out flesh with a ball cutter. Add melon balls and bell peppers to shrimp in bowl; toss gently to mix. Spoon shrimp mixture evenly over chicory. Set aside. Prepare Cocktail Dressing.
To make dressing, in a small bowl, stir together cream, 1/2 teaspoon lemon juice, hot-pepper sauce, sherry and salt.
To serve, spoon dressing over cocktails. If desired, garnish each cocktail with 1 lemon slice. Makes 4 servings.

Individual Cheese Soufflés

2 tablespoons butter or margarine	Salt and freshly ground pepper to taste
1 small celery stalk, thinly sliced	Pinch of ground nutmeg
3 tablespoons all-purpose flour	3 egg whites
1 cup milk	2 egg yolks
1 cup shredded Cheddar or Emmentaler cheese (4 oz.)	

Preheat oven to 350F (175C). Grease 4 individual 3-inch-deep soufflé dishes. Melt butter or margarine in a medium saucepan. Add celery and cook, stirring, until tender. Sprinkle flour over celery; cook over low heat, stirring, about 1 minute. Gradually add milk, stirring constantly; continue to cook, stirring, until bubbly and thickened. Then add cheese and stir until melted. Season with salt, pepper and nutmeg. Remove from heat and cool slightly. In a bowl, beat egg whites until stiff. Gradually beat egg yolks into sauce; stir in a little of the egg whites, then carefully fold in remaining egg whites. Spoon mixture evenly into greased soufflé dishes. Bake 30 minutes or until puffed and golden brown. *Do not open oven door* during first 15 minutes of baking. Serve immediately. Makes 4 servings.

Ham Soufflés

1/2 lb. lean cooked ham	Salt to taste
2 tablespoons butter or margarine	1 teaspoon paprika
3 tablespoons all-purpose flour	3 egg whites
1 cup milk	2 egg yolks

Preheat oven to 350F (175C). Grease 4 individual 3-inch-deep soufflé dishes. Trim any excess fat from ham. Cut ham in cubes; then process in a blender or food processor fitted with a metal blade until finely ground. (Or chop very finely with a knife.) Set ham aside. Melt butter or margarine in a medium saucepan. Sprinkle in flour; cook over low heat, stirring, about 1 minute. Gradually add milk, stirring constantly; continue to cook, stirring, until bubbly and thickened. Remove from heat, stir in ham and season with salt and paprika. Cool slightly. In a bowl, beat egg whites until stiff. Beat egg yolks into sauce; stir in a little of the egg whites, then carefully fold in remaining egg whites. Spoon mixture evenly into greased soufflé dishes. Bake 30 minutes or until puffed and golden brown. *Do not open oven door* during first 15 minutes of baking. Serve immediately. Makes 4 servings.

Mini Quiches

Pastry:
1 cup all-purpose flour
1/4 teaspoon salt

1/4 cup butter or margarine
About 3 tablespoons cold water

Filling:
3 bacon slices, finely diced
4 eggs
2/3 cup whipping cream

1/4 cup shredded Emmentaler
cheese (1 oz.)
Salt and pepper to taste
4 teaspoons butter or margarine

To make pastry, in a bowl, stir together flour and 1/4 teaspoon salt. Using a pastry blender or 2 knives, cut in 1/4 cup butter or margarine until mixture resembles coarse crumbs. Sprinkle cold water over mixture, 1 tablespoon at a time, stirring with a fork until dough holds together. Gather dough into a ball with your hands, wrap in wax paper and refrigerate 30 minutes.
To fill and bake quiches, preheat oven to 400F (205C). Lightly grease 4 quiche dishes or tart pans, 3 to 4 inches in diameter. Divide dough into 4 equal portions. On a lightly floured board, roll out each portion to a 5- to 6-inch circle. Fit dough into pans. In a skillet, cook bacon until lightly browned; drain on paper towels. Sprinkle over pastry. In a bowl, beat together eggs, cream, cheese, salt and pepper. Pour mixture over bacon. Dot quiches with butter or margarine. Bake about 20 minutes or until filling is firm. Makes 4 servings.

Individual Broccoli Tarts

Double recipe Mini Quiches
pastry, opposite
2 lbs. fresh broccoli
(5-1/2 cups,
coarsely chopped)
Salt and pepper to taste
1/4 teaspoon dried and
crumbled leaf thyme

1/4 teaspoon dried and
crumbled leaf basil
2/3 cup whipping cream
4 egg whites
3 tablespoons freshly grated
Parmesan cheese

Prepare pastry. Preheat oven to 400F (205C). Lightly grease 12 tart pans or muffin cups, 3 inches in diameter. Divide chilled dough into 12 equal portions; roll out very thin to about 5 inch circles. Fit circles into greased tart pans, prick pastry shells all over with a fork. Bake 15 minutes or until light golden. Cool. In a medium saucepan, bring 2 cups lightly salted water to a boil. Add broccoli, reduce heat, cover and simmer 20 minutes or until very tender. Drain broccoli; cool. Puree broccoli in a blender, small batches at a time, or in a food processor with a metal blade. Season with thyme, basil, salt and pepper to taste. Set aside. In a small bowl, beat cream until stiff, then fold into the broccoli mixture. Preheat oven to 450F (230C). Fill baked pastry shells with broccoli mixture. Beat egg whites until stiff. Top each tart with beaten whites; sprinkle with cheese. Bake about 5 minutes or until meringue is golden brown. Serve hot or slightly cooled. Makes 12 tarts.

Baked Mushrooms with Eggs

3/4 lb. fresh mushrooms
1/4 lb. lean cooked ham
2 tablespoons butter or
    margarine
1 small onion, finely diced
1/4 cup whipping cream
Salt and freshly ground white
    pepper to taste
12 pitted black olives,
    if desired, whole or sliced
4 eggs
1/4 cup shredded Gouda cheese
    (1 oz.)
1 tablespoon chopped parsley

Preheat oven to 400F (205C).
Grease 4 individual baking dishes. Slice any large mushrooms;
cut smaller ones in half. Trim any
excess fat from ham, then finely
dice ham. Set ham and mushrooms aside. Melt butter or margarine in a medium skillet; add
onion and cook, stirring, until
soft. Stir in ham and mushrooms;
cook about 3 minutes, stirring
occasionally. Stir in cream; season with salt and white pepper.
Spoon mushroom mixture into
greased baking dishes. Make a
shallow well in center of mushroom mixture in each dish; crack
an egg into each well. Sprinkle
each egg lightly with salt; then
sprinkle eggs with cheese. Garnish with olives, if desired. Bake
about 12 minutes or until eggs are
set but yolks are still soft.

To serve, sprinkle baked eggs
with parsley and serve immediately. Makes 4 servings.

Chinese Spring Rolls

3 large dried Chinese mushrooms	All-purpose flour
3 tablespoons vegetable oil	6 tablespoons chicken stock
1 (8-oz.) can bamboo shoots, drained, chopped	1 teaspoon cornstarch mixed with 2 teaspoons cold water
3 tablespoons soy sauce	8 purchased egg roll wrappers
3/4 lb. lean boneless pork, cut in 1/2-inch-thick slices	1 egg white, slightly beaten
	Vegetable oil for deep-frying

To make filling, soak mushrooms in hot water to cover about 1 hour; then drain. Cut out and discard hard stems; thinly slice caps. Heat 2 tablespoons oil in a small skillet; add mushrooms and bamboo shoots. Cook, stirring, 2 minutes. Stir in soy sauce; cook 3 minutes longer. Remove from heat. Cut each pork slice in thin strips; toss in flour to coat lightly. Heat remaining 1 tablespoon oil in another skillet; add pork and cook, stirring, until lightly browned. Stir in stock and mushroom mixture. Stir in cornstarch-water mixture; cook, stirring, until filling is thickened. Remove from heat and cool.

To complete, divide filling equally among wrappers, spooning filling on bottom corner. Fold lower corner of wrapper up over filling; roll once. Brush all corners with egg white; fold both sides in. Roll again; press firmly to seal. In a deep, heavy pan, heat about 2 inches of oil to 325F (165C). Lower rolls into oil, 1 at a time; cook 4 to 6 minutes on each side or until golden brown. Drain on paper towels. Serve hot. Makes 4 servings.

Turkey Vol-au-Vent

4 frozen patty shells (from a 10-oz. pkg.)	1/4 cup whipping cream
2 tablespoons vegetable oil	1 teaspoon lemon juice
1 onion, finely diced	Few drops of Worcestershire sauce
1/4 lb. fresh mushrooms, sliced	Salt, freshly ground white pepper and sugar to taste
1 tablespoon all-purpose flour	1/2 lemon, thinly sliced
2/3 cup dry white wine	1 tomato, cut in wedges
2/3 cup homemade or canned chicken stock	
2 cups diced cooked turkey breast	

Bake patty shells according to package directions. While patty shells are baking, heat oil in a large skillet. Add onion and cook, stirring, until soft. Add mushrooms, sprinkle in flour and cook a few minutes longer, stirring occasionally. Stir in wine and stock. Simmer over low heat until sauce is slightly thickened. Stir in turkey; simmer until heated through. Stir in cream, lemon juice and Worcestershire sauce; season with salt, white pepper and sugar.

To serve, spoon turkey filling into hot patty shells. Garnish with lemon slices and tomato wedges. Makes 4 servings.

Consommé with Pancake Swirls

1 cup all-purpose flour	1/4 lb. calf's liver, minced
Pinch of salt	1 large onion, finely diced
1 egg, slightly beaten	1/8 teaspoon celery salt
2/3 cup milk	Salt and pepper to taste
2/3 cup sparkling water	1 qt. homemade or canned
About 2-1/2 tablespoons	regular-strength consommé
vegetable oil	(4 cups)
1/2 lb. bulk pork sausage	1 tablespoon chopped parsley

In a bowl, stir together flour and salt. Beat in egg, milk and sparkling water to make a smooth batter. Heat a little oil in a 6- or 7-inch skillet. Add about 3 tablespoons batter, or enough to make a thin layer. Cook pancakes, turning once, until lightly browned on both sides. Add more oil as needed. Keep cooked pancakes warm. In a bowl, combine sausage, liver and onion. Heat about 1 tablespoon oil in a large skillet; add sausage mixture and cook, stirring frequently, until sausage is no longer pink. Spoon off fat. Stir in celery salt; season with salt and pepper.

To serve, heat consommé until steaming. Spread sausage mixture on pancakes; roll up pancakes. Cut in 1/2-inch-thick slices. Place pancake slices in individual soup bowls; ladle in hot consommé. Sprinkle with parsley. Makes 4 servings.

Liver-Dumpling Soup

2 day-old dinner rolls	1/2 teaspoon grated lemon peel
2/3 cup lukewarm milk	Salt and freshly ground pepper
2 eggs, beaten	to taste
1 onion, finely chopped	1 tablespoon fine dry
3/4 lb. calf's liver or	breadcrumbs
lamb's liver, minced	1 qt. homemade or canned
1 tablespoon chopped parsley	regular-strength consommé
Pinch of dried leaf marjoram	(4 cups)

Tear rolls in small pieces and soften in a little cold water, then squeeze out any excess moisture. Place softened rolls in a bowl and stir in milk and eggs. Stir in onion, liver, parsley, marjoram, lemon peel, salt, pepper and breadcrumbs. With a wooden spoon, work ingredients together until smooth. Divide mixture into 12 pieces; form each piece into a ball. In a large saucepan, bring about 1-1/2 quarts lightly salted water to a boil. Add dumplings. Reduce heat, cover and simmer about 20 minutes or until dumplings are cooked through. Meanwhile, heat consommé until steaming.

To serve, ladle hot consommé into individual soup bowls. Lift cooked dumplings from water with a slotted spoon; place 3 dumplings in each bowl of consommé. Makes 4 servings.

Minestrone

1/4 lb. leeks
1/4 lb. potatoes
2 medium carrots
1/4 lb. cabbage
1/4 lb. celeriac
2 tablespoons vegetable oil
3 bacon slices, diced
1 garlic clove, finely chopped
1 onion, sliced
1 qt. homemade or canned
  beef stock (4 cups)

About 3/4 cup frozen green beans
About 3/4 cup frozen green peas
Salt and freshly ground white
  pepper to taste
1/4 cup chopped parsley
1 tablespoon chopped celery
  leaves
3/4 cup cooked long-grain
  white rice
1-1/3 cups freshly grated
  Parmesan cheese (4 oz.)

Trim roots and green tops of leeks, then split leeks lengthwise and wash thoroughly to remove sand. Slice leek halves crosswise. Peel potatoes and carrots, then cut in julienne strips. Cut cabbage in thin shreds. Peel and finely dice celeriac. Heat oil in a large saucepan, then add bacon and cook until browned. Add leeks, potatoes, carrots, cabbage, celeriac, garlic and onion; cook, stirring, 5 minutes. Pour in stock. Stir in beans and peas; bring to a boil. Reduce heat, cover and simmer 20 minutes or until all vegetables are tender. Season with salt and white pepper. Stir in parsley, celery leaves and rice. Heat through.

To serve, skim and discard fat from soup. Ladle soup into a tureen or individual soup bowls. Pass cheese at the table to sprinkle over soup. Makes 4 servings.

Dutch Fish Soup

Fish Stock:
1-1/2 lbs. fish trimmings
  (tails, fins and heads)
1 bunch parsley, chopped
1 onion, sliced

1 bay leaf
6 black peppercorns
1 cup dry white wine
4-3/4 cups water

Soup:
1/4 cup butter or margarine
1/2 lb. celery, thinly sliced
About 3/4 lb. each prepared
  carp, pike and eel; or
  2 to 3 lbs. firm white-fish
  fillets, such as cod,
  haddock or halibut

1/2 teaspoon dried leaf thyme
Salt and freshly ground white
  pepper to taste

To make stock, wash fish trimmings and place in a large saucepan. Add parsley, onion, bay leaf and peppercorns to saucepan. Stir in wine and water; bring to a boil. Reduce heat, cover and simmer 30 minutes. Strain stock; set aside.

To make soup, melt butter or margarine in a large saucepan; add celery. Cover and cook about 10 minutes, stirring occasionally. Stir in strained fish stock. Cut fish in bite-size pieces; stir into stock. Cover and simmer about 10 minutes or until fish turns from transparent to opaque. Do not overcook or fish will fall apart. Season with thyme, salt and white pepper. Makes 6 servings.

Sprout Soup with Croutons

Croutons:

2 slices white bread	1 tablespoon butter or margarine

Soup:

2 boxes radish or alfalfa sprouts	Salt and white pepper to taste
3 tablespoons butter or margarine	Pinch of ground nutmeg
1 onion, finely chopped	3 tablespoons dry white wine
1 tablespoon chopped chives	2 egg yolks
2-3/4 cups chicken stock	2/3 cup half and half

To make croutons, cut bread slices in cubes. Melt 1 tablespoon butter or margarine in a skillet; add bread cubes. Cook, stirring frequently, until golden brown all over. Set aside.

To make soup, wash sprouts in cold water, then drain in a colander and coarsely chop; reserve 2 tablespoons. Melt 3 tablespoons butter or margarine in a saucepan. Add remaining sprouts and onion; cook until onion is soft, stirring occasionally. Stir in chives and stock; bring to a boil. Season with salt, white pepper and nutmeg. In a small bowl, beat together wine, egg yolks and half and half; then beat in 4 to 5 tablespoons of the hot soup. Remove soup from heat; stir in egg-yolk mixture. Return soup to heat; reheat, stirring constantly, but do not boil.

To serve, ladle soup into individual soup bowls. Garnish with croutons and reserved chopped sprouts. Makes 4 servings.

Cream of Mushroom Soup

4 tablespoons butter or margarine	1/4 cup all-purpose flour
3/4 lb. fresh mushrooms, thinly sliced	2-3/4 cups homemade or canned beef or chicken stock
1 onion, finely diced	2/3 cup half and half
3 tablespoons chopped parsley	Salt and freshly ground white pepper to taste

Melt 2 tablespoons butter or margarine in a heavy saucepan. Add mushrooms and onion; cook until vegetables are soft, stirring frequently. Stir in 1-1/2 tablespoons parsley. Remove mushroom mixture from pan and set aside. Melt remaining 2 tablespoons butter or margarine in saucepan; sprinkle in flour and cook over low heat, stirring, about 1 minute. Gradually stir in stock. Bring to a boil; boil several minutes, stirring constantly. Reduce heat and stir in mushroom mixture; then stir in half and half. Heat gently 1 to 2 minutes, but do not boil. Season with salt and white pepper.

To serve, ladle soup into a tureen or individual bowls. Sprinkle with remaining 1-1/2 tablespoons parsley. Makes 4 servings.

Health tip

You may substitute plain low-fat yogurt for the half and half in this recipe.

Sardinian Celery Soup

2 tablespoons olive oil	2 tablespoons tomato paste mixed
1 onion, finely chopped	with 2 tablespoons water
1 garlic clove, finely chopped	1 bunch celery
1 medium carrot, peeled,	1 qt. hot water (4 cups)
finely diced	Salt to taste
3/4 lb. beef stew meat,	1/8 teaspoon red (cayenne)
cut in small cubes	pepper

Croutons:

2 slices white bread	1-1/3 cups freshly grated
1 tablespoon butter or margarine	Parmesan or pecorino cheese
	(4 oz.)

Heat oil in a large saucepan. Add onion, garlic, carrot and beef; cook 3 to 4 minutes, stirring occasionally. Stir in tomato-paste-water mixture. Reduce heat, cover and simmer gently 20 minutes, adding a little water if necessary. Separate celery stalks; trim ends and leafy tops. Wash stalks in cold water, then cut in 1/2-inch slices. Add celery to beef mixture and simmer 5 minutes longer. Add hot water, salt and red pepper; simmer 30 to 35 minutes longer or until meat is tender.

To make croutons, cut bread slices in cubes. Melt butter or margarine in a skillet; add bread cubes. Cook, stirring frequently, until golden brown all over. Remove from heat.

To serve, stir croutons into hot soup. Ladle soup into a tureen or individual soup bowls and serve at once. Pass cheese at the table to sprinkle over soup. Makes 4 servings.

Sorrel Soup

Fried Bread:

2 slices white bread	1 tablespoon butter or margarine

Soup:

1 lb. tender young sorrel leaves	2 egg yolks
3 tablespoons butter or margarine	2/3 cup half and half
1 qt. homemade or canned	Red (cayenne) pepper
chicken stock (4 cups)	Salt to taste

To make fried bread, cut bread slices in half. Melt 1 tablespoon butter or margarine in a skillet; add bread. Cook until golden brown on both sides. Keep warm.

To make soup, wash sorrel in lukewarm water; shake dry and cut in thin strips. Reserve 2 tablespoons sorrel strips for garnish. Melt 3 tablespoons butter or margarine in a large saucepan over low heat; add remaining sorrel and cook a few minutes. Stir in stock; cover and simmer gently 15 minutes. In a small bowl, beat together egg yolks, half and half and a pinch of red pepper; then beat in 4 to 5 tablespoons of the hot soup. Remove soup from heat; stir in egg-yolk mixture. Strain soup into another saucepan and season with salt and red pepper. Reheat, but do not boil.

To serve, ladle soup into individual soup bowls. Break fried bread into pieces and add to each serving; sprinkle with reserved sorrel strips. Makes 4 servings.

Hearty Goulash Soup

3/4 lb. lean boneless pork
  (shoulder or leg)
1/2 lb. beef brisket
1 lb. tomatoes
2 tablespoons vegetable oil
2 onions, sliced, separated
  into rings
1/4 lb. carrots, peeled, sliced
1 green bell pepper, seeded,
  cut in strips
1 qt. hot water (4 cups)
1 tablespoon paprika
Salt and freshly ground black
  pepper to taste
Pinch of hot paprika
Pinch of garlic powder
1/4 cup half and half

Cut pork and beef in small, even cubes. Peel and dice tomatoes, making sure not to lose the juice. Set meat and tomatoes aside. Heat oil in a large saucepan; add onions and cook several minutes. Add meat and cook, stirring frequently, 5 minutes or until browned on all sides. Add carrots, bell pepper and tomatoes and their juice. Cook a few minutes, stirring; then stir in hot water and paprika. Reduce heat, cover and simmer 1 hour or until meat is tender. Season with salt, black pepper, hot paprika and garlic powder.

To serve, stir in half and half. Ladle soup into a tureen or individual soup bowls. Makes 4 servings.

Tomato Soup with Rice

2 tablespoons olive oil	Salt and freshly ground black
2 onions, finely diced	pepper to taste
1/2 lb. lean ground beef	1 teaspoon caraway seeds
3/4 cup uncooked long-grain	Pinch of sugar
white rice	Pinch of red (cayenne) pepper
1 qt. tomato juice (4 cups)	2 tablespoons chopped parsley

Heat oil in a large saucepan. Add onions and cook, stirring, until soft. Crumble in beef, then add rice. Cook a few minutes, stirring occasionally. Stir in tomato juice. Bring to a boil; then reduce heat, cover and simmer 20 minutes or until rice is tender. Season with salt and black pepper; stir in caraway seeds, sugar and red pepper.

To serve, skim and discard fat from soup. Ladle soup into a tureen or individual soup bowls. Sprinkle with parsley. Makes 4 servings.

Cook's tip

If you plan to serve the soup as a meal in itself, increase the quantity of beef and add a few diced tomatoes. Enrich the soup with sour cream just before serving.

Potato Soup with Meat Dumplings

1 lb. leeks, washed	3 tomatoes
2 lbs. potatoes	1/8 teaspoon dried leaf marjoram
2 tablespoons vegetable oil	1/8 teaspoon celery salt
1 large onion, finely diced	1 tablespoon chopped parsley
1 qt. beef stock (4 cups)	

Meatballs:

1 day-old dinner roll	1 medium onion, finely diced
1 egg, beaten	Pinch of ground nutmeg
3/4 lb. lean ground beef or pork	Salt and freshly ground pepper

Slice leeks crosswise. Cut potatoes in 1-inch cubes; place in bowl of cold water. Heat oil in a large saucepan; add leeks and onion. Cook 5 minutes, stirring occasionally. Stir in drained potatoes and stock. Reduce heat, cover and simmer 20 minutes or until potatoes are tender. Meanwhile, prepare meatballs.

To make meatballs, tear roll in small pieces. Soften in a little cold water; squeeze out excess moisture. In a bowl, mix softened roll, egg, beef or pork, onion, nutmeg, salt and pepper. Work ingredients together thoroughly. Shape mixture into walnut-size balls.

To complete, drop meatballs into hot soup; simmer about 10 minutes or until cooked through. Cut tomatoes in thin wedges, add to soup and simmer until heated through. Stir in marjoram and celery salt. Ladle soup into a tureen or individual soup bowls. Sprinkle with parsley. Makes 4 servings.

Pearl-Barley Soup

6 tablespoons pearl barley
1-1/2 qts. water
1/2 lb. leeks
1/2 lb. celeriac
1 tablespoon vegetable oil
2 carrots, chopped
1 lb. cabbage, chopped
3 white peppercorns, crushed
1 bay leaf
3 whole cloves
6 bacon slices
3/4 lb. lean smoked
  picnic shoulder
1/2 lb. round steak
1/2 lb. potatoes, diced
Salt to taste
3 tablespoons chopped parsley

Wash barley. In a saucepan, bring 1-1/2 quarts water to a boil. Stir in barley. Reduce heat, cover and simmer 30 minutes or until barley is tender. Set aside (do not drain). Trim roots and green tops of leeks, then split leeks lengthwise and wash thoroughly to remove sand. Chop leek halves. Peel and chop celeriac. Heat oil in a large saucepan; add leeks, celeriac, carrots and cabbage. Cook a few minutes, stirring occasionally. Add crushed peppercorns, bay leaf and cloves. Dice bacon, pork and steak and stir into vegetables. Stir in barley with its cooking water. Reduce heat, cover and simmer 40 minutes. Stir potatoes into soup. Cover and simmer 20 minutes longer or until meat and potatoes are tender, adding a little water as necessary.

To serve, skim and discard fat from soup. Remove bay leaf and cloves. Season soup with salt, then ladle into a tureen or individual soup bowls. Sprinkle with parsley. Makes 4 servings.

Hungarian Bean Soup

1/2 lb. dried navy beans
1 bunch parsley
2 tablespoons vegetable oil
2 onions, diced
2 garlic cloves, finely chopped
2 green bell peppers, seeded,
  cut in strips
1 lb. firm tomatoes
4 cooked smoked sausages
Salt and freshly ground white
  pepper to taste
1/8 teaspoon hot paprika
Pinch of sugar
2 tablespoons chopped chives

Rinse and sort beans. Then soak beans in 4-3/4 cups water 12 hours. Drain beans, place in a saucepan and add 3 cups water. Bring to a boil; reduce heat, cover and simmer 1-1/2 to 2 hours adding a little more water as necessary. Remove from heat. Trim parsley stems. Wash parsley in cold water, shake dry and chop. Heat oil in a large saucepan; add onions, garlic and parsley and cook a few minutes. Add bell peppers and undrained beans. Stir well, then cover and simmer 20 minutes. Peel and chop tomatoes; stir into soup. Slice sausages, add to soup and cook until heated through. Season soup with salt, white pepper, paprika and sugar.

To serve, ladle soup into a tureen or individual soup bowls. Sprinkle with chives. Makes 4 servings.

Cabbage Soup with Beef

5-1/2 cups water
3/4 lb. beef brisket
1/2 onion, unpeeled
1 bay leaf
4 white peppercorns
1/4 lb. leeks
3 bacon slices, diced
3/4 lb. cabbage, cut in strips
1 large pickled beet
1 tablespoon tomato paste
2 to 3 tablespoons wine vinegar
Salt, freshly ground white
  pepper and sugar to taste
1/2 cup dairy sour cream

In a large saucepan, bring water to a boil. Add beef and return to a boil; skim and discard any scum that forms on surface of water. Brown cut side of unpeeled onion half in a lightly greased skillet. (Or skewer onion half on a fork; hold cut side over a gas flame or electric burner until browned.) Add onion half to beef with bay leaf and peppercorns. Reduce heat, partially cover and simmer about 2 hours or until beef is tender. Lift out beef; strain and reserve stock. Cool beef, then thinly slice. Trim roots and green tops of leeks, then split lengthwise and wash thoroughly to remove sand. Slice leek halves crosswise. Set aside. In a large saucepan, cook bacon until browned. Add leeks and cabbage and cook until leeks are soft, stirring frequently. Cut beet in cubes, reserving any juice; stir beet and its juice and tomato paste into leek mixture. Skim and discard fat from strained beef stock; gradually stir stock into leek mixture. Stir in sliced beef and vinegar. Season with salt, white pepper and sugar. Heat through.

To serve, ladle soup into individual bowls; add a spoonful of sour cream to each serving. Makes 4 servings.

Mixed Iceberg Salad

1 head iceberg lettuce	3 small tomatoes, cut in wedges
1 garlic clove, halved	2 tablespoons vegetable oil
1 medium cucumber (unpeeled), very thinly sliced	

Sour-Cream Dressing:

2 tablespoons white-wine tarragon vinegar	Salt and freshly ground white pepper to taste
1/4 cup dairy sour cream	
2 tablespoons chopped mixed fresh herbs, such as parsley, dill, chives and burnet	

Separate lettuce leaves. Wash leaves in cold water, drain well and pat dry. Tear or cut leaves in small pieces. Rub cut sides of garlic around inside of a salad bowl. Arrange lettuce, cucumber and tomatoes in salad bowl; set aside.

To make dressing, in a small bowl, beat together vinegar, sour cream, herbs, salt and white pepper.

To serve, sprinkle oil over salad and toss to coat; then pour dressing over salad. Makes 4 servings.

Radicchio Salad with Orange

3/4 lb. radicchio (red chicory)	2 teaspoons butter or margarine
1/4 lb. chicory	1 tablespoon sliced almonds
1 orange	

Simple Cream Dressing:

1/2 cup whipping cream	1/8 teaspoon sugar
Salt and pepper to taste	

Separate radicchio and chicory leaves. Wash leaves in cold water; shake dry. Tear large radicchio leaves in pieces; cut chicory leaves in 1/2-inch-wide strips. Remove peel and all white membrane from orange. Cut between segments; lift out segments, cut in half crosswise and remove seeds. Arrange radicchio, chicory and halved orange segments in a salad bowl. Set aside.

To make dressing, in a small bowl, stir together cream, salt, pepper and sugar.

To serve, melt butter or margarine in a small skillet. Add almonds. Cook, stirring, until lightly toasted; cool. Pour dressing over salad; sprinkle with toasted almonds. Makes 4 servings.

Cook's tip

To bring out the radicchio's slightly bitter flavor, finely chop some of the stalk and mix it into the salad.

Spinach with Bacon Dressing

1/3 to 1/2 lb. young spinach
2 small white onions, thinly
  sliced, separated into rings

2 hard-cooked eggs,
  cut in wedges

Bacon Dressing:
3 bacon slices, finely diced
1 garlic clove, finely chopped
2 tablespoons white-wine vinegar
2 tablespoons vegetable oil

1 tablespoon orange juice
Salt and freshly ground pepper
  to taste
Pinch of sugar

Remove stems and any tough leaves from spinach; then wash spinach thoroughly in cold water. Shake dry. Tear spinach leaves in pieces. Arrange spinach and onions in a salad bowl; set aside.
To make dressing, in a medium skillet, cook bacon until crisp; drain, reserving drippings. Crumble bacon and set aside. In a bowl, beat together reserved bacon drippings, garlic, vinegar, oil, orange juice, salt, pepper and sugar.
To serve, pour dressing over salad, sprinkle in cooked bacon and toss gently. Garnish with egg wedges. Makes 4 servings.

Cook's tip

As an alternative to the bacon dressing, try this cottage-cheese dressing. In a bowl, combine 1/4 cup small-curd cottage cheese, 2 tablespoons vegetable oil, juice of 1 lemon, 2 tablespoons milk, a pinch of salt and 1/2 teaspoon sugar. Beat thoroughly; then stir in 1 small grated onion.

Cucumber Salad with Yogurt Dressing

1 medium cucumber, unpeeled

1 onion

Yogurt Dressing:
2/3 cup plain whole-milk
  yogurt
1/4 cup chopped fresh dill
Salt and pepper to taste

1 tablespoon lemon juice
1 teaspoon maple syrup

Cut cucumber in half lengthwise; then cut each half in 1/2-inch-thick strips about 2 inches long. Thinly slice onion and separate into rings; cut each ring in quarters. Place cucumber and onion in a salad bowl; set aside.
To make dressing, in a small bowl, beat together yogurt, dill, salt, pepper, lemon juice and maple syrup.
To serve, pour dressing over cucumber and onion; mix gently. Let stand 10 minutes. Makes 4 servings.

Variation
Cucumber & Shrimp Salad: Prepare cucumber as directed above. Omit onion; instead, sprinkle 3/4 lb. cooked, shelled, deveined large shrimp with orange juice and let stand while you make the dressing. To make dressing, beat together 3 tablespoons vegetable oil, juice of 1 lemon, salt to taste, 1/8 teaspoon white pepper, 1/8 teaspoon garlic salt, and 1 teaspoon sugar. Mix dressing with the cucumber strips and shrimp; sprinkle salad with chopped dill.

Belgian Endive with Mandarin Oranges

4 small heads Belgian endive	Peel of 1/2 orange, cut in very
Juice of 1 lemon	thin strips
3 seedless mandarin oranges or	1 teaspoon bottled green
small navel oranges	peppercorns, coarsely chopped

Dressing:

1 teaspoon white-wine vinegar	2 tablespoons walnut oil
Juice of 1 mandarin orange or	Salt and freshly ground white
small navel orange	pepper to taste

Remove any damaged outer leaves from each head of endive; trim root end. With a sharp knife, cut a small wedge out of root end; discard. Cut endive in 1/2-inch-wide strips. Place endive strips in a salad bowl; sprinkle with lemon juice. Remove peel and all white membrane from oranges. Separate oranges into segments; cut each segment in half lengthwise. Sprinkle orange segments over endive. Set aside.

To make dressing, in a small bowl, beat together vinegar, orange juice, oil, salt and white pepper.

To serve, pour dressing over salad; toss to coat. Sprinkle orange peel and chopped peppercorns over salad. Makes 4 servings.

Dandelion Salad

1/4 lb. small, tender	1 lettuce heart
dandelion leaves	1/2 cup walnut halves

Yogurt-Parsley Dressing:

1 tablespoon white-wine	
vinegar	Freshly ground pepper
Salt to taste	to taste
1 teaspoon maple syrup	2 tablespoons chopped parsley
2/3 cup plain low-fat yogurt	or watercress
	2 tablespoons walnut oil

Throughly wash dandelion leaves in lukewarm water, then rinse in cold water and drain well. Separate lettuce leaves; wash in cold water and drain well. Pat dandelion and lettuce leaves dry, then cut in 1-1/2-inch-wide strips. Place in a salad bowl and set aside.

To make dressing, in a small bowl, stir together vinegar, salt and maple syrup until salt is dissolved. Set aside. In another small bowl, beat together yogurt, pepper and parsley or watercress.

To serve, pour vinegar mixture over salad and toss to coat; then sprinkle oil over salad. Pour yogurt mixture over salad; sprinkle salad with walnuts. Makes 4 servings.

Tomato Salad

4 large tomatoes, peeled, sliced
Salt and freshly ground pepper
1 onion, finely chopped
1/2 garlic clove, finely chopped
3 tablespoons olive oil
2 tablespoons white-wine vinegar
2 tablespoons chopped chives, if desired

Arrange tomato slices on a rimmed serving plate. Sprinkle with salt, pepper, onion and garlic. In a small bowl, beat together oil and vinegar; pour evenly over tomatoes. Sprinkle with chives, if desired. Makes 4 servings.

Cauliflower Salad

1 medium cauliflower
1 hard-cooked egg, chopped
1 egg yolk
1/2 teaspoon dry mustard
Pinch of sugar
2 tablespoons white-wine tarragon vinegar
1 tablespoon vegetable oil
2 tablespoons whipping cream
Salt and freshly ground white pepper to taste
2 tablespoons chopped chives

Separate cauliflower into flowerets. Cook cauliflowerets in boiling water until tender. Drain, cool and place in a salad bowl; set aside. In a small bowl, beat together hard-cooked egg, egg yolk, mustard, sugar, vinegar, oil, cream, salt and white pepper. Pour dressing over cauliflowerets; sprinkle with chives. Makes 4 servings.

Bean Salad

1-3/4 lb. fresh green beans
Dried leaf savory to taste
1 onion, thinly sliced, separated into rings
3 bacon slices, diced
2 tablespoons white-wine vinegar
Salt to taste
1/8 teaspoon paprika

Trim ends from beans; remove any strings. Cook beans in boiling lightly salted water seasoned with savory until crisp-tender. Drain beans; cool. Cut large beans in half. Arrange beans and onion in a salad bowl; set aside. In a skillet, cook bacon until crisp. In a small bowl, stir together cooked bacon, bacon drippings, vinegar, salt and paprika. Pour dressing over beans and onion; toss to coat. Makes 4 servings.

Iceberg Salad

1 small head iceberg lettuce
2 small seedless mandarin oranges
1/4 cup orange juice
1/8 teaspoon sugar
1 teaspoon orange peel
2/3 cup whipping cream
Salt to taste
1/2 cup chopped hazelnuts

Separate lettuce leaves. Wash leaves, drain well, pat dry and cut in strips. Remove peel and all white membrane from oranges. Separate oranges into segments; cut each segment in half lengthwise. Arrange lettuce and orange segments in a salad bowl; set aside. In a small bowl, stir together orange juice, sugar and orange peel. In another bowl, beat cream until it holds soft peaks; fold in orange-juice mixture. Season with salt. Pour dressing over salad. Sprinkle with nuts. Makes 4 servings.

Fish Salad with Peas

2 tablespoons white-wine
  vinegar
2 parsley sprigs
3/4 lb. cod fillets
1 (10-oz.) pkg. frozen
  green peas

Butter-lettuce leaves
2 hard-cooked eggs, sliced
1/2 red bell pepper, seeded,
  cut in strips

Curry Dressing:
1/4 cup mayonnaise
2/3 cup plain low-fat yogurt
1 to 2 teaspoons curry powder
1 garlic clove, finely chopped

Salt to taste
1 teaspoon paprika
2 shallots, peeled, grated

In a large saucepan, bring about 2-1/2 quarts lightly salted water
to a boil. Add vinegar, parsley sprigs and fish. Reduce heat,
cover and simmer 10 minutes or until fish flakes readily when
prodded. Lift out fish, cool completely and cut in 1-3/4-inch
cubes. Set aside. Cook peas according to package directions until
tender; drain, cool and set aside. Wash lettuce leaves in cold
water, shake dry and use to line a salad bowl. Arrange alternate
layers of hard-cooked egg slices, fish cubes, bell-pepper strips
and cooled peas in lettuce-lined bowl. Set aside.
To make dressing, in a small bowl, beat together mayonnaise,
yogurt and curry powder. Crush garlic together with salt; then
stir garlic-salt mixture into dressing. Stir in paprika and shallots.
To serve, pour dressing over salad. Makes 4 servings.

Chicken Salad with Grapes

1/2 lb. purple grapes
1/2 lb. iceberg lettuce
3 to 4 cups diced, cooked chicken
3 small cucumbers (unpeeled),
  very thinly sliced

4 small tomatoes, cut in wedges
1 onion, thinly sliced,
  separated into rings
1 tablespoon chopped fresh dill

Grape-Juice Dressing:
3 tablespoons white-wine
  vinegar
2 tablespoons unsweetened
  grape juice

Few drops of maple syrup
3 tablespoons vegetable oil
Salt and freshly ground white
  pepper to taste

Peel and halve grapes, if desired; remove seeds. Separate lettuce
leaves; wash leaves in cold water, drain well, pat dry and tear in
small pieces. Combine chicken, lettuce, grapes, cucumbers,
tomatoes and onion in a salad bowl. Set aside.
To make dressing, in a small bowl, beat together vinegar, grape
juice, maple syrup, oil, salt and white pepper.
To serve, pour dressing over salad; mix gently. Sprinkle with
dill. Makes 4 servings.

Chicken Salad with Green Beans

1-3/4 lbs. cooked chicken
1 (16-oz.) pkg. frozen
   green beans
1 large onion, thinly sliced,
   separated into rings

4 tomatoes, cut in wedges
10 pimento-stuffed green olives,
   sliced

Dressing:
6 tablespoons half and half
3 tablespoons white-wine vinegar
1 teaspoon Dijon-style mustard

1/2 teaspoon sugar
Salt to taste

Remove any skin and bones from chicken; cut meat in bite-size pieces. Cook beans according to package directions until crisp-tender. Drain beans; cool. Combine chicken, cooled beans, onion, tomatoes and olives in a salad bowl. Set aside.
To make dressing, in a small bowl, beat together half and half, vinegar, mustard, sugar and salt.
To serve, pour dressing over salad; mix gently. Let stand 1 hour to allow flavors to blend. Makes 4 servings.

Cook's tip

For a more filling dish, add cooked diced potatoes to the salad.

Spicy Beef Salad

2 onions
1 small bunch parsley
1-3/4 lbs. beef brisket
1 apple, peeled, sliced

5 or 6 sweet pickles, sliced
1 red bell pepper,
   cut in strips
1/4 lb. small mushrooms,

Piquant Dressing:
2 tablespoons wine vinegar
Few dashes of Worcestershire
   sauce

2 tablespoons sweet-pickle juice
2 tablespoons vegetable oil
Salt and pepper to taste

Cut 1 unpeeled onion in half. Brown cut sides of onion halves in a lightly greased skillet. In a large saucepan, bring 2 quarts lightly salted water to a boil; add parsley, onion halves and beef. Return to a boil; skim and discard any scum that forms on surface of water. Reduce heat, cover and simmer about 2 hours or until beef is tender. Strain and reserve cooking liquid. Cool beef, then cut in strips. Peel remaining onion, thinly slice and separate into rings. Combine beef, onion, apple, pickles, bell pepper and mushrooms. Set aside.
To make dressing, boil strained meat cooking liquid, uncovered, until slightly reduced. Pour 1/4 cup of the reduced stock into a small bowl; beat in vinegar, Worcestershire sauce, oil, sweet-pickle juice, salt and pepper.
To serve, pour dressing over salad; mix gently. Let stand 20 minutes. Makes 4 servings.

Cheese & Sausage Salad

8 oz. Emmentaler cheese
3/4 lb. cooked smoked sausage
1 apple
About 4 sweet pickles, diced

1 (about 8-oz.) can whole-kernel
  corn, drained
1/2 bunch chives

Vinaigrette Dressing:
1 onion, finely diced
1 garlic clove, finely chopped
3 tablespoons vegetable oil
2 tablespoons red-wine vinegar

Salt and freshly ground white
  pepper to taste
1 teaspoon prepared mustard
1/8 teaspoon hot paprika

Cut cheese in very thin strips. Skin and thinly slice sausage. Peel, quarter, core and finely dice apple. Combine cheese, sausage, apple, pickles and corn in a salad bowl. Set aside.
To make dressing, in a small bowl, stir together onion, garlic, oil, vinegar, salt, white pepper, mustard and paprika.
To serve, pour dressing over salad; mix gently. Wash chives in cold water, shake dry and chop. Sprinkle chopped chives over salad. Makes 4 servings.

Chicken Salad with Avocado

1-3/4 lbs. cooked chicken
1/2 lb. purple grapes
2 seedless mandarin oranges or
  small navel oranges

1 ripe avocado
Orange juice
Butter-lettuce leaves
1/2 cup chopped walnuts

Orange-Sherry Dressing:
2 tablespoons mayonnaise
3 tablespoons half and half
1 tablespoon dry sherry

3 tablespoons orange juice
Salt to taste

Remove any skin and bones from chicken; cut meat in bite-size pieces. Peel grapes, if desired; then halve grapes and remove seeds. Remove peel and all white membrane from oranges. Separate oranges into segments. Halve, pit and peel avocado; slice each half crosswise and sprinkle slices lightly with orange juice to prevent darkening. Place chicken, grapes, orange segments and avocado in a bowl; toss gently.
To make dressing, in a small bowl, beat together mayonnaise, half and half, sherry, 3 tablespoons orange juice and salt.
To serve, wash lettuce leaves in cold water, shake dry and use to line a salad bowl. Spoon salad into lettuce-lined bowl. Pour dressing over salad and sprinkle with walnuts. Makes 4 servings.

Carrot Salad

1 lb. carrots
2 medium oranges
**5 to 7 tablespoons fresh
     lemon juice**
1 tablespoon powdered sugar
Pinch of ground cinnamon
1 tablespoon vegetable oil

Peel carrots, then cut in very thin julienne strips. Cut peel and all white membrane from oranges. Cut between segments; lift out segments and remove seeds. In a salad bowl, gently mix orange segments with carrots. In a small bowl, stir together lemon juice, powdered sugar, cinnamon and oil; pour over salad. Makes 4 servings.

Fennel Salad

3/4 lb. fennel bulbs
1 bunch radishes
**2 medium cucumbers, peeled,
     thinly sliced**
3 tablespoons vegetable oil
1 tablespoon lemon juice
**Salt and freshly ground white
     pepper to taste**
**1 tablespoon chopped mixed
     fresh herbs, such as chives,
     parsley and mint**

Trim feathery leaves from fennel. Wash leaves in cold water, shake dry and chop enough to make 1 tablespoon. Reserve chopped leaves for garnish. Slice fennel bulbs very thinly. Wash and slice radishes. In a salad bowl, combine fennel, radishes and cucumbers. In a small bowl, beat together oil, lemon juice, salt and white pepper; mix into salad. Sprinkle reserved chopped fennel leaves and herbs over salad. Makes 4 servings.

Seafood Salad

**1 lb. fresh white or
   green asparagus tips**
1 (8-3/4-oz.) can mussels
**3/4 lb. cooked, shelled,
   deveined large shrimp**
5 tablespoons half and half
2 tablespoons mayonnaise
Few drops of lemon juice
Salt and pepper to taste
Pinch of sugar
1 teaspoon paprika
Lettuce leaves
2 teaspoons chopped fresh dill

Cook asparagus tips in boiling lightly salted water until tender. Drain, rinse in cold running water and drain again. Drain mussels, reserving 2 tablespoons liquid. Combine shrimp, asparagus and mussels; set aside. In a small bowl, beat together half and half, mayonnaise, reserved 2 tablespoons mussel liquid, lemon juice, salt, white pepper, sugar and paprika.

Wash lettuce leaves in cold water, shake dry and use to line 4 individual salad plates. Pour dressing over salad; mix gently; spoon onto lettuce. Sprinkle with dill. Makes 4 servings.

Windsor Salad

1/4 cup mayonnaise
1 teaspoon lemon juice
**2 teaspoons grated fresh
   horseradish**
Salt to taste
1/8 teaspoon sugar
**Few drops of Worcestershire
   sauce**
**1 lb. cooked, boned,
   skinned chicken breasts**
3/4 lb. celeriac
1/2 lb. mushrooms, sliced
**3 small dill pickles,
   cut in julienne strips**
Lettuce leaves

In a small bowl, combine mayonnaise, lemon juice, horseradish, salt, sugar and Worcestershire sauce. Set aside. Cut chicken in strips. Peel celeriac; cut in very thin slices, then cut each slice in thin strips. Combine chicken, celeriac, mushrooms and pickles in a bowl. Pour dressing over salad; mix gently. Cover and let stand 20 minutes. Arrange lettuce leaves around rim of a platter. Spoon salad into center. Makes 4 servings.

Normandy Rice Salad

1 celery stalk
1 tart apple
**About 1-1/3 cups cooked
   long-grain white rice**
2/3 cup half and half
**Salt and freshly ground white
   pepper to taste**
1 tablespoon lemon juice

Thinly slice celery stalk. Quarter and core apple; thinly slice each quarter crosswise. Combine apple, celery and rice in a salad bowl. In a small bowl, beat together half and half, salt, white pepper and lemon juice; pour over salad and toss gently. Sprinkle reserved chopped celery leaves over salad. Makes 4 servings.

Tuna Salad

2 (7-oz.) cans tuna	**Lemon juice**
1/2 grapefruit, peeled,	**3 hard-cooked eggs**
segmented	**Butter-lettuce leaves**
1 banana	

Dressing:

3 tablespoons mayonnaise	**1/8 teaspoon salt**
2/3 cup plain low-fat yogurt	**About 1/2 teaspoon paprika**

Drain tuna; break in equal-size pieces. Carefully remove all membrane from each grapefruit segment, then remove seeds and cut segments in half crosswise. Slice banana; sprinkle slices lightly with lemon juice. Chop 2 hard-cooked eggs; cut remaining egg in wedges and reserve for garnish. Combine tuna, grapefruit, banana and chopped eggs in a bowl; set aside.

To make dressing, in a small bowl, beat together mayonnaise, yogurt, salt and 1/2 teaspoon paprika.

To serve, wash lettuce leaves in cold water, shake dry and use to line a salad bowl. Pour dressing over tuna mixture; mix gently. Spoon tuna salad into lettuce-lined bowl; garnish with reserved hard-cooked egg wedges and sprinkle with paprika. Makes 4 servings.

Cook's tip

For a more filling tuna salad, add a few spoonfuls of cooked rice.

Mushroom Salad

3/4 lb. small fresh mushrooms	**Chicory or leaf-lettuce leaves**
2 teaspoons lemon juice	**Red (cayenne) pepper to taste**
1/2 lb. lean cooked ham	

Cream Dressing:

2 tablespoons mayonnaise	**Salt to taste**
1/4 cup half and half	**1/8 teaspoon sugar**
1 tablespoon white-wine vinegar	

Cut larger mushrooms in halves or quarters; leave smaller ones whole. Place mushrooms in a bowl and sprinkle with lemon juice. Trim any excess fat from ham; then dice ham and stir into mushrooms. Set aside.

To make dressing, in a small bowl, beat together mayonnaise, half and half, vinegar, salt and sugar.

To serve, wash chicory or lettuce leaves in cold water, shake dry and use to line 4 individual salad bowls. Stir dressing into mushroom mixture; spoon into lettuce-lined bowls. Sprinkle with red pepper. Makes 4 servings.

Cook's tip

For a more filling meal, add 2 or 3 chopped hard-cooked eggs to the salad.

Corn & Sausage Salad

1/2 lb. cooked smoked sausage
4 oz. Gouda cheese
2 small onions, thinly sliced,
　separated into rings
1/2 red bell pepper, seeded,
　cut in strips

1/2 green bell pepper, seeded,
　cut in strips
4 medium tomatoes, sliced
2 sweet pickles, thinly sliced
1 (12-oz.) can whole-kernel
　corn, drained

Spicy Dressing:

2 tablespoons red-wine vinegar
3 tablespoons vegetable oil
1/2 teaspoon prepared mustard
1/2 teaspoon paprika

Salt and freshly ground black
　pepper to taste
Pinch of sugar
Pinch of red (cayenne) pepper

Skin sausage; then cut sausage and cheese in julienne strips. Combine sausage, cheese, onions, red and green bell pepper, tomatoes, pickles and corn in a salad bowl. Set aside.
To make dressing, in a small bowl, beat together vinegar, oil, mustard, paprika, salt, black pepper, sugar and red pepper.
To serve, pour dressing over salad and mix gently. Let stand 20 minutes. Makes 4 servings.

Spaghetti Salad

7 to 8 oz. uncooked spaghetti
3/4 lb. cooked, boned,
　skinned turkey breast
12 oz. Emmentaler cheese
2 bunches radishes

2 green bell peppers, seeded,
　cut in strips
4 tomatoes, cut in wedges
2 hard-cooked eggs, sliced
2 tablespoons chopped chives

Nippy Yogurt Dressing:

1/4 cup half and half
2/3 cup plain low-fat yogurt
3 tablespoons ketchup
Dash of hot-pepper sauce

1 tablespoon white-wine vinegar
Salt to taste
1/2 teaspoon paprika

In a large saucepan, bring 3 quarts salted water to a boil. Break spaghetti in halves or thirds; drop into boiling salted water. Boil about 12 minutes or until tender but still firm to the bite. Drain, rinse under cold running water and drain again. Set aside. Cut turkey and cheese in julienne strips. Wash and slice radishes. Combine cooked spaghetti, turkey, cheese, radishes, bell peppers, tomatoes and hard-cooked egg slices in a salad bowl. Set aside.
To make dressing, in a small bowl, beat together half and half, yogurt, ketchup, hot-pepper sauce, vinegar, salt and paprika.
To serve, pour dressing over salad; mix gently. Sprinkle with chives. Makes 4 servings.

Special Luncheon Salad

Romaine-lettuce leaves
1 bunch radishes
2 small cucumbers, thinly sliced
2 tomatoes, cut in wedges

10 bottled cocktail onions
8 miniature corn-on-the-cob
1/2 lb. thinly sliced mortadella
 or other cold cut

Green-Peppercorn Dressing:
1/2 cup dairy sour cream
1 tablespoon soy sauce
Celery salt to taste

Pinch of sugar
1 teaspoon bottled green
 peppercorns, drained

Line a salad bowl or platter with lettuce. Thinly slice radishes. Arrange radishes, cucumbers, tomatoes, onions and miniature corn-on-the-cob over lettuce. Cut to the center of each cold cut slice; roll each slice into a cone. Arrange atop salad.
To make dressing, in a small bowl, beat together sour cream, soy sauce, celery salt, sugar and green peppercorns.
To serve, pour dressing over salad. Makes 4 servings.

Variation
Cervelat Salad (shown at top): Slice cervelat (or other cold cut or cooked, smoked sausage) and sweet pickles; place in a bowl. Cut cheese and red bell pepper in strips and add to salad; toss. For dressing, beat together 1 tablespoon *each* oil, wine vinegar, prepared mustard and chopped onion. Season with salt and pepper. Add to salad; toss. Top with hard-cooked egg wedges.

Egg Salad

1 cup frozen green peas
1/2 lb. lean cooked ham
1/2 lb. purple grapes

4 hard-cooked eggs,
 cut in wedges
4 tomatoes, cut in wedges
1/4 cup chopped parsley

Dressing:
2 tablespoons mayonnaise
2/3 cup plain low-fat yogurt
2 tablespoons ketchup
2 tablespoons white-wine vinegar

1/4 cup chicken stock
Salt to taste
1 teaspoon paprika

In a small saucepan, bring 1/4 cup lightly salted water to a boil. Add peas; reduce heat, cover and simmer until tender. Drain peas; cool. Trim any excess fat from ham, then cut ham in strips. Halve grapes and remove seeds. Combine cooled peas, ham, grapes, hard-cooked egg wedges and tomatoes in a salad bowl. Set aside.
To make dressing, in a small bowl, beat together mayonnaise, yogurt, ketchup, vinegar, stock, salt and paprika.
To serve, pour dressing over salad; mix gently. Cover and refrigerate about 10 minutes. Then sprinkle parsley over salad. Makes 4 servings.

Potato Salad with Herring

1-1/4 lbs. new potatoes, scrubbed	2 or 3 fresh dill pickles, sliced
1/2 lb. pickled herring	1 large onion, thinly sliced, separated into rings
1 large tart apple	
1 (16-oz.) can beets	

Dressing:

3 tablespoons mayonnaise	Freshly ground white pepper to taste
1/3 cup plain low-fat yogurt	Salt to taste
1 tablespoon white-wine vinegar	

Cook unpeeled potatoes in boiling lightly salted water until tender. Drain potatoes; cool, peel and slice. Set aside. Rinse herring in cold water, pat dry and cut in squares. Peel, quarter, core and dice apple. Drain beets, reserving 2 tablespoons of the liquid. Cut drained beets in cubes. Combine sliced cooled potatoes, herring, apple, beets, pickles and onion in a large salad bowl. Set aside.

To make dressing, in a small bowl, beat together mayonnaise, yogurt, reserved 2 tablespoons beet liquid, vinegar and white pepper.

To serve, pour dressing over salad; mix gently. Let stand a few minutes. Season with salt before serving. Makes 4 servings.

Potato Salad with Pork

1-3/4 lbs. new potatoes, scrubbed	1 tablespoon white-wine vinegar
1 (10-oz.) pkg. frozen green peas	Salt
3 bacon slices, diced	Garlic salt to taste
6 tablespoons homemade or canned beef stock	3/4 lb. cooked lean pork loin roast, diced
	1 onion, diced
	2 tablespoons vegetable oil

Cook unpeeled potatoes in boiling lightly salted water until tender. Drain potatoes; cool, peel and slice. Set aside. Cook peas according to package directions until tender; drain, cool and set aside. In a medium skillet, cook bacon until crisp. Drain and set aside. In a small saucepan, heat stock; add vinegar and a pinch of salt. Place sliced cooled potatoes in a large salad bowl; add stock mixture and stir gently. Sprinkle with garlic salt. Gently mix in pork, onion, cooled peas, cooked bacon and oil. Cover and let stand a few minutes. Season with salt before serving. Makes 4 servings.

Italian Salad

1-1/4 lbs. new potatoes, scrubbed	2 tablespoons red-wine vinegar
1 small cauliflower	Salt and freshly ground white pepper to taste
1/4 lb. fresh green beans	3 tablespoons olive oil or vegetable oil
1/4 lb. carrots, diced	
1 cup frozen green peas	2 hard-cooked eggs, cut in wedges
1/4 lb. fresh mushrooms	
10 anchovy fillets	2 tablespoons chopped parsley

Cook unpeeled potatoes in boiling lightly salted water until tender. Drain potatoes; cool. Peel and slice. Set aside. Separate cauliflower into flowerets. Cook cauliflowerets in boiling water until tender; drain and cool. Set aside. Trim ends from beans and remove any strings, then cut beans in 2-inch lengths. Cook beans and carrots in boiling lightly salted water until crisp-tender. Drain, cool and set aside. Cook peas in 1/4 cup boiling lightly salted water until tender; drain, cool and set aside. Cut any large mushrooms in halves or quarters; leave smaller ones whole. Cut anchovy fillets in strips.

To serve, in a large bowl, beat together vinegar, salt and white pepper. Add sliced cooled potatoes, cauliflowerets, beans, carrots, peas, mushrooms and anchovies. Toss gently to mix; correct seasoning. Gently stir in oil. Arrange hard-cooked egg wedges atop salad; sprinkle with parsley. Makes 4 servings.

Pasta Salad with Salami

1-1/3 cups uncooked macaroni	1 red bell pepper, seeded, diced
1/2 lb. thinly sliced salami	1 green bell pepper, seeded, diced
1 cup diced Emmentaler cheese (4 oz.)	About 2 dill pickles, diced

Creamy Paprika Dressing:

3 tablespoons mayonnaise	1/8 teaspoon sugar
1/4 cup half and half	1/2 teaspoon hot paprika
1 teaspoon lemon juice	2 to 3 tablespoons milk, if desired
Salt and freshly ground pepper to taste	

In a large saucepan, bring 3 quarts salted water to a boil. Sprinkle in macaroni; boil about 12 minutes or until macaroni is tender but still firm to the bite. Drain macaroni, rinse under cold running water and drain again. Cut salami slices in 1/2-inch-wide strips. Combine cooled macaroni, salami, cheese, bell peppers and pickles in a large salad bowl. Set aside.

To make dressing, in a small bowl, beat together mayonnaise, half and half, lemon juice, salt, pepper, sugar and paprika. For a thinner dressing, stir in milk.

To serve, pour dressing over salad; mix gently. Let stand about 20 minutes. Makes 4 servings.

Melon Cup

Juice of 1 lemon
2 tablespoons honey
1 (2-1/4-lb.) honeydew melon
2 seedless mandarin oranges
  or small navel oranges
1 apple
1 banana
1/2 lb. purple grapes
1/3 cup whipping cream
2 teaspoons sugar
1/4 teaspoon vanilla extract

In a small bowl, stir together lemon juice and honey. Set aside. Cut off top 1/3 of melon—in a zigzag pattern, if you wish—and remove seeds. Scoop out melon flesh with a ball cutter. Reserve hollowed melon shell for a serving "bowl." Remove peel and all white membrane from oranges, then separate oranges into segments. Peel, quarter and core apple; slice quarters crosswise. Cut banana in half lengthwise; slice halves crosswise. Halve grapes and remove seeds. Combine melon, orange segments, apple, banana and grapes in a bowl; stir in honey mixture. In another bowl, beat cream until it holds soft peaks; beat in sugar and vanilla.
To serve, fold cream mixture into fruit; spoon into melon bowl. Makes 4 servings.

Mixed Fruit Salad

(Behind melon in photograph)

Cut fruit of your choice in equal-size cubes or slices. Sweeten with a little powdered sugar; then stir in orange or apple juice. If desired, flavor juice with the liqueur of your choice.

Raspberry Cups

(Top right of photograph)

Mix lightly sweetened fresh raspberries with 1 part whipped cream and 1 part plain low-fat yogurt. Serve in glasses.

Strawberry Curd

(Front right of photograph)

Gently mix lightly sweetened fresh strawberries with cottage cheese.

Fruit Salad with Cream

2 tart apples
2 large navel oranges
1/2 lb. purple grapes
3 tablespoons coarsely
    chopped walnuts
2/3 cup whipping cream
2 teaspoons sugar
1/4 teaspoon vanilla extract
2 tablespoons orange juice
1-1/2 tablespoons
    orange-flavored liqueur

Quarter, core and slice apples. Cut peel and all white membrane from oranges; then slice oranges crosswise, making round slices. Cut each slice in quarters. If desired, cut grapes in half and remove seeds. Combine apples, orange slices, grapes and walnuts in a bowl. In another bowl, beat cream until it holds soft peaks; sprinkle in sugar and vanilla and continue to beat until stiff. Fold in orange juice and liqueur.

To serve, spoon cream mixture over fruit. Makes 4 servings.

Cook's tip

This is an adaptable recipe; you can alter it to use any fresh fruit in season. Vary the liqueur depending on your choice of fruit.

Exotic Fruit Salad

3/4 lb. ripe fresh pineapple
    (about 1/4 of a small
    pineapple)
1 mango
1 kiwifruit
1 small cantaloupe or
    1 lb. other melon of
    your choice
1 or 2 ripe figs
1-1/2 tablespoons grenadine
    syrup
1-1/2 tablespoons
    orange-flavored liqueur
Juice of 1/2 lemon
1/2 vanilla bean or
    1/2 teaspoon vanilla extract
2/3 cup whipping cream
1-1/2 teaspoons powdered sugar

Peel pineapple; cut out core. Cut pineapple flesh in bite-size chunks. Peel mango; slice flesh from pit, then cut flesh in bite-size pieces. Peel and thinly slice kiwifruit. Halve melon and remove seeds; scoop out flesh with a ball cutter. Slice figs. Combine pineapple, mango, kiwifruit and melon in a serving bowl (for the most attractive presentation, use a clear glass bowl). Set aside. In a small bowl, stir together grenadine syrup, liqueur and lemon juice; gently fold into fruit. Cover and refrigerate about 30 minutes.

To serve, slit vanilla bean lengthwise with a sharp knife; scrape out pith, if using. In a bowl, beat cream with vanilla pith or vanilla extract until it holds stiff peaks; sprinkle in powdered sugar and continue to beat until stiff. Spoon whipped cream over fruit salad. Makes 4 servings.

Asparagus Omelet with Shrimp

1 lb. fresh white or
    green asparagus
6 eggs
1/4 cup half and half
Salt and freshly ground white
    pepper to taste
About 1/4 cup butter or
    margarine
1/2 lb. cooked, shelled
    small shrimp

Wash asparagus. Snap off and discard woody ends of stalks. Peel bases of stalks, then tie stalks into a bundle. In a large saucepan, bring about 2 quarts lightly salted water to a boil. Add asparagus; reduce heat, cover and simmer briskly 20 to 30 minutes or until tender. Drain asparagus and keep warm. In a bowl, beat together eggs, half and half, salt and white pepper. Melt about 2 teaspoons butter or margarine in a 7- to 8-inch skillet. Pour in 1/4 of egg mixture; tilt skillet to distribute evenly. Cook until eggs are set but top surface is still moist and shiny. Slide omelet onto a warm plate; cover and keep warm in a 200F (95C) oven. Repeat with remaining egg mixture and 6 more teaspoons butter or margarine, make 3 more omelets. Melt remaining butter or margarine in a skillet over low heat; add shrimp and heat through, stirring often.

To serve, arrange 1/4 of drained asparagus on each omelet. Fold each omelet over asparagus; top evenly with shrimp. Makes 4 servings.

Cook's tip

If you are unable to find fresh asparagus, use tender broccoli instead.

Chinese-Style Shrimp

1 (10-oz.) pkg. frozen green peas	1/8 teaspoon red (cayenne) pepper
1/4 lb. leeks	Celery salt to taste
1/4 cup vegetable oil	1/2 teaspoon ground ginger
1 lb. cooked, shelled, deveined large shrimp	1 teaspoon sugar

Cook peas according to package directions until tender. Drain; set aside. Trim off roots and green tops of leeks; then split leeks lengthwise and wash thoroughly to remove sand. Thinly slice leek halves crosswise. Heat oil in a large skillet; add leeks and cook until soft, stirring frequently. Add shrimp; continue to cook, stirring, until shrimp are heated through. Stir in drained peas and heat through. Stir in red pepper, celery salt, ginger and sugar; serve immediately. Makes 4 servings.

Shrimp Fritters

2 slices white bread	1/2 teaspoon finely chopped fresh gingerroot
1/4 cup homemade or canned chicken stock	2 tablespoons all-purpose flour
6 canned water chestnuts, finely chopped	1 lb. cooked, shelled, deveined small shrimp
2 eggs, separated	Vegetable oil for deep-frying
Salt to taste	

Cut crusts off bread; then tear bread in small pieces, place in a bowl and moisten with stock. Let stand a few minutes; squeeze out any excess moisture. Stir water chestnuts, egg yolks, salt, gingerroot and flour into softened bread; then stir in shrimp. In another bowl, beat egg whites until stiff; fold into shrimp mixture. Shape mixture into small balls.

To cook, in a deep, heavy saucepan, heat about 2 inches of oil to 350F (175C) or until a 1-inch bread cube turns golden brown in about 65 seconds. Lower about 6 fritters into oil, making sure they do not touch each other. Cook, turning occasionally, 4 to 5 minutes or until golden brown. Drain on paper towels; keep hot. Repeat with remaining fritters. Makes 4 servings.

Rice with Seafood

1 lb. mussels
1/4 lb. leeks
2 tablespoons vegetable oil
1/4 lb. carrots, peeled,
  cut in julienne strips
1 onion, finely chopped
1 garlic clove, finely chopped
1 cup uncooked long-grain
  white rice

1/8 teaspoon saffron threads
2 cups chicken stock
2/3 cup dry white wine
1 bay leaf
3/4 lb. cooked, shelled,
  deveined large shrimp
1/4 lb. cooked squid
Thyme sprig

Soak a clay casserole in cold water 20 minutes. Drain well. Scrub mussels under cold running water; discard beards. In a large saucepan, bring 1 quart water to a boil; add mussels and boil until shells open. Drain mussels, discarding any with unopened shells; set aside. Trim leeks, then split leeks lengthwise and wash thoroughly to remove sand. Slice leeks crosswise. Heat oil in a skillet; stir in leeks, carrots, onion and garlic. Cover; cook 5 minutes, stirring occasionally. Transfer vegetables casserole; stir in rice and salt. Soften saffron in stock; add with wine to casserole. Add bay leaf. Cover casserole and place on lowest rack of a cold oven. Bake 50 minutes, in a 400F (205C) oven, or until rice is tender. Arrange shrimp, squid, thyme sprig and cooked mussels over rice. Cover; cook 20 minutes or until seafood is hot. Remove bay leaf; stir well. Makes 4 servings.

Shrimp Fricassee

1 tablespoon butter or
  margarine
1 teaspoon sugar
3/4 lb. carrots, peeled,
  cut in julienne strips
1 small onion, finely diced
1 tablespoon all-purpose flour
2/3 cup homemade or
  canned chicken stock

3 medium tomatoes
2/3 cup half and half
1-3/4 lbs. cooked, shelled,
  deveined medium shrimp
Salt and freshly ground
  white pepper to taste
3 tablepoons chopped fresh dill

Melt butter or margarine in a saucepan; sprinkle in sugar. Cook, stirring, until sugar dissolves and begins to caramelize. Add carrots and onion; toss lightly to coat. Cook a few minutes, stirring constantly; then sprinkle in flour and cook, stirring, until golden. Gradually stir in stock. Bring to a simmer; cover and simmer 20 minutes. Peel, seed and dice tomatoes; add diced tomatoes and any juice to pan. Stir in half and half and shrimp; simmer gently 10 minutes or until shrimp are heated through. Do not allow fricassee to boil.

To serve, season with salt and white pepper; then stir in dill. Makes 4 servings.

Shrimp with Scrambled Eggs

Croutons:
2 slices white bread   1 tablespoon butter or margarine

Shrimp with Scrambled Eggs:
1/2 lb. new potatoes, scrubbed	3 eggs
2 tablespoons vegetable oil	3 tablespoons half and half
3 bacon slices, finely diced	Salt and freshly ground white
1 onion, diced	pepper to taste
1 lb. cooked, shelled,	2 tablespoons chopped fresh dill
deveined medium shrimp	

To make croutons, cut bread slices in cubes. Melt butter or margarine in a skillet; add bread cubes. Cook, stirring frequently, until golden brown all over.
To make shrimp with eggs, cook unpeeled potatoes in boiling lightly salted water until tender. Drain potatoes; cool, peel, dice and set aside. Heat oil in a large skillet; add bacon and cook until crisp. Remove bacon from pan; add onion to drippings and cook, stirring, until soft. Return cooked bacon to pan with potatoes and shrimp. Continue to cook, stirring frequently, until shrimp are heated through. In a bowl, beat together eggs, half and half, salt, white pepper and dill. Pour egg mixture over shrimp mixture and stir gently until eggs are set but still moist.
To serve, spoon onto individual plates; sprinkle with croutons. Makes 4 servings.

Provençal-Style Shrimp

1 qt. water (4 cups)	1 large onion, finely chopped
Salt	4 garlic cloves, finely chopped
Parsley sprig	1 red bell pepper, seeded,
1-1/3 lbs. cooked, shelled,	finely chopped
deveined large shrimp	2 tablespoons chopped mixed
Juice of 1/2 lemon	fresh herbs, such as parsley,
1-1/2 tablespoons cognac	chervil and lovage
Few dashes of Worcestershire	3 tablespoons butter or
sauce	margarine
1 tablespoon vegetable oil	

In a large saucepan, bring water to a boil with a pinch of salt and parsley sprig. Add shrimp and simmer 1 minute. Lift out shrimp, drain, and place in a large bowl. Stir in lemon juice, cognac and Worcestershire sauce; cover and refrigerate 30 minutes. Heat oil in a skillet; add onion, garlic, bell pepper and herbs. Cook 2 minutes, stirring constantly. Season with salt; keep warm. Melt butter or margarine in another skillet. Drain shrimp and pat dry; add to skillet and cook, stirring, until very lightly browned on all sides.
To serve, spoon shrimp onto individual plates; top evenly with vegetable mixture. Makes 4 servings.

Oven-Baked Haddock

1 (2-1/4 lb.) piece haddock	Freshly ground white pepper
1 tablespoon lemon juice	to taste
Salt to taste	1/4 teaspoon paprika
Large dill sprig	2/3 cup dry white wine
6 bacon slices, diced	4 medium tomatoes
1 green bell pepper, seeded,	1 tablespoon butter or margarine
cut in strips	
1-3/4 lbs. small potatoes,	
peeled	

Preheat oven to 400F (205C). Wash fish inside and out with cold water; cut off fins. Pat fish dry. Sprinkle with lemon juice, then sprinkle inside and out with salt. Place dill sprig in fish cavity. Set fish aside. In a large skillet, cook bacon until crisp. Scrape cooked bacon and drippings into a baking pan; distribute evenly over pan bottom. Place fish on 1 side of pan; arrange bell pepper and potatoes next to fish. Sprinkle vegetables with salt, white pepper and paprika. Pour wine around vegetables and fish. Cover and bake on next-to-lowest oven rack about 40 minutes or until potatoes are fork-tender and fish turns from transparent to opaque. Meanwhile, cut a cross in stem end of each tomato; sprinkle with salt and dot with butter or margarine. Place tomatoes in pan with fish during last 10 minutes of baking. Makes 4 servings.

Flounder with Bacon

4 (about 8-oz.) flounder	2 tablespoons chopped parsley
fillets	Freshly ground white pepper
4 teaspoons lemon juice	to taste
3 bacon slices, finely diced	Salt to taste
4 small onions, diced	1/4 cup all-purpose flour
1/4 lb. small fresh mushrooms,	1/2 cup butter or margarine
chopped	

Wash fish in cold water, pat dry and sprinkle with lemon juice. Set aside. In a small skillet, cook bacon until crisp. Remove from pan; add onions to drippings and cook, stirring frequently, until golden. Return cooked bacon to pan with mushrooms and parsley; cook, stirring, until mushrooms are soft. Season with white pepper, cover and keep warm over lowest heat. Sprinkle fish with salt, then dip in flour to coat both sides; shake off any excess. Melt 2 tablespoons butter or margarine in a large skillet; add 1 fish fillet and cook about 4 minutes on each side or until fish turns from transparent to opaque. Transfer to a warm plate, top with 1/4 of mushroom mixture and keep warm. Repeat with remaining 6 tablespoons butter or margarine, remaining 3 fish fillets and remaining mushroom mixture. Makes 4 servings.

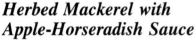

Herbed Mackerel with Apple-Horseradish Sauce

2 bunches mixed fresh herbs, such as parsley, chives, thyme, rosemary and sage	Salt and freshly ground white pepper to taste
1 tablespoon butter or margarine, room temperature	4 small tomatoes 2 (9 oz.) smoked mackerel

Apple-Horseradish Sauce:

1-2 teaspoons lemon juice	2/3 cup whipping cream
About 1-1/2 tablespoons grated fresh horseradish	1 large apple

Preheat oven to 400F (205C). Trim herb stems; then wash herbs in cold water, shake dry and coarsely chop. Blend 1 teaspoon chopped herbs with butter or margarine; season with salt and white pepper. Cut a deep cross in stem end of each tomato; fill each cross with 1/4 of herb butter. Place fish in center of a large sheet of foil; sprinkle with remaining chopped herbs. Arrange tomatoes next to fish. Bring up all sides of foil to enclose fish and tomatoes loosely. Place in a baking pan; bake 15 to 20 minutes.
To make sauce, in a small bowl, stir together lemon juice, horseradish and cream. Peel, core and finely grate apple; stir into cream mixture.
To serve, place 1 tomato and a portion of fish on each individual plate. Pass sauce at the table. Makes 4 servings.

Pike Cooked in Stock

1 (2-1/4-lb.) cleaned, dressed pike	1 teaspoon mustard seeds 1/2 teaspoon white peppercorns
2-1/2 qts. water (10 cups)	Pinch of salt
1/3 cup white-wine vinegar	1/2 cup butter
1 onion, cut in quarters	1 teaspoon lime juice
1 celery stalk, chopped	2 tablespoons chopped parsley
Small dill sprig	Small parsley sprigs
1 bay leaf	1/2 lemon, sliced

Wash fish inside and out with cold water; set aside. In a large saucepan, bring 2-1/2 quarts water and vinegar to a boil. Add onion, celery, dill sprig, bay leaf, mustard seeds, peppercorns and salt. Reduce heat, cover and simmer 15 minutes. Place fish in simmering stock; cover and simmer 40 to 45 minutes or until fish turns from transparent to opaque. Do not allow stock to boil.
To serve, melt butter in a small saucepan; stir in lime juice and chopped parsley. Lift fish from stock, drain briefly and transfer to a warm platter. Sprinkle a few drops of the melted-butter mixture over fish; serve remaining melted-butter mixture separately. Garnish fish with parsley sprig and lemon slices. Makes 4 servings.

Trout with Bacon

4 (about 8-oz.) cleaned,
   dressed trout
Juice of 1 lemon
Salt to taste
1 (3-oz.) pkg. cream cheese,
   room temperature
2 tablespoons milk
1 garlic clove, finely chopped
4 teaspoons chopped fresh dill

4 teaspoons chopped parsley
12 thin bacon slices
1 tablespoon butter or margarine
2 shallots, peeled,
   finely chopped
2/3 cup homemade or
   canned chicken stock
About 1/2 teaspoon chopped
   fresh rosemary

Preheat oven to 425F (220C). Wash fish inside and out with cold water; pat dry. Season lemon juice with salt and rub mixture into both sides of each fish. Set fish aside. In a small bowl, beat cream cheese and milk until smooth; stir in garlic, dill and parsley. Spoon 1/4 of cream-cheese mixture into body cavity of each fish. Wrap each fish in 3 bacon slices. Arrange bacon-wrapped fish side by side in a large baking dish; bake on center oven rack about 20 minutes. Meanwhile, melt butter or margarine in a small skillet; add shallots and cook, stirring, until soft. Stir in stock and rosemary; simmer gently 5 minutes. After fish have baked 20 minutes, pour stock mixture over them; bake 10 minutes longer or until fish turns from transparent to opaque. Makes 4 servings.

Foil-Baked Cod

1 (1-3/4-lb.) piece cod
Juice of 1 lemon
Salt and freshly ground white
   pepper to taste
1 teaspoon Dijon-style mustard
1/4 lb. leeks
2 bunches green onions, sliced

1/4 lb. carrots, peeled,
   cut in julienne strips
About 1/2 cup chopped parsley
2 tablespoons butter or
   margarine
3 bacon slices

Preheat oven to 425F (220C). Wash fish inside and out with cold water; pat dry. Sprinkle inside and out with lemon juice; rub with salt and white pepper. Spread mustard over outside of fish, then set fish aside. Trim roots and green tops of leeks, then split leeks lengthwise and wash thoroughly to remove sand. Slice leek halves crosswise. In a bowl, mix leeks, green onions and carrots. Lightly grease a large sheet of foil; lay fish in center of foil. Spoon 1/2 of vegetable mixture into cavity of fish; combine remaining mixture with parsley and sprinkle over fish. Dot with butter or margarine, then top with bacon. Bring up all sides of foil to enclose fish loosely. Place in a baking pan; bake about 40 minutes or until fish turns from transparent to opaque. Makes 4 servings.

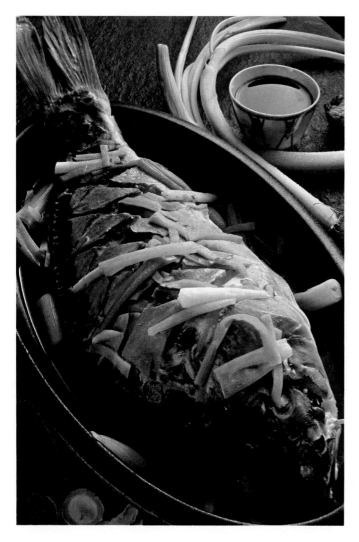

Chinese-Style Carp

1 (2-lb.) cleaned, dressed carp	2 tablespoons vegetable oil
Salt to taste	1 teaspoon sugar
1 tablespoon soy sauce	1 tablespoon shredded fresh gingerroot
2 tablespoons dry sherry	2 green onions

Wash fish inside and out with cold water; remove any large scales. Pat fish dry. Using a sharp knife, score both sides of fish in a diagonal crisscross pattern, making cuts 1/4 inch deep and 1/2 inch apart. Sprinkle fish inside and out with salt; place in a heatproof dish that will fit inside a large steamer. Stir together soy sauce, sherry, oil and sugar. Sprinkle soy-sauce mixture and gingerroot over fish. Cut green onions in 2-inch lengths; arrange over fish. Fill steamer with water to just below rack; bring to a boil. Water should not bubble up through rack. Place dish with fish on steamer rack; cover and steam 15 to 20 minutes or until fish turns from transparent to opaque. Add more boiling water to steamer if necessary. Lift rack from steamer. Slide hot dish with fish on another, slightly larger dish for easier handling. Makes 4 servings.

Blue Trout

4 (about 8-oz.) trout	2 parsley sprigs
1 leek	2/3 cup dry white wine
1 onion, thinly sliced, separated into rings	1/4 cup white-wine vinegar
1 celery stalk, sliced	1 lime
2 dill sprigs	1/2 bunch parsley
	1/2 cup butter or margarine

Clean trout, but do not remove heads and tails. Wash trout inside and out with cold water; be careful not to damage the outermost layer, which gives the fish its blue color. Set fish aside. Trim roots and green top of leek, then split leek lengthwise and wash thoroughly to remove sand. Slice leek halves crosswise. In a large saucepan, bring about 3 quarts lightly salted water to a boil. Add leek, onion, celery, dill sprigs and parsley sprigs; reduce heat and simmer 10 minutes. Stir in wine and vinegar; bring to a boil. Lower fish into boiling stock; reduce heat, cover and simmer 12 minutes. Meanwhile, thinly slice lime; set aside. Trim parsley stems, then wash parsley in cold water, shake dry and separate into sprigs. Set aside. In a small saucepan, heat butter or margarine until slightly browned; pour into a serving dish and keep warm.

To serve, lift fish from stock, drain and arrange on a warm platter. Garnish with lime slices and parsley sprigs. Pass browned butter at the table to spoon over fish. Makes 4 servings.

Redfish with Tomatoes

1-3/4 lbs. redfish fillets	6 bacon slices, finely diced
1 teaspoon lemon juice	1 onion, finely diced
Salt to taste	1/4 cup dry white wine
6 tomatoes	

Sauce:

1/2 cup mayonnaise	2 shallots, peeled,
3 tablespoons plain low-fat	finely chopped
yogurt	4 teaspoons Dijon-style mustard
1 hard-cooked egg,	Salt and freshly ground pepper
finely chopped	to taste

Preheat oven to 400F (205C). Lightly oil a baking dish. Wash fish in cold water, pat dry and sprinkle with lemon juice and salt. Cut a cross in stem end of 4 tomatoes; sprinkle lightly with salt; then arrange in oiled baking dish with fish. Set aside. Peel, seed and dice remaining 2 tomatoes; set aside. In a large skillet, cook bacon until crisp. Remove from pan; add onion to drippings and cook, stirring frequently, until golden. Return cooked bacon to pan with diced tomatoes; stir well. Stir in wine, then pour mixture over fish. Bake 10 to 15 minutes or until fish turns from transparent to opaque. Meanwhile, prepare sauce.
To make sauce, in a small bowl, stir together mayonnaise, yogurt, hard-cooked egg, shallots, mustard, salt and pepper.
To serve, place 1 tomato and a portion of fish on each individual plate. Pass sauce separately. Makes 4 servings.

Cod in Mustard Sauce

1-3/4 lbs. cod fillets	1 teaspoon paprika
Juice of 1 lemon	1/2 lemon, thinly sliced
Salt to taste	Parsley sprigs

Mustard Sauce:

2 tablespoons butter or	Salt and freshly ground pepper
margarine	to taste
1 tablespoon all-purpose flour	1/8 teaspoon ground nutmeg
1 cup milk	1 tablespoon chopped parsley
2 tablespoons prepared mustard	

Preheat oven to 425F (220C). Grease a baking dish. Wash fish in cold water, pat dry and sprinkle with lemon juice and salt. Place fish in greased baking dish, sprinkle with paprika and set aside.
To make sauce, melt 1 tablespoon butter or margarine in a saucepan. Sprinkle in flour and cook over low heat, stirring about 1 minute. Gradually add milk, stirring constantly; continue to cook, stirring, until sauce is bubbly and slightly thickened. Stir in mustard, salt, pepper, nutmeg and chopped parsley. Remove from heat.
To complete, pour sauce over fish and dot with remaining 1 tablespoon butter or margarine. Bake on center oven rack about 15 minutes or until fish turns from transparent to opaque. Garnish baked fish with lemon slices and parsley sprigs. Makes 4 servings.

Haddock with Mushrooms

1-3/4 lbs. haddock fillets	Onion salt, freshly ground white
Juice of 1 lemon	pepper and soy sauce
Salt to taste	to taste
3 bacon slices, diced	Parsley sprigs
1/2 lb. small fresh mushrooms	1 lemon, cut in wedges
2/3 cup dry white wine	1 tomato, sliced
1/2 cup half and half	1 tablespoon chopped chives

Preheat oven to 425F (220C). Grease a baking dish. Wash fish in cold water, pat dry and sprinkle with lemon juice and salt. Place fish in greased baking dish; set aside. In a skillet, fry bacon until crisp. Drain and set aside. Cut larger mushrooms in halves or quarters; leave smaller ones whole. Spoon mushrooms over fish; sprinkle with cooked bacon, then pour wine into dish. Cover and bake on center oven rack about 15 minutes or until fish turns from transparent to opaque. Lift fish from baking dish, place on a warm platter and keep warm. Stir half and half into mushrooms and cooking juices in baking dish; season with onion salt, white pepper and soy sauce. Pour sauce over fish.
To serve, garnish fish with parsley sprigs, lemon wedges and tomato slices; sprinkle with chives. Makes 4 servings.

Salmon Steaks with Mixed Vegetables

4 (8-oz.) salmon steaks	1/2 teaspoon salt
Juice of 1 lemon	1 bay leaf
2 cups plus 2 tablespoons water	3 black peppercorns
2/3 cup white-wine vinegar	1 (16-oz.) pkg. frozen mixed
1/2 lemon, sliced	vegetables
1 onion, thinly sliced	

Sauce:

1 tablespoon cornstarch mixed	1 tablespoon chopped fresh dill
with 2 tablespoons cold water	1 tablespoon chopped parsley
1 tomato, peeled, seeded, diced	1/4 teaspoon sugar
1/4 cup half and half	Salt to taste

Wash fish in cold water, pat dry and sprinkle with lemon juice. Set aside. In a large saucepan, combine water, vinegar, lemon slices, onion, 1/2 teaspoon salt, bay leaf and peppercorns. Bring to a boil; boil 10 minutes. Add fish, reduce heat, cover and simmer about 10 minutes or until fish turns from transparent to opaque. Meanwhile cook mixed vegetables according to package directions. Drain vegetables; place in a warm serving dish. Lift cooked fish from stock; arrange on top of vegetables. Cover; keep warm in a 200F (95C) oven. Strain stock.
To make sauce, pour 1 cup stock into a small saucepan. Stir in cornstarch mixture. Bring to a boil, stirring; stir in tomato, half and half, parsley, dill, sugar and salt. Heat through.
To serve, spoon sauce over fish. Makes 4 servings.

Pickled Herring

4 cleaned, dressed fresh herring	1/4 cup all-purpose flour
1/4 cup fresh lemon juice	6 tablespoons vegetable oil
Salt to taste	

Pickling Liquid:

2 cups plus 2 tablespoons white-wine vinegar	8 black peppercorns
	2 whole allspice
2 cups plus 2 tablespoons water	1/2 lb. onions, thinly sliced,
3 bay leaves	separated into rings

Wash fish inside and out with cold water; pat dry. Sprinkle fish cavities with lemon juice; then sprinkle fish inside and out with salt. Let fish stand a few minutes to dry slightly. Dip fish in flour to coat both sides; shake off excess. Heat oil in a skillet. Cook fish, 1 at a time, about 6 minutes on each side. (Turn fish carefully; the flesh is fairly fragile and will break easily.) Transfer cooked fish to a large, shallow dish; cool.

To make pickling liquid, in a large saucepan, combine vinegar, water, bay leaves, peppercorns and allspice. Bring to a boil; stir in onions and boil 5 minutes. Remove pan from heat. Cool pickling liquid, then pour over cooled fish. Cover and refrigerate 24 hours. Makes 4 servings.

Dutch-Style Fried Herring

4 cleaned, dressed fresh young herring	1/4 cup all-purpose flour
	1/4 cup vegetable oil
Salt and freshly ground white pepper to taste	

Wash fish inside and out with cold water and pat dry. Mix salt and white pepper; rub into fish inside and out. Dip fish in flour to coat both sides; shake off excess. Heat oil in a large skillet; add fish and cook about 6 minutes on each side or until browned and crisp. Makes 4 servings.

House-Style Salted Herring

4 salted herring fillets	2 dill pickles, sliced
1 large onion, thinly sliced, separated into rings	1 tablespoon chopped mixed fresh herbs, such as
1 tart apple	parsley, dill and rosemary

Creamy Dressing:

2/3 cup dairy sour cream	1 teaspoon Dijon-style mustard
2/3 cup plain low-fat yogurt	1 teaspoon sugar
1/4 cup half and half	1 to 2 teaspoons lemon juice
1/2 teaspoon mustard seeds	

Soak herring in cold water overnight. Drain, pat dry and cut in 1-inch-wide strips. Set aside. Place onion in a wire strainer; lower into a saucepan filled with boiling water and blanch 2 minutes. Drain, rinse under cold running water and drain again. Set aside. Quarter and core apple; slice each quarter crosswise. Place herring, onion, apple and pickles in a bowl; set aside.
To make dressing, in a small bowl, beat together sour cream, yogurt, half and half, mustard seeds, mustard and sugar. Stir in enough lemon juice to give a distinct sweet-sour flavor.
To complete, pour dressing over herring mixture; mix gently, cover and refrigerate 2 to 3 days. Sprinkle with herbs before serving. Makes 4 servings.

Salted Herring in Yogurt Sauce

6 salted herring fillets	10 pimento-stuffed green olives, sliced
1 tart apple	
2 dill pickles, cut in julienne strips	2 tablespoons chopped fresh dill

Yogurt Sauce:

2/3 cup half and half	1 teaspoon sugar
2/3 cup plain low-fat yogurt	1/8 teaspoon freshly ground white pepper
1 tablespoon white-wine vinegar	

Soak herring in cold water overnight. Drain, pat dry and cut in 1-inch squares. Set aside. Cut apple in wedges; core wedges and slice crosswise. Combine herring, apple, pickles and olives in a large bowl. Set aside.
To make sauce, in a small bowl, beat together half and half, yogurt, vinegar, sugar and white pepper.
To complete, pour sauce over herring mixture; mix gently. Cover and refrigerate 24 hours. Sprinkle with dill before serving. Makes 4 servings.

Cook's tip

If desired, do not use olives; instead, stir in 1/2 to 1 banana, sliced and liberally sprinkled with lemon juice, just before serving.

Classic Steaks

4 (7-oz.) tenderloin or
   sirloin steaks,
   cut 1 inch thick
1/4 cup vegetable oil
Salt and freshly ground white
   pepper to taste
1 large onion, thinly sliced
   and sautéed (optional)

Slash edge fat of steaks at about 1-inch intervals to prevent curling. Heat a large skillet until hot; add 1 tablespoon oil for each steak (you may need to cook steaks in batches). Reduce heat, add steaks and cook 1 minute on each side. Reduce heat even further; cook steaks 1 to 4 minutes longer on each side. (For rare steaks, cook only 1 to 2 minutes total on each side; for well-done steaks, cook about 5 minutes total on each side.) Sprinkle steaks with salt and white pepper. Top with sautéed onion, if desired. Makes 4 servings.

Variations

Tournedos (lower left of photograph): Tournedos are cut from the narrow end of the tenderloin; a 1-1/4-inch-thick steak should weigh only about 4-1/2 oz. Before cooking tournedos, tie string around the sides so meat will hold its shape and cook evenly. Cook tournedos over medium heat 5 to 6 minutes on each side or until done to your liking; serve with herb butter.

Porterhouse Steaks (top left of photograph): Porterhouse steaks contain a section of rib bone; the tenderloin is the largest section of muscle. These steaks weigh about 1-3/4 lbs. To cook, brush with oil; cook over medium heat 5 to 7 minutes on each side or until done to your liking. Top with sautéed mushrooms, if desired.

Entrecôte Cavour
(Italian-Style Rib Steak)

1/4 lb. bone marrow	Salt and freshly ground pepper
1/4 cup vegetable oil	to taste
2 onions, thinly sliced,	10 bottled cocktail onions
separated into rings	2 tablespoons butter or
3 tomatoes, peeled, seeded,	margarine
diced	3 tablespoons chopped parsley
4 (7-oz.) rib steaks	

In a small saucepan, bring a small amount of lightly salted water to a boil. Cut marrow in 4 equal slices, place in a wire strainer, lower into boiling water and boil 3 minutes. Lift out; cool. Heat 1 tablespoon oil in a large skillet. Add onion; cook until golden, stirring frequently. Stir in tomatoes; cook 5 minutes longer, stirring often. Remove onion rings and tomatoes from skillet and keep warm. Heat remaining 3 tablespoons oil in skillet; add steaks and cook 3 minutes on each side or until done to your liking. Transfer steaks to warm plates; sprinkle with salt and pepper and keep warm. Add cocktail onions to pan juices; heat through.

To serve, spoon marrow and cocktail onions over steaks; top with onion-tomato mixture. Melt butter or margarine in skillet; sprinkle melted butter or margarine and parsley over steaks. Makes 4 servings.

Flambéed Pepper Steak

4 (7-oz.) tenderloin steaks	Salt to taste
1 tablespoon black peppercorns	3 tablespoons cognac
3 tablespoons vegetable oil	2 tablespoons butter or
1 small onion, finely diced	margarine

Trim any excess fat from steaks. Tie string around sides of steaks so meat will hold its shape and cook evenly. Coarsely crush peppercorns with a mortar and pestle, or place between 2 sheets of wax paper and roll with a rolling pin until crushed. Lightly brush both sides of each steak with oil, then sprinkle steaks with crushed peppercorns. Heat remaining oil in a large skillet. When oil is very hot, add steaks and cook 2 minutes. Turn steaks over; add onion. Cook until onion is soft and steaks are done to your liking, stirring onion frequently. Sprinkle steaks with salt.

To serve, pour cognac into a small saucepan and warm over a low flame. Pour warmed cognac over steaks; carefully ignite. Let flames die down. Add butter or margarine; heat until melted. Turn steaks to coat with pan juices, then transfer to warm plates. Spoon sauce from pan over steaks. Makes 4 servings.

Viennese Tafelspitz

1 large onion
2 whole cloves
1 bay leaf
5 black peppercorns
2-1/4 lbs. beef top round
2 large carrots
2 leeks
1/2 medium celeriac
Salt to taste

Cut unpeeled onion in half; stick cloves into 1 half. In a large saucepan, bring 2-1/2 quarts lightly salted water to a boil; add onion halves, bay leaf, peppercorns and beef. Reduce heat slightly and simmer briskly 20 minutes, skimming and discarding any scum that forms on surface of water. Then reduce heat to low; simmer, uncovered, 1-1/2 hours. Meanwhile, peel carrots and cut lengthwise in quarters; cut each quarter in half crosswise. Trim roots and green tops of leeks, then split leeks lengthwise and wash thoroughly to remove sand. Cut leek halves crosswise in thick slices. Peel and dice celeriac. After meat has simmered 1-1/2 hours, add carrots, leeks and celeriac to pan. Cover; simmer 30 minutes longer or until meat and vegetables are tender. **To serve,** cut meat across the grain in thick slices; arrange on a warm platter. Arrange vegetables alongside meat. Strain stock, then skim and discard fat and season stock with salt. Spoon some of the strained stock over meat and vegetables to moisten. Makes 6 servings.

Rolled Beef with Mushroom Filling

2-1/4 lbs. chuck steak	Salt and freshly ground pepper
3 tablespoons vegetable oil	1 teaspoon dry mustard
6 bacon slices, diced	About 2 cups beef stock
1/2 lb. mushrooms, thinly sliced	2/3 cup half and half
1 onion, finely chopped	1 teaspoon cornstarch mixed with
1/2 teaspoon dried leaf thyme	2 teaspoons cold water

Place steak between 2 large sheets of plastic wrap. With a mallet, pound steak firmly and evenly to flatten. Set aside. Heat 1 teaspoon oil in a skillet. Add bacon; cook until crisp. Remove bacon from pan. Add mushrooms to drippings; cook, stirring, 3 minutes. Stir in cooked bacon; set aside. Mix onion, thyme, salt, pepper, mustard and 1 teaspoon oil. Spread over meat; spread 3/4 of mushroom mixture over meat. Roll up meat; tie in several places with string. Heat remaining oil in a large saucepan; add rolled meat and brown on all sides. Add about 1 cup of stock. Bring to a simmer; cover and simmer 1 to 1-1/4 hours or until tender, adding stock as needed and turning meat roll occasionally. About 5 minutes before end of cooking time, stir in half and half and remaining 1/4 of mushroom mixture.

To serve, lift meat roll from pan and transfer to a warm platter; keep warm. Stir cornstarch mixture into pan; cook, stirring, until sauce is thickened. Spoon some of the sauce over meat roll; pass remaining sauce at the table. To carve meat, cut crosswise in thick slices. Makes 6 servings.

Rolled Beef with Ham

4 (5-oz.) slices chuck steak	1/4 teaspoon dried leaf marjoram
1 small bunch mixed herbs, such as parsley, chives and basil	1/4 teaspoon dried leaf lovage
	Salt and freshly ground pepper
	4 (1-oz.) slices lean cooked ham
1 small leek	2 tablespoons vegetable oil
1 onion, finely chopped	1-3/4 cups beef stock
1 garlic clove, finely chopped	

Place each slice of steak between 2 sheets of plastic wrap. With a mallet, pound firmly and evenly to flatten. Set aside. Trim herb stems. Wash herbs in cold water; shake dry and finely chop. Set aside. Trim off roots and green top of leek, then split leek lengthwise and wash thoroughly to remove sand. Thinly slice leek halves crosswise. In a small bowl, mix leek, onion, garlic, marjoram, lovage, salt and pepper. Trim away any excess fat from ham slices. Place a slice of ham on each steak; spread leek mixture over ham. Roll up steak slices; tie securely with string or fasten with wooden picks. Heat oil in a saucepan. Add chopped herbs; cook briefly. Add beef rolls; brown on all sides. Add 1/2 of stock; bring to a simmer. Cover and simmer 50 to 60 minutes or until tender, adding remaining stock as necessary.

To serve, remove string or wooden picks; place meat rolls on a platter or individual plates. Skim and discard fat from pan juices; spoon juices over meat rolls. Makes 4 servings.

Beef Stroganoff

1-3/4 lbs. beef tenderloin
2 sweet dill pickles
1/4 cup canned sliced beets
3 tablespoons vegetable oil
2 onions, thinly sliced,
  separated into rings
1/2 cup small fresh mushrooms,
  very thinly sliced

2 tablespoons capers
1 teaspoon sugar
Salt and freshly ground pepper
  to taste
1/4 cup dairy sour cream

Trim any excess fat from beef, then cut meat in strips and set aside. Pare outer skin from pickles; cut pickles in julienne strips. Drain and dice beets. Set pickles and beets aside. Heat oil in a large skillet; add onions and cook until golden brown, stirring frequently. Remove onions from pan. Add meat, a portion at a time, and brown on all sides. When last portion of meat has been browned, return all meat to pan with onions, mushrooms, pickles, beets, capers and sugar. Stir well. Cover and cook over low heat 10 minutes, stirring occasionally.

To serve, season with salt and pepper. Stir in sour cream; heat through, but do not boil. Makes 4 servings.

North German Pepper Pot

1/4 lb. lean cooked ham
1-1/3 lbs. beef round steak
3 tablespoons vegetable oil
2 onions, sliced, separated
  into rings
1 tablespoon paprika

Salt and freshly ground black
  pepper to taste
1 red chili pepper
1 cup dry red wine
1/2 lb. potatoes
1 to 1-1/2 teaspoons sugar

Trim any excess fat from ham; cut ham in 1-inch cubes. Cut steak in 1-inch cubes. Heat oil in large saucepan over high heat. Add onions, ham and beef; cook 5 minutes, stirring constantly. Stir in paprika, salt, black pepper, chili pepper and wine. Reduce heat, cover and simmer 40 minutes. Peel potatoes and cut in 1-inch cubes; stir into stew. Simmer, uncovered, 20 minutes longer or until beef and potatoes are tender. Season with sugar; add more salt and black pepper, if desired. Makes 4 servings.

Beef Stew with Corn

1-1/4 lbs. beef stew meat	1 bay leaf
3 tablespoons vegetable oil	Pinch of red (cayenne) pepper
3 onions, diced	2/3 cup beef stock
1 garlic clove, diced	1 (8-oz.) can whole-kernel
1 green bell pepper, seeded,	corn, drained
cut in strips	4 sweet dill pickles, diced
1 red bell pepper, seeded,	2/3 cup whipping cream
cut in strips	
Salt and freshly ground black	
pepper to taste	

Cut beef in 1-1/2-inch cubes; set aside. Heat oil in a large saucepan; add onions and garlic. Cook, stirring, until onions are soft. Remove from pan. Add beef and brown on all sides. Return onions to pan with bell peppers, salt, black pepper, bay leaf, red pepper and stock. Stir well. Reduce heat, cover and simmer 1-1/4 to 1-1/2 hours or until meat is tender, adding hot water as needed. Stir in corn and pickles about 10 minutes before end of cooking time.

To serve, remove bay leaf. Stir cream into stew; heat through. Add more salt and black pepper, if desired. Makes 4 servings.

Oxtail Stew

2 tablespoons olive oil	2 celery stalks, cut in
3 bacon slices, diced	1-1/2-inch lengths
1 onion, finely chopped	4 tomatoes
1 garlic clove, finely chopped	Salt and freshly ground pepper
2 lbs. oxtail, cut in	to taste
2-inch lengths	1 tablespoon chopped parsley,
1 cup dry white wine	if desired
1 to 2 cups beef stock	

Heat oil in a large saucepan. Add bacon, onion and garlic; cook, stirring, until onion is soft. Add oxtail pieces; brown on all sides. Stir in wine. Reduce heat, cover and simmer 1-1/2 hours, shaking pan occasionally and adding stock as needed. Stir in celery; cook 20 minutes longer. Peel and quarter tomatoes. Stir into stew; cook 10 minutes longer or until meat is tender.

To serve, skim and discard fat from stew. Season with salt and pepper, then sprinkle with parsley, if desired. Makes 4 servings.

Roast Beef

1 (2-lb.) beef sirloin
  tip roast
Freshly ground white pepper
  to taste
2 tablespoons Worcestershire
  sauce

1/4 cup vegetable oil
2 tablespoons cognac
1/2 teaspoon red (cayenne)
  pepper
Salt to taste

Score fat on top of beef in a crisscross pattern. Place beef in a deep bowl. In a small bowl, mix white pepper, Worcestershire sauce, 3 tablespoons oil, cognac and red pepper; pour evenly over meat. Cover and refrigerate 1 hour, turning meat over occasionally. Preheat oven to 475F (245C). Brush a roasting rack with remaining 1 tablespoon oil; rinse roasting pan in cold water. Lift meat from marinade and pat dry; rub with salt. Place meat on rack in roasting pan. Roast on next-to-lowest oven rack 25 minutes or until a meat thermometer inserted in thickest part registers 140F (60C) for rare.

To serve, lift meat from pan, transfer to a warm platter and let stand about 10 minutes. Meanwhile, skim and discard fat from pan juices. Thinly slice meat across the grain; pour juices over meat. Makes 6 servings.

Roast Beef with Mustard

2 lbs. beef rump roast
Salt and freshly ground pepper
  to taste
1/4 cup orange marmalade
1/4 cup applesauce
1/4 cup prepared mustard
2 to 3 tablespoons raspberry or
  other fruit vinegar

1 teaspoon finely chopped
  fresh thyme
1 tablespoon chopped parsley
2/3 cup dry white wine
1 cup beef stock
1/4 lb. celeriac
1 small carrot, peeled, diced
2 onions, diced
1/4 cup whipping cream

Preheat oven to 325F (160C). Rub beef with salt and pepper. In a small bowl, stir together marmalade, applesauce, mustard, vinegar, thyme and parsley. Spread mixture thickly over top of meat. Place meat in a roasting pan. Roast on center oven rack 20 minutes; then pour 1/3 cup wine and 1/2 cup stock around meat. Roast 20 minutes longer. Peel and dice celeriac; sprinkle around meat with carrot and onions. Pour in remaining 1/2 cup stock. Roast about 30 minutes longer or until meat is tender.

To serve, lift meat from roasting pan, transfer to a warm platter and let stand about 10 minutes. Meanwhile, dilute pan juices with a little hot water. Strain juices into a saucepan; skim and discard fat. Stir in cream and remaining 1/3 cup wine; heat, stirring, until sauce is slightly thickened. Slice meat across the grain; pass sauce to accompany meat. Makes 6 servings.

Sweet & Sour Beef with Red-Wine Sauce

1-3/4 lbs. beef top round
1 carrot, peeled,
**   coarsely chopped**
1 celeriac, peeled,
**   coarsely chopped**
1 bay leaf
4 whole allspice
4 black peppercorns
Thyme sprig
2 cups red Burgundy wine
2/3 cup red-wine vinegar
1 cup water
Salt and freshly ground pepper
**   to taste**
3 bacon slices, diced
1/4 cup vegetable oil
2 tablespoons tomato paste
Sugar and red-wine vinegar
**   to taste**

Place beef in a large, deep bowl. Sprinkle with carrot, celeriac, bay leaf, allspice, peppercorns and thyme sprig. Pour in wine. In a saucepan, bring 2/3 cup vinegar and water to a boil; remove from heat. Cool, then pour over meat. Cover and refrigerate 1 to 2 days, turning meat over occasionally. Preheat oven to 425F (220C). Lift meat from marinade; pat dry and rub with salt and pepper. Strain marinade, reserving vegetables and seasonings. In a roasting pan, cook bacon until crisp; remove from pan. Add oil to drippings; when oil is hot, add meat and brown on all sides. Add vegetables and seasonings strained from marinade; then stir in cooked bacon and tomato paste. Gradually stir in strained marinade. Cover roasting pan. Roast on lowest oven rack 2 hours or until meat is very tender.
To serve, lift meat from roasting pan, transfer to a warm platter and let stand about 10 minutes. Meanwhile, strain pan juices; skim and discard fat. Adjust sweet-and-sour flavoring with sugar and vinegar. Slice meat across the grain; spoon pan juices over meat. Makes 4 servings.

Wiener Schnitzel

4 (5-oz.) veal cutlets	2 eggs
Salt and freshly ground white pepper to taste	1 tablespoon water
	1 cup fine dry bread crumbs
About 2 tablespoons all-purpose flour	1/4 cup butter or margarine
	1 lemon

Trim any membrane from veal cutlets. Place each cutlet between 2 sheets of plastic wrap; pound lightly with a flat-surfaced mallet to flatten evenly. Rub salt and white pepper into both sides of each cutlet. Place flour in a shallow dish. In another shallow dish, beat together eggs and water. Place bread crumbs in a third shallow dish. Dip cutlets, 1 at a time, in flour to coat both sides; shake off any excess. Dip in egg mixture, then dip in crumbs to coat both sides. Shake off excess. Melt 2 tablespoons butter or margarine in a large skillet. Add cutlets, reduce heat and cook 3 to 4 minutes. Melt remaining butter or margarine in pan. Turn cutlets over; cook 3 to 4 minutes longer or until browned and crisp. Remove cutlets from pan, transfer to a warm platter or individual plates and keep warm.

To serve, cut 4 center slices from lemon. Squeeze a little juice from remaining lemon into pan juices; stir to mix. Sprinkle each cutlet with a little of the pan juices; garnish each with a lemon slice. Makes 4 servings.

Veal Medallions with Sorrel

4 (4-oz.) veal medallions (veal tenderloin steaks)	2/3 cup plain low-fat yogurt
	2 teaspoons lemon juice
1 cup tender young sorrel leaves	1 teaspoon sugar
1/4 cup butter or margarine	
Salt and freshly ground white pepper to taste	

Tie string around sides of veal medallions so meat with hold its shape. Set aside. Wash sorrel in lukewarm water, shake dry and cut in strips. Set aside. Melt butter or margarine in a large skillet; add veal and cook 4 minutes on each side or until golden brown. Sprinkle with salt and white pepper. Transfer to a warm platter; keep warm. Stir yogurt into pan juices, then stir in sorrel. Heat about 2 minutes over low heat, stirring constantly. Do not allow mixture to boil. Stir in lemon juice, sugar and a little salt, if needed.

To serve, place veal medallions in sauce and turn to coat. Return veal to platter; spoon sauce over veal. Makes 4 servings.

Veal Cutlets in Cream

4 (5-oz.) veal cutlets
3 tablespoons butter or
  margarine
Salt and freshly ground white
  pepper to taste
2/3 cup beef stock
1/3 cup whipping cream
1/8 teaspoon dried leaf lovage

Trim any membrane from veal cutlets. Place each cutlet between
2 sheets of plastic wrap; pound lightly with a flat-surfaced mallet
to flatten evenly. Melt butter or margarine in a large skillet. Add
cutlets; cook 3 to 4 minutes on each side or until golden brown.
Sprinkle with salt and white pepper. Remove cutlets from pan,
transfer to a warm platter or individual plates and keep warm.
To serve, pour stock into pan juices; bring to a simmer. Stir in
cream and bring to a boil. Crumble lovage and stir into sauce.
Season sauce with salt and white pepper. Spoon cream sauce
over cutlets. Makes 4 servings.

Cook's tip

**If you wish, substitute plain low-fat yogurt for half the cream in the sauce. In
this case, do not bring sauce to a boil after adding cream and yogurt; heat
through over low heat, stirring constantly.**

Saltimbocca (Veal Cutlets with Sage)

8 small (2- to 2-1/2 oz.)
  veal cutlets
1/4 lb. prosciutto, cut in 8
  thin slices
8 fresh sage leaves
1/4 cup vegetable oil
Salt and freshly ground white
  pepper to taste
1/4 cup dry white wine
2 tablespoons butter or
  margarine

Trim any membrane from veal cutlets. Place each cutlet between
2 sheets of plastic wrap; pound lightly with a flat-surfaced mallet
to flatten evenly. Top each cutlet with 1 prosciutto slice and 1
sage leaf; hold prosciutto and sage in place with a wooden pick;
see photograph above. Heat oil in a large skillet over medium
heat. Add cutlets, sage-side down; sprinkle with salt and white
pepper. Cook 2 to 3 minutes. Turn cutlets over and cook 2 to 3
minutes longer. Sprinkle about 1 tablespoon wine over cutlets.
Lift cutlets from pan, transfer to warm platter or individual plates
and keep warm.
To serve, add remaining wine and butter or margarine to pan
juices. Heat, stirring, until butter is melted. Pour sauce over
cutlets. Makes 4 servings.

Veal Rolls

4 (4-oz.) slices boneless
  veal round
1 teaspoon prepared mustard
Salt and freshly ground white
  pepper to taste
1/2 lb. ground veal
1 egg, beaten
1 tablespoon chopped parsley
1/4 lb. leeks
3 tablespoons vegetable oil

1/4 lb. carrots, peeled, chopped
1 onion, chopped
1 cup beef stock
1 bay leaf
2 whole cloves
3 black peppercorns
1 teaspoon capers
2/3 cup dry white wine
4 bacon slices

Spread veal slices with mustard; sprinkle with salt and white
pepper. In a bowl, mix ground veal, egg and parsley; spread
mixture on veal slices. Roll up slices and tie in several places
with string. Set aside. Trim roots and green tops of leeks, then
split leeks lengthwise and wash thoroughly to remove sand.
Chop leek halves; set aside. Heat oil in a large skillet; add veal
rolls and brown on all sides. Remove from pan. Add leeks,
carrots and onion to pan; cook, stirring, until onion is soft.
Return veal rolls to pan. Stir in stock, bay leaf, cloves, peppercorns and capers. Reduce heat, cover and simmer about 30
minutes or until meat is tender, adding wine as needed.
To serve, in a medium skillet, cook bacon until crisp. Drain; set
aside. Lift veal rolls onto a warm platter; remove string. Strain
cooking juices; pour over veal rolls. Garnish with bacon. Makes
4 servings.

Osso Buco
(Braised Veal Shanks)

4 lbs. meaty veal shanks,
  cut through bone in
  4 to 8 pieces
All-purpose flour
Salt and freshly ground white
  pepper to taste
Pinch of dried leaf marjoram
1/4 cup butter or margarine

1 onion, sliced, separated
  into rings
1 garlic clove, finely chopped
1/4 cup dry white wine
1 (1-inch) square orange peel
1 (1-inch) square lemon peel
About 1 cup beef stock
Pinch of ground nutmeg

Dip veal pieces in flour to coat lightly; shake off excess. Sprinkle
veal with salt, white pepper and marjoram. Melt 2 tablespoons
butter or margarine in a large skillet; add veal and brown on all
sides. Remove from pan. Add onion and garlic and cook, stirring, until onion is soft. Return veal to pan. Stir in wine, orange
peel, lemon peel, and 1/3 cup stock. Reduce heat, cover and
simmer about 1-1/2 hours or until meat is tender; add more stock
as needed.
To serve, lift cooked veal from pan, transfer to a warm platter
and keep warm. Strain pan juices; skim and discard fat. Add
remaining 2 tablespoons butter or margarine to strained juices;
heat, stirring, until melted. Season with nutmeg and a little salt,
if desired. Spoon sauce over veal. Makes 4 servings.

Zurich-Style Veal Stew

1 tablespoon all-purpose flour
1 tablespoon butter or
  margarine, room temperature
1/4 cup vegetable oil
1-1/4 lbs. veal stew meat,
  cut in thin slices
1 onion, finely diced
3/4 lb. small fresh mushrooms,
  thinly sliced
2/3 cup dry white wine
1/2 pint half and half (1 cup)
Salt and freshly ground white
  pepper to taste
1 tablespoon chopped mixed
  fresh herbs, such as
  parsley, chives and sage

Thoroughly mix flour with butter or margarine; set aside. Heat oil in a large skillet. Add veal, a portion at a time, and brown on all sides. Remove meat when it is cooked, keep warm. Add onion to pan drippings; cook, stirring, until soft. Add mushrooms and cook until soft, stirring frequently. Stir in wine and half and half; then add flour-butter mixture and stir until dissolved. Cook a few minutes, stirring constantly; season with salt and white pepper. Mix in meat and any juices that have drained into bowl; heat through.

To serve, sprinkle stew with herbs. Makes 4 servings.

Cook's tip

There are several recipes for Zurich-Style Veal Stew; not all versions include mushrooms. If you don't have fresh mushrooms, it's best simply to omit them—don't substitute canned mushrooms. The traditional accompaniment for this stew is Potato Cake, page 124.

Roast Veal Knuckle

3 onions
1 bunch mixed herbs,
  such as parsley,
  chives and basil
1 bay leaf
3 juniper berries
3 white peppercorns
1 (2-lb.) meaty veal knuckle
  (heel of round)
Salt and pepper to taste

1/2 teaspoon hot paprika
2 tablespoons vegetable oil
2 tablespoons butter or
  margarine
1/2 lb. mushrooms, sliced
1 lb. zucchini, diced
4 tomatoes, cut in quarters
1/8 teaspooon dried leaf basil
1/8 teaspoon dried leaf thyme
1/2 cup whipping cream

Cut 1 unpeeled onion in half. In a large saucepan, combine 3 quarts salted water, herbs, onion halves, bay leaf, juniper berries and peppercorns. Bring to a boil. Add veal; reduce heat. Simmer 30 minutes. Lift meat from pan; strain and reserve stock. Preheat oven to 425F (220C). Pat meat dry; rub with salt, pepper and paprika. Heat oil in a roasting pan on top of range; add meat and brown on all sides. Roast 45 minutes or until a meat thermometer inserted in thickest part registers 170F (75C). During roasting, gradually add 2 cups stock to roasting pan. Chop remaining 2 onions. Melt butter or margarine in a saucepan; add onions, mushrooms, zucchini and tomatoes. Cover and cook until tender. Season with salt, pepper, basil and thyme. Place meat on a platter; surround with vegetables. Skim and discard fat from pan juices. Stir cream into juices; heat, stirring, until slightly thickened. Pass sauce separately. Makes 4 servings.

Stuffed Breast of Veal

1 day-old dinner roll
1 cup milk
2 large onions
3/4 lb. mixed ground meat
  (veal, pork and beef)
2 eggs, beaten
Salt and freshly ground pepper
2 tablespoons chopped parsley

1 (2-lb.) boned breast of veal,
  with pocket for stuffing
  cut in it
1/4 cup vegetable oil
2 carrots
1/2 small celeriac
2 cups beef stock
1/4 cup whipping cream

Preheat oven to 425F (220C). Tear roll in small pieces, place in a bowl and pour in milk. Let stand a few minutes. Dice 1 onion. Add diced onion, ground meat, eggs, salt, pepper and parsley to softened roll; mix well. Sprinkle veal with salt and pepper, then stuff with meat mixture. Sew closed with strong thread or dental floss. Heat oil in a roasting pan on top of range. Add stuffed veal; brown on all sides. Roast 1 hour. Peel and chop carrots and celeriac; cut remaining onion in wedges. Arrange vegetables around meat, reduce oven temperature to 400F (205C) and pour a little stock into pan. Roast about 30 minutes or until meat is fork-tender.

To serve, place on a platter; let stand 10 minutes. Strain pan juices into a saucepan; skim and discard fat. Stir remaining stock and cream into juices. Heat, stirring, until slightly thickened. Slice meat across grain; pass sauce separately. Makes 6 servings.

Roast Loin of Veal

1 (3-lb.) rolled veal loin
  roast with kidney
Salt and freshly ground white
  pepper to taste
1/4 cup vegetable oil
2 bunches mixed fresh herbs,
  such as parsley,
  chives and thyme

1 onion, cut in wedges
1 tomato, cut in quarters
1 bay leaf
2 cups beef stock
1 teaspoon paprika
1/4 cup whipping cream

Preheat oven to 400F (205C). Rub veal with salt and white pepper. Heat oil in a roasting pan on top of the range. Add meat; brown on all sides. Then roast on lowest oven rack 30 minutes. Trim herb stems. Wash herbs in cold water, shake dry and coarsely chop. Distribute herbs, onion, tomato and bay leaf in pan around meat. Roast 30 minutes longer, basting meat occasionally with some of stock. Reduce oven temperature to 400F (205C) and roast, basting occasionally, 30 minutes longer or until meat is tender and thermometer inserted in thickest part of meat registers 170F (75C).

To serve, lift meat from pan, transfer to a warm platter and let stand about 10 minutes. Meanwhile, stir remaining stock into pan juices. Strain juices into a saucepan; skim and discard fat. Stir in paprika and cream. Heat, stirring, until sauce is slightly thickened. Slice meat across the grain; pass sauce at the table to accompany meat. Makes 6 servings.

Veal Roast with Herbs

1 (2-lb.) veal rump roast
Salt and white pepper
1 tablespoon chopped parsley
1 tablespoon chopped chives
2 cups beef stock

1 medium cauliflower
1/4 cup butter or margarine
Pinch of ground nutmeg
2 large tomatoes, halved, seeded
2/3 cup whipping cream

Preheat oven to 400F (205C). Rub veal with salt and white pepper. Sprinkle 1/2 of parsley and chives over meat; press in gently. Place meat in a roasting pan; roast 20 minutes or until golden brown, adding stock occasionally. Cover meat with foil; roast 30 minutes. Meanwhile, separate cauliflower into flowerets. Cook in salted water until soft; drain and mash with a fork. Mix butter or margarine, salt and nutmeg into mashed cauliflower. Stuff into tomato halves; arrange in a shallow baking dish. Remove foil from meat. Sprinkle meat with remaining parsley and chives; pour remaining stock in to pan. Bake 10 minutes longer or until a meat thermometer registers 170F (75C). Transfer to warm platter. Bake tomatoes until heated through, about 10 minutes.

To serve, arrange tomatoes around meat; keep warm. Skim and discard fat from pan juices. Add cream and heat, stirring, until slightly thickened. Thinly slice meat across the grain. Pass sauce separately. Makes 4 servings.

Flemish-Style Pork Chops

4 (5-oz.) pork chops
1 large tart apple
3 tablespoons butter or
  margarine

Salt and freshly ground white
  pepper to taste
2 tablespoons chopped fresh mint
2 tablespoons whipping cream

Preheat oven to 400F (205C). Slash edge fat of chops at about 1-inch intervals to prevent curling. With a sharp knife, loosen meat slightly along bone. Peel, quarter and core apple; thinly slice each quarter lengthwise. Heat 2 tablespoons butter or margarine in a large skillet; add chops and cook until well-browned on both sides, seasoning with salt and white pepper after turning. Transfer chops to a baking dish. Add apple slices to drippings in skillet; cook until lightly browned on both sides. Arrange apples on top of chops; dot with remaining 1 tablespoon butter or margarine. Bake on center oven rack 15 minutes or until apples are tender and meat is no longer pink in center.
To serve, stir together mint and cream; spoon over chops. Makes 4 servings.

Pork Chops aux Fines Herbes (Pork Chops Stuffed with Herbs)

4 (5-oz.) pork chops
2 tablespoons crumbled
  Roquefort cheese
1 onion, finely chopped
2 garlic cloves, finely chopped
2 tablespoons chopped
  fresh rosemary

1 tablespoon chopped parsley
1 tablespoon chopped
  fresh lovage (optional)
1 tablespoon chopped chives
2 tablespoons vegetable oil
Salt to taste

Slash edge fat of chops at about 1-inch intervals to prevent curling. With a sharp knife, loosen meat slightly along bone. Cut a horizontal pocket in thickest part of each chop; set chops aside. Place cheese in a small bowl; mash with a fork. Mix in onion, garlic, rosemary, parsley, lovage and chives. Stuff chops with herb mixture; fasten closed with wooden picks. Heat oil in a large skillet. Add chops; cook until browned on both sides, seasoning with salt after turning. Reduce heat; cook chops until meat is no longer pink in center, about 15 minutes. Makes 4 servings.

Bohemian Schnitzel

**4 (5-oz.) slices boneless
  pork shoulder
2 teaspoons prepared mustard
2 tablespoons all-purpose flour
1 tablespoon paprika**

**1 tablespoon vegetable oil
3 bacon slices, finely diced
2 onions, thinly sliced,
  separated into rings**

Trim any membrane or fat from pork slices; press each slice firmly with your hand to flatten evenly. Thinly spread meat with mustard. Mix flour and paprika; dip meat in flour mixture to coat both sides. Place meat on a wire rack and let dry slightly. Heat oil in a large skillet; add bacon and cook until crisp. Remove from pan. Add onions to drippings; cook, stirring, until soft. Remove from pan and set aside with cooked bacon. Add meat to drippings; cook 2 to 3 minutes on each side or until well-browned. Reduce heat; cook 4 minutes longer on each side or until meat is no longer pink in center. Return cooked bacon and onions to pan; heat through. Makes 4 servings.

Stuffed Pork Tenderloin

**4 thick (7-oz.) slices pork
  tenderloin
2 slices white bread
2 garlic cloves, finely chopped
1 tablespoon chopped parsley
1 tablespoon chopped
  fresh chervil**

**1 tablespoon chopped chives
1 tablespoon half and half
Salt and freshly ground white
  pepper to taste
3 tablespoons vegetable oil**

Preheat broiler. With a sharp knife, cut each pork slice almost in half horizontally (stop just short of 1 edge). Tear bread in small pieces and soften in a little cold water; squeeze out excess moisture. In a small bowl, mix softened bread, garlic, parsley, chervil, chives, half and half, salt and white pepper. Fill pork slices evenly with herb mixture; press meat firmly together. Brush a broiler pan with oil; broil pork slices about 20 minutes or until meat is no longer pink in center, turning and brushing with oil frequently. Makes 4 servings.

Cook's tip

This recipe is just as good with beef rib steaks or lamb leg steaks.

Pork Tenderloin in Yogurt Sauce

2 (3/4-lb.) pork tenderloins, trimmed of excess fat	All-purpose flour
Salt to taste	2 tablespoons butter or margarine
1 teaspoon paprika	1 onion, diced
4 oz. Emmentaler cheese or Gouda cheese	1-1/3 cups plain low-fat yogurt
	2 tablespoons chopped parsley

Trim any membrane from pork with a sharp knife. Rub salt and paprika into meat. Cut cheese in thin, 2-inch-long strips. Cut small, evenly spaced slits in meat and insert cheese strips, leaving about 1/2 inch of each strip showing. Sprinkle meat with flour to coat lightly. Melt butter or margarine in a large saucepan; add meat and cook until golden brown on all sides (cheese will melt during cooking). Add onion and cook a few minutes, then stir in yogurt. Reduce heat to low. Cover and simmer 40 minutes or until meat is no longer pink in center, stirring frequently.
To serve, lift meat to a warm platter; keep warm. Stir parsley into yogurt sauce and spoon over meat. Makes 4 servings.

Sweet & Sour Pork

1-1/4 lbs. pork tenderloin, trimmed	2 tablespoons vegetable oil
3 tablespoons soy sauce	5 tablespoons distilled white vinegar
Freshly ground pepper to taste	2 tablespoons sugar
Cornstarch	2 tablespoons cold water
1 (8-oz.) can pineapple slices, juice pack	Vegetable oil for deep-frying

Cut meat in 1-inch cubes. In a small bowl, mix 2 tablespoons soy sauce and pepper. Dip pork cubes in soy sauce, then in cornstarch to coat all sides. Shake off any excess and set aside. Drain pineapple, reserving 1/4 cup juice. Cut up pineapple slices. Set aside. Heat 2 tablespoons oil in a saucepan; stir in vinegar, sugar, remaining 1 tablespoon soy sauce, reserved 1/4 cup pineapple juice and cut-up pineapple slices. Simmer 1 minute. Stir together 1-1/2 teaspoons cornstarch and cold water; stir into sauce. Cook, stirring, until thickened. Remove from heat, cover and set aside. In a deep, heavy saucepan, heat about 2 inches of oil to 350F (175C) or until a 1-inch bread cube turns golden brown in about 65 seconds. Add meat, a few pieces at a time; cook about 6 minutes or until golden brown and crisp. Drain on paper towels; keep hot.
To serve, reheat sauce until bubbly; stir in cooked meat and serve at once. Makes 4 servings.

Pork Stew with Rice

2 tablespoons vegetable oil	3 cups beef stock
1 onion, diced	1/2 cup plus 1 tablespoon
2 garlic cloves, finely diced	long-grain white rice
1-1/4 lbs. lean boneless pork	4 firm tomatoes
cut in 1-1/2-inch cubes	1/4 teaspoon caraway seeds
Salt to taste	2/3 cup dairy sour cream
1 tablespoon paprika	

Heat oil in a large saucepan; add onion and garlic. Cook a few minutes. Add pork; cook until pork is lightly browned on all sides. Stir in salt, paprika and 1-1/2 cups stock. Bring to a simmer; cover and simmer 30 minutes. Stir in rice and remaining 1-1/2 cups stock; simmer 20 minutes longer. Peel tomatoes, cut in wedges and remove seeds. Add tomatoes and caraway seeds to stew; stir gently and simmer 20 minutes longer or until meat is tender.

To serve, stir in sour cream; heat through, but do not boil. Add more salt, if desired. Makes 4 servings.

Silesian Heaven (Boiled Pork with Fruit)

1 (8-oz.) pkg. mixed	1/2 (3-inch) cinnamon stick
dried fruit	1 tablespoon lemon juice
3/4 lb. boneless lean smoked	1 tablespoon cornstarch mixed
picnic shoulder	with 2 tablespoons cold water
1 tablespoon sugar	

Pour about 2 cups hot water into a bowl. Stir in fruit, cover and let stand 12 hours. In a large saucepan, bring about 2 cups lightly salted water to a boil. Add pork, reduce heat to medium, cover loosely and simmer briskly 45 minutes, adding more water as needed. Drain fruit; add fruit, sugar, cinnamon stick and lemon juice to simmering pork. Simmer briskly 30 minutes longer, adding a little water if needed. Lift pork from pan, cut in thick slices and keep hot. Stir cornstarch-water mixture into fruit mixture in pan; heat, stirring, until thickened.

To serve, remove cinnamon stick from thickened fruit mixture; pour fruit mixture into a serving dish. Top with sliced pork. Makes 4 servings.

Pork Shoulder with Prunes

6 pitted prunes
1 (2-lb.) boned fresh pork
  shoulder with skin
Salt to taste
2 tablespoons vegetable oil

1-3/4 cups hot water
1 onion
2 whole cloves
2/3 cup whipping cream

Place prunes in a small bowl; add enough water to cover. Cover and set aside. Preheat oven to 475F (245C). Score pork skin in a crisscross pattern; rub pork with salt. Heat oil in a roasting pan on top of the range; place pork in pan, scored-side down. Carefully pour 1 cup hot water around pork. Roast on lowest oven rack 20 minutes. Cut onion in half; stick 1 clove in each half. Turn meat over, add clove-studded onion halves to pan. Roast 1 hour longer or until a meat thermometer inserted in thickest part of meat registers 170F (75C). During roasting, gradually add remaining 3/4 cup hot water; baste meat occasionally.

To serve, lift meat from pan, transfer to a warm platter and let stand about 10 minutes. Meanwhile, dilute pan juices with a little hot water, then strain into a saucepan. Skim and discard fat. Stir in cream; heat, stirring, until slightly thickened. Drain prunes, cut in quarters and stir into sauce. Thinly slice meat across the grain; pass sauce at the table to accompany meat. Makes 6 servings.

Stuffed Rolled Pork

2 lbs. boned leg of pork,
  ready for rolling
1 teaspoon prepared mustard
Salt to taste
1/2 teaspoon dried leaf thyme
1/2 teaspoon dried leaf rosemary
1/2 teaspoon paprika
1/2 lb. celery, sliced

1/2 red bell pepper, seeded,
  cut in strips
1 garlic clove, chopped
3 tablespoons vegetable oil
1 cup beef stock
2/3 cup dairy sour cream
1 teaspoon cornstarch mixed with
  2 teaspoons cold water

Preheat oven to 475F (245C). Spread pork with mustard; sprinkle with salt, thyme, rosemary and paprika. Sprinkle celery and bell pepper evenly over meat, then sprinkle with garlic. Roll up meat and tie in several places with string. Heat oil in a roasting pan on top of range; add meat and brown on all sides. Pour 1/2 cup stock around meat. Roast 20 minutes, then pour in remaining 1/2 cup stock. Reduce oven temperature to 400F (205C) and roast 40 to 50 minutes longer or until a meat thermometer inserted in thickest part of meat registers 170F (75C).

To serve, place meat on a platter; let stand about 10 minutes. Meanwhile, dilute pan juices with a little hot water; skim and discard fat. Stir together sour cream and cornstarch-water mixture, then stir into juices. Heat, stirring, until slightly thickened. Slice meat across the grain; pass sauce separately. Makes 6 servings.

Pork in Puff Pastry

1/2 (17-1/4 oz.) pkg. frozen puff pastry, thawed	1 egg, separated
1 (2-lb.) cooked lean boneless pork loin roast or 1 (2-lb.) piece Canadian bacon	3 tomatoes, if desired Salt and freshly ground pepper to taste, if desired

Preheat oven to 425F (220C). Unfold thawed pastry sheet. On a lightly floured board, roll out pastry to 2 times original size. Using a pastry wheel, cut off a 1/2-inch wide strip from around edges; set aside. Place meat in center of pastry. Slightly beat egg white; brush edges of pastry with a little egg white. Fold pastry over meat to enclose; press firmly to seal. Place meat, seam-side down, on an ungreased baking sheet. Beat any remaining egg white with egg yolk; brush over pastry. Arrange pastry trimmings in a lattice pattern over pastry. Brush lattice with egg mixture. Bake in preheated oven on next-to-lowest oven rack 30 minutes or until golden brown. If desired, 15 minutes before end of baking time, cut tomatoes in half, sprinkle with salt and pepper and arrange in a shallow baking dish. Bake alongside meat until heated through.
To serve, cut meat and pastry crosswise in thick slices. Accompany each serving with a tomato half, if desired. Makes 6 servings.

Stuffed Picnic Shoulder

3 medium tart apples	1/8 teaspoon sugar
1/2 lb. pitted prunes (about 1-1/2 cups lightly packed)	1 teaspoon finely chopped fresh rosemary
2 tablespoons fine dry bread crumbs	2 lbs. boned fresh picnic shoulder, with pocket for stuffing cut in it
Salt and freshly ground white pepper to taste	2/3 cup whipping cream

Preheat oven to 425F (220C). Rinse a roasting pan and rack in cold water. Peel, quarter, core and slice apples. Cut up prunes. In a bowl, mix apples, prunes, bread crumbs, salt, white pepper, sugar and rosemary. Stuff pork with fruit mixture; sew closed with strong thread or dental floss, making stitches about 1/2 inch apart. Score pork skin in a diagonal crisscross pattern. Place pork, scored-side up, on rack in roasting pan. Roast 1-1/2 hours or until a meat thermometer inserted in thickest part of meat (not in stuffing) registers 170F (75C). During roasting, add a little hot water to pan and baste meat occasionally.
To serve, lift meat from pan, transfer to a warm platter and let stand about 10 minutes. Meanwhile, dilute pan juices with hot water; skim and discard fat. Stir cream into juices; heat, stirring, until sauce is slightly thickened. Cut meat crosswise in thick slices; pass sauce at the table to accompany meat. Makes 6 servings.

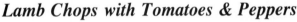

Lamb Chops with Tomatoes & Peppers

8 (3-oz.) lamb chops	1/2 lb. red bell peppers,
1/4 cup olive oil	seeded, cut in thin strips
1/4 teaspoon black pepper	4 small tomatoes, peeled, diced
Pinch of dried leaf rosemary	2 tablespoons tomato paste
Pinch of dried leaf sage	2/3 cup chicken stock
1 garlic clove	Salt and white pepper to taste
1 onion, diced	3/4 teaspoon dried leaf basil

Slash edge fat of chops at about 1-inch intervals to prevent curling. Place chops in a shallow dish; set aside. In a small bowl, mix 2 tablespoons oil, black pepper, rosemary and sage. Cut garlic clove in half; press 1 half through a garlic press into oil mixture. Stir to mix. Brush seasoned oil over chops, cover and refrigerate 3 hours. Dice remaining 1/2 garlic clove. Heat 1 tablespoon oil in a large skillet; add diced garlic and onion. Cook until onion is golden brown, stirring frequently. Stir in bell peppers and cook a few minutes; then stir in tomatoes, tomato paste and stock. Mix well; season with salt, white pepper and basil. Reduce heat, cover and simmer 25 minutes. After sauce has simmered 15 to 20 minutes, heat remaining 1 tablespoon oil in another large skillet. Add chops; cook 3 to 4 minutes on each side or until done to your liking.
To serve, place 2 chops on each individual plate; spoon tomato-pepper sauce over chops. Makes 4 servings.

Lamb Rib Chops

4 (5-oz.) lamb rib chops	1/2 teaspoon dried leaf mint
3 tablespoons vegetable oil	
Salt and freshly ground white	
pepper to taste	

Slash edge fat of chops at about 1-inch intervals to prevent curling. In a small bowl, mix 2 tablespoons oil, salt, white pepper and mint. Brush seasoned oil over chops. Heat remaining 1 tablespoon oil in a large skillet over medium-high heat. Add chops and cook a few seconds on each side; then reduce heat and cook 3 minutes longer on each side or until done to your liking. Makes 4 servings.

Cook's tip

Lamb rib chops are also an excellent choice for grilling or broiling.

Shashlik

2 teaspoons dried leaf rosemary
4 onions, cut in wedges
6 bacon slices
1/2 teaspoon freshly ground
  pepper
1 lb. lean boneless lamb (leg or
  shoulder), cut
  in 1-1/2-inch cubes

1 garlic clove, finely chopped
Salt to taste
2 tablespoons vegetable oil

Crush rosemary with a mortar and pestle; coat onion wedges in rosemary. Cut bacon slices in fairly large pieces; dip bacon pieces in pepper. On 4 sturdy metal skewers, thread lamb cubes alternately with onions and bacon. Place kebabs in a shallow baking dish. Crush garlic together with salt; place in a small bowl and stir in oil. Brush seasoned oil over kebabs, cover and refrigerate 3 hours. Preheat a cast-iron broiler pan. Place kebabs on hot pan; broil about 3 inches below heat 10 to 15 minutes or until meat is well-browned on outside but still pink in center. Turn frequently during broiling. Makes 4 servings.

Lamb Kebabs

3 yellow or red bell peppers
4 green bell peppers
2 lbs. lean boneless lamb (leg
  or shoulder), cut in
  2-1/4-inch cubes
Salt and freshly ground white
  pepper to taste

1 tablespoon paprika
3 onions, thickly sliced
4 tomatoes, cut in wedges
About 3 tablespoons
  vegetable oil

Seed bell peppers. Cut in quarters lengthwise and cut each quarter in half crosswise. Set aside. Sprinkle lamb with salt, white pepper and paprika. On sturdy metal skewers, thread lamb alternately with bell peppers, onions and tomatoes; brush generously with oil. Arrange kebabs on a lightly greased grill over a solid bed of hot coals. Cook 25 minutes or until meat is well-browned on outside but still pink in center; turn and brush frequently with oil. If broiled about 3 inches below heat, kebabs will cook in about 15 minutes.

To serve, slide meat and vegetables from skewers into a large serving bowl. Makes 4 servings.

Cook's tip

Authentic Yugoslav lamb kebabs are cooked over hot coals, but you may also broil these large kebabs.

Barbecued Saddle of Lamb with Coconut Pears

1 (3-lb.) saddle of lamb	2 tablespoons lemon juice
5 tablespoons honey	2 tablespoons vegetable oil
1 teaspoon curry powder	

Coconut Pears:

4 medium pears	1-1/3 cups sweetened shredded
2 tablespoons butter or	coconut
margarine	1 teaspoon sugar

Score side of lamb above ribs in a diagonal crisscross pattern, making cuts 1 inch deep and about 1-1/2 inches apart. Place meat in a large baking dish. In a small bowl, mix honey, curry powder, lemon juice and oil. Brush honey marinade generously over lamb; cover and refrigerate 4 hours. Preheat gril. Just before grilling meat, begin baking pears.

To make pears, preheat oven to 400F (205C). Peel, halve and core pears. Place pear halves side by side in a baking dish. Melt butter or margarine in a skillet; add coconut and cook, stirring, until golden. Sprinkle coconut over pears, then sprinkle evenly with sugar. Bake about 20 minutes or until pears are tender; turn off oven and keep pears warm. While pears are baking, cook meat.

To cook meat, lift meat from dish; reserve any marinade. Place meat on a lightly greased grill about 4 inches above a solid bed of hot coals. Cook 25 to 30 minutes or until a meat thermometer inserted in thickest part (not touching bone) registers 160F (70C) for medium. During cooking, turn meat often and brush with marinade, making sure scored side of meat is well-coated.

To serve, place cooked meat in turned-off oven with pears. Let stand 15 minutes, then slice across the grain. Serve with pears. Makes 8 servings.

Roast Leg of Lamb

1 (3-lb.) leg of lamb
3 garlic cloves, cut in slivers
2 tablespoons tomato paste
1 tablespoon all-purpose flour
2 tablespoons lemon juice
1/8 teaspoon ground
  caraway seeds
4 black peppercorns, crushed

Salt to taste
3 tablespoons vegetable oil
3 small onions, cut in quarters
1 cup beef stock
2/3 cup dry white wine
1 teaspoon cornstarch mixed with
  2 teaspoons cold water

Score lamb skin in a crisscross pattern. With tip of a sharp knife, cut small gashes in flesh under skin; insert garlic slivers. In a small bowl, mix tomato paste, flour, lemon juice, caraway seeds, salt and peppercorns. Brush mixture over lamb. Place lamb in a deep bowl, cover and refrigerate 12 hours. Preheat oven to 475F (245C). Heat oil in a roasting pan on top of range; add lamb and brown on all sides. Add onions to pan; pour in 1/2 cup stock. Roast 15 minutes, then reduce oven temperature to 400F (205C). Roast 40 minutes longer or until a meat thermometer inserted in thickest part of meat (not touching bone) registers 160F (70C) for medium. During roasting, gradually add wine and remaining 1/2 cup stock and baste with pan juices.
To serve, place meat on a platter; let stand 10 minutes. Dilute pan juices with a little hot water; strain juices into a saucepan. Stir in cornstarch mixture; heat, stirring, until slightly thickened. Thinly slice meat; pass gravy separately. Makes 4 servings.

Rolled Lamb Shoulder

Pinch of dried leaf marjoram
Pinch of dried leaf oregano
Pinch of dried leaf thyme
2 garlic cloves, finely chopped
1/4 cup olive oil
2 lbs. boned lamb shoulder,
  ready for rolling

Salt and freshly ground pepper
  to taste
2/3 cup beef stock
2/3 cup dry white wine
1/4 cup dairy sour cream

Preheat oven to 425F (220C). Crumble marjoram, oregano and thyme into a small bowl; mix in garlic and oil. Rub 3 tablespoons of the seasoned oil into lamb; sprinkle lamb with salt and pepper. Roll up meat; tie in several places with string. Place in a roasting pan; sprinkle with remaining seasoned oil. Roast on next-to-lowest oven rack about 40 minutes or until a meat thermometer inserted in thickest part of meat registers 160F (70C) for medium. During roasting, gradually add stock to pan and baste meat occasionally. Ten minutes before end of cooking time, pour wine over meat.
To serve, lift cooked meat from pan, transfer to a warm platter and let stand about 10 minutes. Meanwhile, mix sour cream into pan juices; heat through, but do not boil. Add salt and pepper, if desired. Slice meat across the grain; pass sauce at the table to accompany meat. Makes 6 servings.

Milan-Style Calf's Liver

2 tablespoons all-purpose flour	1-1/3 cups uncooked macaroni
Salt and freshly ground white pepper to taste	1/4 cup butter or margarine, melted
Pinch of dried leaf marjoram	2/3 cup freshly grated Parmesan cheese (2 oz.)
4 (5-oz.) slices calf's liver	
1 cup milk	3 tablespoons vegetable oil

On a shallow plate, stir together flour, salt, white pepper and marjoram. Set aside. Wash liver in cold water, pat dry and remove any membranes and large veins. Drip liver slices in milk; let excess drip off. Then dip liver slices in seasoned flour to coat both sides; shake off any excess. Place liver on a wire rack and let dry a few minutes. Meanwhile, in a large saucepan, bring 3 quarts salted water to a boil. Sprinkle in macaroni and boil about 12 minutes or until tender but still firm to the bite. Drain and transfer to a warm platter. Pour melted butter or margarine over macaroni, then sprinkle on cheese; toss to mix. Keep warm. Heat oil in a large skillet. Add liver and cook 3 to 4 minutes on each side or until cooked through but still slightly pink in center.
To serve, arrange cooked liver on top of macaroni. Makes 4 servings.

Berlin-Style Calf's Liver

4 (5-oz.) slices calf's liver	2 onions, thinly sliced, separated into rings
2 tablespoons all-purpose flour	
2 apples	Salt and freshly ground white pepper to taste
1/4 cup butter or margarine	

Wash liver in cold water, pat dry and remove any membranes and large veins. Dip liver slices in flour to coat both sides; shake off any excess. Place liver on a wire rack and let dry several minutes. Meanwhile, peel and core apples, then cut crosswise in 8 equal-size rings. Melt 2 tablespoons butter or margarine in a large skillet; add apple rings and cook until golden on both sides. Remove from pan and keep warm. Add onions to butter in pan; cook until crisp and golden brown, stirring frequently. Remove from pan and keep warm with apples. Melt remaining 2 tablespoons butter or margarine in skillet. Add liver; cook 3 to 4 minutes on each side or until cooked through but still slightly pink in center. Sprinkle with salt and white pepper.
To serve, arrange liver on a warm platter; top with apples and onions. Makes 4 servings.

Normandy-Style Veal Kidneys

1-1/4 lbs. small veal or pork kidneys, without fat	1 tablespoon butter or margarine
Salt	1-1/2 tablespoons Calvados
1 tart apple	5 tablespoons half and half
3 tablespoons vegetable oil	Freshly ground pepper to taste
1 onion, diced	1/2 teaspoon sugar
	Chopped parsley, if desired

Wash kidneys in cold water, pat dry and cut in half. Cut out white membranes. Rub sliced kidneys with salt and let stand 30 minutes; then rinse in lukewarm water and pat dry. Set aside. Peel and core apple, then cut crosswise in thick rings. Set aside. Heat oil in a skillet; add onion and cook, stirring, until soft. Stir in kidneys; add butter or margarine and stir until melted. Pour Calvados into a small saucepan and warm over a low flame; pour over kidneys and carefully ignite. Let flames die down. Season half and half with salt and pepper and pour over kidneys. Sprinkle apple rings with sugar, add to pan and stir gently to mix. Simmer over low heat 5 minutes.

To serve, sprinkle with parsley, if desired. Makes 4 servings.

Flambéed Kidneys

1-1/4 lbs. veal kidneys, without fat	1 garlic clove, finely diced
Salt	3 tablespoons cognac
Freshly ground pepper to taste	1/4 cup half and half
About 1/4 cup all-purpose flour	1 tablespoon butter or margarine
3 tablespoons vegetable oil	1 teaspoon sugar
1 onion, finely diced	2 teaspoons Dijon-style mustard

Wash kidneys in cold water, pat dry and cut in half. Cut out white membranes; slice kidneys. Rub sliced kidneys with salt and let stand 30 minutes; then rinse in lukewarm water and pat dry. Sprinkle kidneys with pepper; dip in flour to coat and shake off any excess. Set aside. Heat oil in a large skillet; add onion and garlic. Cook, stirring, until onion is soft. Add kidneys and cook 5 minutes, turning frequently. Pour cognac into a small saucepan and warm over a low flame. Pour over kidneys; carefully ignite. Let flames die down. Season half and half with salt and stir into kidneys. Add butter or margarine, sugar and mustard; stir until butter or margarine is melted. Then simmer over low heat 8 minutes; do not allow sauce to boil. Makes 4 servings.

Spanish-Style Hamburgers

1 day-old dinner roll
1 onion, chopped
10 pimento-stuffed green olives,
   chopped
2 eggs, beaten
1 lb. mixed lean ground beef
   and pork
Salt and white pepper
1/8 teaspoon garlic salt
2 tablespoons vegetable oil
1 tomato, cut in 4 thick slices
4 rolled anchovy fillets stuffed
   with capers
2/3 cup dry red wine
3 tablespoons tomato paste
Sugar to taste
1 (8-oz.) can tomato sauce
1 to 2 teaspoons curry powder
1/2 teaspoon dried leaf oregano

Tear roll in small pieces and soften in a little cold water. Squeeze out excess moisture. In a bowl, mix softened roll, onion, olives, eggs, meat, salt, white pepper and garlic salt. With wet hands, shape meat mixture into 4 equal patties. Heat oil in a large skillet; add patties and brown quickly on both sides. Then reduce heat and cook about 7 minutes longer on each side or until done to your liking. Remove patties from pan, transfer to a warm rimmed platter and keep warm. Add tomato slices to drippings in pan; brown lightly on both sides. Place 1 tomato slice on each meat patty; top each tomato slice with an anchovy fillet. Pour wine into pan; stir to loosen browned bits. In a bowl, mix tomato paste, sugar, tomato sauce, curry powder and oregano; stir into wine in pan. Bring to a boil, stirring; season with salt and white pepper.

To serve, pour sauce evenly around meat patties. Makes 4 servings.

Pork Patties with Corn

1/2 cup finely diced Edam cheese (2 oz.)	2 tablespoons vegetable oil
3/4 lb. lean ground pork	1 tablespoon butter or margarine
2 oz. liverwurst	1 (12-oz.) can whole-kernel corn, drained
1/4 lb. bulk pork sausage	1 tomato, cut in wedges
1/4 cup chopped parsley	Parsley sprigs
2 eggs, beaten	

In a bowl, mix cheese, ground pork, liverwurst, pork sausage, chopped parsley and eggs. With wet hands, shape meat mixture into 8 flat patties. Heat oil in a large skillet; add patties and brown quickly on both sides. Then reduce heat and cook about 10 minutes longer or until no longer pink in center, turning frequently. Meanwhile, melt butter or margarine in a saucepan. Add corn; cover and heat through, stirring occasionally.

To serve, pour corn into a warm serving dish; top with meat patties. Garnish with tomato wedges and parsley sprigs. Makes 4 servings.

Variation
Hamburgers Albani: Serve meat patties with canned white beans instead of corn. Warm beans in melted butter or margarine, then stir in tomato paste and ketchup to taste. Pour into a serving dish and sprinkle with parsley.

Hamburgers with Herb Butter

1 lb. lean ground beef	1 tablespoon lemon juice
Salt and freshly ground white pepper to taste	1/2 teaspoon celery salt
	1 day-old dinner roll
2 teaspoons paprika	2 egg yolks
1/4 cup butter or margarine, room temperature	2 tablespoons vegetable oil
	1 tomato, cut in wedges
1 tablespoon chopped parsley	Dill sprigs
1 tablespoon chopped fresh dill	

In a bowl, mix beef, salt, white pepper and paprika. Cover and refrigerate 15 minutes. In a small bowl, beat together butter or margarine, parsley, chopped dill, lemon juice and celery salt. Refrigerate until firm. Tear roll in small pieces and soften in a little cold water; squeeze out excess moisture. Work softened roll and egg yolks into beef mixture. With wet hands, shape mixture into 8 thick patties. Heat oil in a large skillet; add patties and brown quickly on both sides. Then reduce heat and cook 10 minutes longer or until done to your liking, turning frequently.

To serve, arrange meat patties on a warm platter. Cut a cross in top of each patty; fill with chilled herb butter. Garnish with tomato wedges and dill sprigs. Makes 4 servings.

Stuffed Meatballs

1/4 cup chopped chives	1/4 cup half and half
1 teaspoon paprika	Salt and freshly ground white
2 tablespoons butter or	pepper to taste
margarine, room temperature	Pinch of garlic powder
1 lb. lean ground beef	Vegetable oil
1/4 lb. lean ground pork	
3 tablespoons fine dry	
bread crumbs	

In a small bowl, mix chives, paprika and butter or margarine; divide into 4 equal portions. In another bowl, mix beef, pork, bread crumbs, half and half, salt, white pepper and garlic powder. Divide meat mixture into 4 equal portions; with wet hands, shape each portion into a ball around 1/4 of butter mixture. Brush meatballs with oil. Cover and refrigerate 30 minutes. Preheat broiler; brush broiler rack with oil. Broil meatballs about 30 minutes or until no longer pink in center, turning and brushing frequently with oil. Makes 4 servings.

Cevapcici
(Ground-Meat Rolls)

1 lb. lean ground beef	1/4 cup vegetable oil
1/2 lb. ground veal sausage	1 teaspoon all-purpose flour
Salt and coarsely ground pepper	1/4 cup chopped parsley
to taste	4 onions, finely chopped
2 garlic cloves, finely chopped	

In a bowl, mix beef, veal, salt, pepper, garlic, 2 tablespoons oil, flour, parsley and 1/4 of chopped onions. Place remaining onions in a serving dish; set aside to serve with meat rolls. With wet hands, shape 1 heaping tablespoon of meat mixture into a small roll; press in ends of roll to flatten. Repeat with remaining meat mixture. Heat remaining 2 tablespoons oil in a skillet. Cook rolls, turning frequently, about 10 minutes or until well-browned on outside but still slightly pink in center.

To serve, arrange meat rolls on a warm platter; pass reserved chopped onions to accompany meat. Makes 4 servings.

Meat Loaf in Puff Pastry

1 small leek	1 teaspoon soy sauce
3/4 lb. cabbage	Salt and white pepper
1 tablespoon butter or margarine	1/2 (17-1/4 oz.) pkg. frozen puff
2 onions, diced	pastry, thawed
3/4 lb. mixed lean ground beef	1 cup shredded Gouda cheese
and pork	(4 oz.)
1/4 lb. mushrooms, thinly sliced	1 egg
2 egg yolks, beaten	

Trim roots and green top of leek, then split leek lengthwise and wash thoroughly to remove sand. Thinly slice leek halves crosswise. Cut cabbage in thin strips. Set leek and cabbage aside. Melt butter or margarine in a large skillet; add onions, then crumble in meat. Cook, stirring, until meat is browned. Spoon off and discard fat. Stir in leek, cabbage and mushrooms. Reduce heat, cover and cook 10 minutes, stirring frequently. Remove from heat. Stir in 2 egg yolks, soy sauce, salt and white pepper. Cool. Preheat oven to 400F (205C). Unfold pastry sheet on a lightly floured board. Roll out about 1-1/2 times original size. Spread cooled meat mixture over rectangle to within 1 inch of edges. Sprinkle with cheese. Separate egg. Lightly beat egg white; brush over pastry edges. Roll up pastry jelly-roll style, starting with a long edge. Press ends and seam to seal. Place roll on an ungreased baking sheet. Beat egg yolk; brush over roll. Bake 35 minutes or until golden brown. Serve hot. Makes 6 servings.

Meat Loaf with Hard-Cooked Eggs

1 day-old dinner roll	2 hard-cooked eggs
1 onion, diced	1 tablespoon all-purpose flour
1/2 lb. lean ground pork	1 small bunch mixed herbs,
1/2 lb. ground veal	such as parsley, chives
3/4 lb. lean ground beef	and basil, chopped
Salt and white pepper	2 cups beef stock
1/4 teaspoon dried leaf thyme	1/4 lb. mushrooms, sliced
1/4 teaspoon dried leaf oregano	1/4 cup dairy sour cream
2 tablespoons chopped parsley	1 teaspoon prepared mustard
2 to 3 tablespoons milk	2 teaspoons ketchup

Preheat oven to 425F (220C). Lightly grease a shallow baking pan. Tear roll in small pieces; soften in a little water. Squeeze out excess moisture. In a bowl, mix softened roll, onion, meat, salt, white pepper, thyme, oregano, parsley and milk. Place 1/2 of meat mixture in greased pan; shape into an oblong. Arrange whole hard-cooked eggs down center of meat, spacing evenly. Pat remaining mixture on top; shape into a smooth loaf. Sprinkle loaf with flour. Bake 5 minutes. Sprinkle mixed herbs around loaf. Bake about 55 minutes, gradually adding stock to pan.
To serve, place meat loaf on a platter; keep warm. Pour pan juices into a small saucepan; skim and discard fat. Stir in mushrooms; simmer 5 minutes. Stir in sour cream, mustard and ketchup; heat through. Do not boil. Slice meat loaf; pass sauce separately. Makes 4 servings.

Meat-Loaf Ring in Cabbage

1-1/4 lbs. Savoy cabbage
1 day-old dinner roll
2 onions, diced
2 eggs, beaten
1-1/4 lbs. mixed lean ground
  beef and pork

Salt and freshly ground white
  pepper to taste
1/2 teaspoon ground caraway
  seeds
1 tablespoon vegetable oil
Tomato sauce

Remove core and any damaged leaves from cabbage, then boil cabbage in salted water 10 minutes. Drain and cool. Separate leaves. Cut out and discard thick stalk bases from outer leaves; set enough outer leaves aside to line mold. Finely chop inner leaves; set aside. Tear roll in small pieces and soften in a little cold water. Squeeze out any excess moisture. In a bowl, mix softened roll, chopped inner cabbage leaves, onions, eggs, beef and pork, salt, white pepper and ground caraway seeds. Brush a ring mold with oil and line with reserved cabbage leaves. Fill lined mold with meat mixture; smooth surface. Cover with remaining outer cabbage leaves. Wrap mold tightly in foil and set in a saucepan of boiling water. Water should come halfway up sides of mold. Simmer 1-1/2 hours, adding more boiling water as needed.

To serve, unwrap mold; then turn out meat loaf onto a warm platter. Pass tomato sauce at the table to accompany meat. Makes 4 servings.

Viennese Meat Loaf

1 day-old dinner roll
2 onions, finely chopped
2 garlic cloves, finely chopped
1 lb. mixed lean ground beef
  and pork
1/4 lb. pork liver, chopped
2 eggs, beaten
Salt and freshly ground pepper
  to taste

1 teaspoon paprika
1 teaspoon Dijon-style mustard
8 thin bacon slices
1 cup beef stock
1 teaspoon cornstarch
2/3 cup dairy sour cream
Crisp-cooked bacon slices,
  if desired

Preheat oven to 425F (220C). Tear roll in small pieces and soften in a little cold water. Squeeze out any excess moisture. In a bowl, mix softened roll, onions, garlic, beef, pork, liver, eggs, salt, pepper, paprika and mustard. Shape mixture into a loaf. Line a shallow baking pan with 4 bacon slices; place meat loaf on top and cover with remaining 4 bacon slices. Bake on next-to-lowest oven rack 45 minutes, basting occasionally with stock.

To serve, lift meat loaf from pan and transfer to a warm platter; keep warm. Discard bacon slices in baking pan. Pour pan juices into a small saucepan. Skim and discard fat, then pour in any remaining stock and a little hot water, if necessary. Bring to a simmer. Stir together cornstarch and sour cream; stir into juices and heat through. Slice meat loaf; pass sauce at the table to accompany meat. Garnish with bacon slices, if desired. Makes 4 servings.

Ground-Meat Pie

Pastry:

3-3/4 cups all-purpose flour	2 to 3 tablespoons cold water
1/2 teaspoon salt	1 egg, beaten
1-1/4 cups firm butter	

Filling:

1 lb. lean ground beef	1/2 teaspoon dried leaf marjoram
1 lb. lean ground pork	3 tablespoons chopped parsley
3 eggs, beaten	1/4 lb. chicken livers
Salt and freshly ground white pepper to taste	1 tablespoon butter or margarine
2 teaspoons paprika	1/4 lb. fresh mushrooms
	2 egg yolks, beaten

To make pastry, in a large bowl, stir together flour and 1/2 teaspoon salt. Using a pastry blender or 2 knives, cut in butter until mixture resembles coarse crumbs. Mix water and 1 egg; add to mixture. Toss with a fork until dough holds together. Then gather dough into a ball with your hands, wrap in wax paper and refrigerate 2 hours.

To make filling, in a bowl, mix beef, pork, 3 eggs, salt, white pepper, paprika, marjoram and parsley. Set aside. Cut any fat from chicken livers. Rinse livers, pat dry and cut in 1-inch cubes. Melt butter or margarine in a skillet. Add cubed chicken livers and cook, turning frequently, until browned on all sides. Remove from heat; cool. Cut larger mushrooms in halves or quarters; leave smaller ones whole.

To complete, preheat oven to 400F (205C). On a lightly floured board, roll 1/2 of pastry to a 12'' x 12'' square. Place pastry square on a baking sheet. Spread ground meat mixture over pastry to within 1 inch of edges. Distribute livers and mushrooms evenly over meat and press in lightly. Smooth surface of meat. Roll out remaining pastry to a 14'' x 14'' square; place over meat. Trim any excess pastry, then firmly press edges together with a fork. Roll out pastry trimmings; cut into rounds with a small fluted cutter. Brush pie with beaten egg yolks; decorate with pastry rounds and brush again with egg yolks. Using a very small (about 1/2-inch-diameter) round cutter, cut a hole in center of each decorative round to allow steam to escape during baking. Bake on next-to-lowest oven rack about 1 hour and 20 minutes or until deep golden brown. Makes 12 servings.

Cook's tip

If desired, you may also sprinkle the meat mixture with diced, crisp-cooked bacon.

Chicken in Red Wine

1 (2-1/2-lb.) chicken, cut up	3 tablespoons vegetable oil
Salt to taste	2/3 cup chicken stock
1/2 teaspoon paprika	1 cup dry red wine
1/8 teaspoon red (cayenne)	3 tomatoes
pepper	1/4 teaspoon dried leaf thyme
1/2 garlic clove	1/2 cup half and half
1 tablespoon butter or margarine	Dairy sour cream

Wash chicken in cold water; pat dry. Remove as much fat as possible. Rub chicken pieces with salt, paprika and red pepper. Rub a large skillet with cut side of garlic clove, then add butter or margarine and oil. Heat until butter or margarine is melted. Add chicken pieces and brown on all sides; transfer chicken and pan drippings to a large saucepan. Pour stock and 1/2 cup wine into saucepan; bring to a simmer. Cover and simmer 25 minutes. Peel, quarter and seed tomatoes; add to chicken along with thyme and remaining 1/2 cup wine. Stir gently. Simmer 10 minutes longer or until meat near bone is no longer pink; cut to test.
To serve, skim and discard fat from sauce. Stir half and half into sauce; heat through. Garnish chicken with a spoonful of sour cream. Makes 4 servings.

Chicken with Almonds

1/4 cup butter or margarine,	Salt to taste
room temperature	1 onion
1/8 teaspoon ground cloves	1 apple
1/8 teaspoon ground ginger	About 1 cup chicken stock
1 tablespoon honey	1 tablespoon sliced almonds
1 (2-1/2-lb.) chicken	

Preheat oven to 375F (190C). In a small bowl, beat together butter or margarine, cloves, ginger and honey. Set aside. Rinse chicken inside and out with cold water; pat dry. Rub body cavity with salt. Cut onion in wedges; cut apple in wedges and remove core. Place apple and onion wedges in body cavity; fasten cavity closed with small metal skewers. Place chicken, breast down, on a rack in a roasting pan. Spread with 1/2 of butter mixture. Roast 20 minutes. Carefully pour about 1/3 cup stock into pan and baste chicken. Turn chicken breast up and spread with remaining butter mixture. Roast 30 to 40 minutes longer or until a meat thermometer inserted in thickest part of thigh (not touching bone) registers 185F (85C). During roasting, add stock to pan as necessary; baste chicken often. Ten minutes before end of roasting time, sprinkle chicken with almonds.
To serve, lift chicken from pan, transfer to a warm platter and let stand 10 minutes before carving. Remove apple and onion wedges from chicken; serve alongside. Makes 4 servings.

Spit-Grilled Herbed Chicken

1 (2-1/2-lb.) chicken	Large rosemary sprig
Salt to taste	1 teaspoon paprika
1/2 bunch parsley	1/4 cup dairy sour cream
1/2 bunch lovage (optional)	1 tablespoon all-purpose flour
1/2 bunch chives	1 tablespoon vegetable oil
Large basil sprig	

Wash chicken in cold water; pat dry. Rub body cavity with salt. Trim parsley and lovage stems. Wash all fresh herbs in cold water, shake dry and place in body cavity. Fasten cavity closed with small metal skewers. In a small bowl, stir together paprika, sour cream, flour and oil. Spread mixture over chicken. Tie legs and wings to body with string. Skewer chicken on spit; secure firmly in place. Grill 1 hour or until a meat thermometer inserted in thickest part of thigh (not touching bone) registers 185F (85C), keeping spit turning constantly. If chicken browns too quickly, reduce heat or move spit farther away from grill. Makes 4 servings.

Stuffed Chicken

1 (2-1/2-lb.) chicken	1/2 teaspoon dried leaf thyme
Salt and freshly ground white pepper to taste	1 egg, beaten
1/2 teaspoon paprika	3 tablespoons fine dry breadcrumbs
1/4 lb. fresh mushrooms, chopped	Melted butter or margarine
8 oz. goose-liver paté, chopped	
About 1/2 cup pistachio nuts, chopped	

Preheat oven to 375F (190C). Wash chicken inside and out with cold water; pat dry. Rub body cavity with salt, white pepper and paprika. In a bowl, mix mushrooms, paté, pistachios, thyme, egg and breadcrumbs. Stuff chicken with paté mixture; sew body cavity closed with strong thread. Tie chicken legs and wings to body with string. Brush chicken all over with melted butter or margarine. Place chicken, breast down, on a rack in a roasting pan. Roast 20 minutes. Turn chicken breast up and brush again with melted butter or margarine; roast 30 to 40 minutes longer or until a meat thermometer inserted in thickest part of thigh (not touching bone) registers 185F (85C).

To serve, lift chicken from pan and transfer to a warm platter. Let stand 10 minutes before carving. Makes 4 servings.

Duck with Fruit Stuffing

1 (about 4-1/2-lb.) duck
Salt and freshly ground white
   pepper to taste
2 large apples
1/4 lb. fresh figs
1 teaspoon curry powder
1 tablespoon firm butter or
   margarine, cut in
   small pieces
3 tablespoons vegetable oil
1 cup hot water

Wash duck inside and out with
cold water; pat dry. Pull off any
large lumps of fat. With a fork,
prick duck skin all over to let fat
escape during roasting. Rub duck
body cavity with salt and white
pepper. Peel, quarter, core and
thickly slice apples. Cut stems
from figs; dice figs. Season apples and figs with salt, white pepper and curry powder; then toss
lightly with butter or margarine.
Spoon stuffing into duck body
cavity. Sew cavity closed with
strong thread; tie duck legs and
wings to body with string. Preheat oven to 375F (190C). Heat
oil in a large roasting pan on top
of the range. Add duck and
brown well on all sides; this
should take about 15 minutes.
Then place duck, breast down, on
a rack in pan. Roast about 40
minutes. Pour off fat. Turn duck
breast up, carefully pour hot
water into pan and roast about 1
hour longer. During roasting,
baste duck frequently with pan
juices, adding more hot water to
pan as necessary.
To serve, lift duck from pan and
transfer to a warm platter. Let
stand 10 minutes before carving.
Makes 4 servings.

Ginger Duck

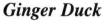

1/4 lb. leeks
2 oz. fresh gingerroot
1 small (about 4-lb.) duck,
  cut up
Salt to taste
3 tablespoons vegetable oil
1 cup dry white wine
1/4 cup soy sauce

1/8 teaspoon red (cayenne)
  pepper
1 teaspoon cornstarch
5 tablespoons canned
  pineapple juice
2 canned pineapple slices,
  cut up

Rub duck with salt. Heat 2 tablespoons oil in a large skillet. Add duck; brown well on all sides, about 10 minutes. Remove from pan and keep warm. Pour off and discard all but 1 tablespoon drippings. Trim off green tops of leeks, then split leeks lengthwise and wash thoroughly to remove sand. Thinly slice leek halves crosswise. Peel and halve gingerroot. Cut 1 half in thin slices; grate remaining half. Heat remaining 1 tablespoon oil with drippings in skillet; add leeks and gingerroot slices. Cook, stirring, until leeks are soft. Add wine, soy sauce and red pepper; simmer 5 minutes. Return duck pieces to pan, cover and simmer 10 minutes or until meat near bone is cooked through, but still pink. Transfer duck pieces to a warm plate; keep warm. Strain cooking liquid; return to pan. Skim and discard fat. In a small bowl, combine cornstarch and pineapple juice; stir into cooking liquid with grated gingerroot. Cook until thickened. Return duck pieces to pan; heat through. Makes 4 servings.

Peking Duck

1 (4-1/2-lb.) duck
2 tablespoons sugar
2 shallots, peeled, chopped

Mandarin Pancakes:
2 cups all-purpose flour
Salt to taste
3/4 cup boiling water

2 bunches green onions, sliced
Soy sauce

About 2 tablespoons
  vegetable oil

Pull off any fat. Dissolve sugar in a little water; brush over duck skin. Make small slits in skin; loosen skin slightly. Using a straw, blow air under skin. Place shallots in duck body cavity. Truss duck. Hang duck in a cool, well-ventilated place about 12 hours or until skin dries out. Preheat oven to 375F (190C). Place duck, breast down, on a rack in a roasting pan; roast 1-3/4 to 2 hours, turning breast up after 45 minutes. Pour off fat as needed.
To make pancakes, sift flour and salt into a large bowl. Stir in water. Knead dough until smooth. Cover; let rest 20 minutes. Cut into 16 pieces. Flatten each piece into a 3-inch circle. Brush 1 side with a little oil. Stack circles in pairs, oiled sides together. Roll out to a 5-inch pancake, rolling both sides. Do not roll edges too thin. Heat an ungreased skillet over medium heat. Cook 1 pancake at a time until pancake puffs up; turn. Cook until small brown spots appear on underside. Peel layers apart.
To serve, carve duck into small, thin slices. Serve onions and soy sauce separately. Makes 4 servings.

Roast Turkey Roll

1/2 lb. pitted prunes (about 1-1/2 cups lightly packed)
1 (2-lbs.) boned turkey breast, ready for rolling
Salt and freshly ground white pepper to taste
1 teaspoon prepared mustard
Few dashes of cider vinegar
2 onions, finely diced
1 garlic clove, finely diced
1 tablespoon chopped lemon balm (optional)
1/4 cup fine dry bread crumbs
1 egg, beaten
3 tablespoons vegetable oil
2 cups boiling water
2/3 cup dry red wine
1/2 cup dairy sour cream

Preheat oven to 425F (220C). Place prunes in a bowl; add enough warm water to cover. Let stand about 4 hours. Rub 1 side of turkey breast with salt and white pepper, spread with mustard and sprinkle with vinegar. Drain and dice prunes. In a medium bowl, combine diced prunes, onions, garlic, lemon balm, bread crumbs and egg. Spread prune mixture over turkey. Roll up meat; tie in several places with string. Heat oil in a roasting pan on top of range; add turkey roll and brown lightly on all sides. Then roast 10 minutes. Carefully pour boiling water into roasting pan; baste meat with pan juices. Roast about 20 minutes longer or until a meat thermometer inserted in center of meat registers 170F (75C); baste frequently with pan juices.

To serve, place turkey on a platter; let stand 10 minutes. Stir wine and cream into pan juices; heat through. Season with salt and white pepper. Slice turkey roll crosswise; pass sauce separately. Makes 6 servings.

Turkey Steaks with Almonds

4 (6-oz.) slices turkey breast
Freshly ground white pepper to taste
2 tablespoons all-purpose flour
Salt to taste
1 teaspoon paprika
1/4 cup butter or margarine
1 cup sliced almonds
2 canned peach halves, drained, sliced

Remove any membrane from turkey; rub each slice with white pepper. Season flour with salt, white pepper and paprika. Dip turkey slices in flour mixture to coat both sides; shake off any excess. Heat 2 tablespoons butter or margarine in a large skillet. Add turkey slices; cook about 30 seconds on each side. Remove turkey from pan; dip slices in almonds to coat both sides. Press almonds firmly onto meat. Melt remaining 2 tablespoons butter or margarine in skillet; add almond-coated slices and cook 3 to 4 minutes longer on each side or until meat is no longer pink in center.

To serve, transfer turkey to a warm platter; keep warm. Add peaches to juices in pan; heat through. Serve with turkey. Makes 4 servings.

Roast Goose with Chestnut Stuffing

3/4 lb. chestnuts	Pinch of dried leaf marjoram
1 (9-lb.) goose with giblets	Pinch of dried leaf tarragon
1 tablespoon butter or margarine	2 teaspoons salt
2 large tart apples	1 cup water
1 dinner roll	2 cups hot water
1 egg yolk	2/3 cup beer
Salt and freshly ground white pepper to taste	2/3 cup dry red wine

Using a sharp knife, cut a slit in rounded side of each chestnut. Cook chestnuts, covered, in boiling salted water 30 minutes. Drain chestnuts. Cool, peel and cut in wedges. Set aside. Preheat oven to 400F (205C). Rinse a roasting pan with cold water. Wash goose inside and out with cold water; pat dry. Pull off any large lumps of fat. Cut off tail. With a fork, prick goose all over to let fat escape during roasting. Set goose aside. Wash goose giblets; pat dry. Remove any fat from heart and liver; finely chop heart and liver. Reserve remaining giblets for other uses, if desired. Melt butter or margarine in a skillet; add chopped heart and liver and cook, stirring, until browned. Set aside. Peel, core and finely dice apples. Set aside. Tear roll in small pieces and soften in a little cold water; squeeze out any excess moisture. In a bowl, mix apples, softened roll, browned goose heart and liver, chestnuts, egg yolk, salt to taste, white pepper, marjoram and tarragon. Stuff goose with apple mixture and sew cavity closed with strong thread. Tie goose legs and wings to body with string. Dissolve 2 teaspoons salt in 1 cup water. Set aside. Place goose, breast down, on a rack in rinsed roasting pan. Roast on lowest oven rack 3 to 3-1/2 hours total, brushing frequently with salt water after the first hour. Pour off fat as needed. After goose has roasted 1 hour, turn goose on its side and carefully pour 2 cups hot water into roasting pan. Roast 30 minutes longer, then turn goose on its other side. Roast 30 minutes longer; turn goose breast up and continue to roast until done. During last 30 minutes of roasting, sprinkle goose several times with beer. When goose is done, turn off oven; let goose rest 20 minutes before removing from oven and carving.

To serve, transfer goose to a warm platter. Dilute pan juices with hot water; pour into a saucepan. Skim and discard fat. Stir in wine; season with salt and white pepper. Heat through. Pass at the table to accompany meat. Makes 8 servings.

Venison Rolls

1 onion, grated
5 tablespoons vegetable oil
2 tablespoons red-wine vinegar
4 (5-oz.) venison leg steaks
Salt to taste
1/2 teaspoon hot paprika
1 teaspoon bottled green
   peppercorns, crushed
1/2 green bell pepper, seeded,
   cut in strips

1 small fresh dill pickle,
   cut in thin strips
6 thin bacon slices
1 cup game stock or homemade or
   canned beef stock
1/2 cup dairy sour cream
1 tablespoon chopped parsley

In a shallow bowl, mix onion, 4 tablespoons oil and vinegar. Add venison; turn to coat. Cover and refrigerate 24 hours. Lift venison from marinade; pat dry. Sprinkle 1 side of each steak with salt, paprika and crushed peppercorns. Arrange bell-pepper and pickle strips diagonally across steaks. Dice 2 bacon slices; sprinkle evenly over steaks. Roll up steaks. Wrap each one in a bacon slice; secure with small metal skewers or wooden picks. Heat remaining 1 tablespoon oil in a skillet; add venison rolls and brown quickly on all sides. Add stock and bring to a boil. Reduce heat, cover and simmer 40 minutes or until meat is tender.
To serve, lift venison from pan, transfer to a warm platter and keep warm. Add cream to pan juices; heat, stirring, until sauce is slightly thickened. Stir in parsley, then spoon sauce over rolls. Makes 4 servings.

Fried Venison Steaks

5 tablespoons vegetable oil
2 tablespoons cider vinegar
6 tablespoons dry red wine
3 juniper berries
1 teaspoon Dijon-style mustard
4 (5-oz.) venison leg steaks
Salt and freshly ground white
   pepper to taste

1/2 cup diced fresh pineapple
1/2 banana
1/2 cup canned red tart
   cherries, drained, plus
   1 tablespoon cherry juice

In a shallow bowl, beat together 3 tablespoons oil, vinegar, wine, juniper berries and mustard. Add venison; turn to coat. Cover and refrigerate 24 hours, turning occasionally. Lift venison from marinade; pat dry. Reserve 2 tablespoons of the marinade. Heat remaining 2 tablespoons oil in a large skillet. Add steaks; cook 5 to 6 minutes each side. Season cooked steaks with salt and white pepper. Remove steaks from pan, transfer to a warm platter and keep warm. Add pineapple to pan drippings; cook, stirring, until heated through. Slice banana into pan; stir in cherries, cherry juice and reserved 2 tablespoons marinade. Heat through over low heat.
To serve, pour fruit sauce over steaks. Makes 4 servings.

Venison Cutlets

2 tablespoons olive oil	1 teaspoon ground cinnamon
2 tablespoons lemon juice	2 tablespoons butter or
1/2 teaspoon ground cloves	margarine
4 (5-oz.) venison cutlets	Salt to taste
2 small ripe pears	2/3 cup game stock or beef stock
1 teaspoon honey	Freshly ground black pepper
3/4 cup plus 2 tablespoons	to taste
dry white wine	

In a small bowl, beat together oil, 1 tablespoon lemon juice and cloves. Rub oil mixture into venison; let stand at room temperature 30 minutes. Meanwhile, peel pears, cut in wedges and remove cores. In a saucepan, stir together remaining 1 tablespoon lemon juice, honey, 1/4 cup wine and cinnamon. Bring to a simmer. Add pears, reduce heat, cover and simmer 15 minutes. Lift pears from pan; keep warm. Reserve pear-cooking liquid. Press cutlets with your hand to flatten slightly. Melt butter or margarine in a skillet over medium heat. Add cutlets; cook 4 minutes on each side. Season cooked cutlets with salt; transfer to a warm platter and keep warm. Stir remaining 10 tablespoons wine, stock and reserved pear-cooking liquid into pan drippings. Bring to a boil; season liberally with pepper.
To serve, return cutlets to pan and simmer in sauce 5 minutes; do not allow sauce to boil. Gently mix in pears. Makes 4 servings.

Venison Cutlets in Juniper Sauce

4 (6-oz.) slices venison	1/4 cup butter or margarine
3 tablespoons olive oil	Salt to taste
5 tablespoons dry red wine	2/3 cup whipping cream
2 tablespoons cider vinegar	6 tablespoons gin
5 juniper berries, crushed	Few drops of lemon juice
4 thick slices firm-textured	Freshly ground pepper to taste
white bread	

Trim any skin from venison. In a shallow bowl, beat together oil, wine, vinegar and 1/2 of juniper berries. Add venison and turn to coat; then cover and refrigerate 2 to 3 hours, stirring occasionally. Cut crusts off bread slices. Melt 2 tablespoons butter or margarine in a large skillet; add bread and cook, turning as needed, until golden brown on both sides. Transfer fried bread to a warm platter; keep warm. Lift venison from marinade and pat dry; reserve 2 tablespoons marinade. Melt remaining 2 tablespoons butter or margarine in skillet; add venison slices and cook 4 to 5 minutes on each side. Season with salt.
To serve, arrange 1 venison slice on each fried bread slice. Keep warm. Beat 2 tablespoons cream until stiff; set aside. Stir gin, reserved 2 tablespoons marinade, remaining cream, remaining crushed juniper berries and lemon juice into pan drippings. Heat, stirring, until slightly thickened; season with pepper. Quickly fold in whipped cream, then spoon over venison and serve at once. Makes 4 servings.

Saddle of Venison with Cherry Sauce

1 (3-lb.) saddle of venison
3 juniper berries, crushed
1/2 teaspoon dried leaf thyme
Salt to taste
3 tablespoons clarified butter
6 bacon slices
About 2 cups game stock or
　beef stock
1 orange

Cherry Sauce:
1 (16-oz.) can red
　tart cherries
Sugar to taste
1 tablespoon cornstarch
3 tablespoons cherry-flavored
　liqueur

Trim skin from meat, then rub meat with crushed juniper berries and thyme. Let stand at room temperature 30 minutes. Preheat oven to 425F (220C). Pat meat dry and sprinkle with salt. Heat clarified butter in a roasting pan on top of range, add meat and brown well on all sides. Then arrange bacon over meat; roast 35 to 45 minutes total. After the first 10 minutes of roasting, pour 1 cup stock into pan; stir to mix with pan drippings. Then baste meat every 8 minutes for remainder of roasting time, adding more stock to pan as necessary. Remove bacon and begin checking for doneness after 30 minutes of roasting time. If meat gives slightly under the pressure of a finger, then returns to its original shape, it is done to the proper point—cooked through, but still slightly pink in center. Place meat on a warm platter; let stand 10 minutes. Meanwhile, prepare sauce.

To make sauce, drain cherries, reserving juice. In a saucepan, stir together sugar, cornstarch and cherry juice. Bring to a boil. Stir in cherries and liqueur, then stir in roasting-pan juices and heat through.

To serve, slice orange; garnish venison with orange slices. If desired, top each orange slice with a small spoonful of cherry sauce. Slice meat across the grain; pass sauce at the table to accompany meat. Makes 8 servings.

Saddle of Hare with Ginger Sauce

2 (14-oz.) larded saddles of hare	1 parsley root, if desired, chopped
Salt and freshly ground white pepper to taste	1/2 teaspoon ground ginger
5 juniper berries, crushed	1/8 teaspoon ground nutmeg
4 black peppercorns, crushed	1 cup dry red wine
1/4 lb. celeriac	2 teaspoons lemon juice
2 tablespoons vegetable oil	1/2 lb. grapes, halved, seeded
1 carrot, diced	2 tablespoons cranberry sauce
2 small onions, diced	1/2 cup dairy sour cream
	2 orange slices, cut in thirds

Preheat oven to 425F (220C). Rub saddles of hare with salt, white pepper, crushed juniper berries and crushed peppercorns. Peel and dice celeriac. Heat oil in a roasting pan on top of range; add hare, celeriac, carrot, onions and parsley root, if desired. Cook, stirring vegetables frequently and turning meat as needed, until meat is browned on all sides. Sprinkle ginger and nutmeg over meat and vegetables, then pour wine and lemon juice into pan. Roast 20 minutes. Turn off oven. Place meat on a heatproof platter; let stand in turned-off oven 10 minutes. Strain pan juices into a small saucepan; bring to a simmer. Reserve 4 grape halves for garnish, then stir remaining grapes into simmering pan juices. Stir in cranberry sauce and sour cream; heat through.
To serve, garnish meat with orange slices and grapes. Slice meat across the grain; pass sauce. Makes 4 servings.

Saddle of Wild Boar

10 juniper berries	8 whole cloves
1 (3-lb.) saddle of wild boar	1 cup beef stock or game stock
Salt to taste	1 tablespoon all-purpose flour
2 teaspoons paprika	1 cup apple juice
2 tablespoons vegetable oil	1/4 cup cranberry sauce
8 thin bacon slices	Freshly ground pepper to taste

Preheat oven to 400F (205C). Soak juniper berries 5 minutes in water to cover. Trim any skin and gristle from boar; rub meat with salt and paprika. Heat oil in a roasting pan on top of the range; add meat and brown quickly on all sides. Arrange bacon over meat; secure each bacon slice in place with a clove. Pour juniper berries and their soaking water into pan. Roast on next-to-lowest oven rack 1 hour. Turn off oven. Remove bacon and cloves from meat. Transfer meat to a warm platter and let stand in turned-off oven 15 minutes. Meanwhile, stir stock into pan juices; then pour mixture into a saucepan. Skim and discard fat. Shake or stir together flour and apple juice until smooth. Pour apple-juice mixture into stock mixture; bring to a boil, stirring constantly. Stir in cranberry sauce. Reduce heat and simmer 5 minutes. Season sauce with salt and pepper. Slice meat across the grain; pass sauce at the table to accompany meat. Makes 6 servings.

Rabbit with Thyme

1 (3-lb.) rabbit, cut up	1 garlic clove, chopped
4 large thyme sprigs	1 (1-inch) square lemon peel
2/3 cup beef stock	3 tablespoons vegetable oil
2 cups dry white wine	Salt and freshly ground pepper
2 bay leaves	to taste
4 black peppercorns, crushed	1/2 teaspoon sugar

Wash rabbit pieces in cold water; pat dry. Place rabbit pieces in a saucepan with thyme sprigs. In another saucepan, combine stock, wine, bay leaves, crushed peppercorns, garlic and lemon peel. Bring to a boil; cool and pour over rabbit. Cover and refrigerate 24 to 48 hours, turning rabbit pieces occasionally. Lift meat from marinade; pat dry. Strain marinade into a saucepan; heat through. Heat oil in a large, heavy saucepan; add meat and brown on all sides. Season 2 cups of the hot marinade with salt, pepper and sugar, then pour over meat. Reduce heat, cover and simmer 50 minutes or until meat is tender, adding remaining marinade as necessary and turning meat occasionally.

To serve, lift meat from sauce and place on a warm platter. Dilute sauce with a little hot water and serve with meat. Makes 4 servings.

Peppered Hare

1 (3-lb.) hare	6 white peppercorns
Salt and freshly ground pepper	2/3 cup dry red wine
to taste	1 tablespoon all-purpose flour
1 teaspoon hot paprika	mixed with 2 tablespoons
3 tablespoons vegetable oil	cold water
2 onions, diced	

Remove bones from hare. Chop bones; place in a saucepan. Pour in enough water to cover. Bring to a boil; reduce heat to low, cover and simmer 2 hours. Strain stock; set aside. Cut hare meat in 2-inch cubes. Sprinkle with salt, pepper and paprika. Heat oil in a large, heavy saucepan; add meat and brown on all sides. Add onions, peppercorns, and 2/3 cup strained stock. Reduce heat to low, cover and simmer about 40 minutes or until meat is tender, gradually adding wine and stirring occasionally. Stir in flour-water mixture; heat, stirring, until sauce is thickened. Makes 4 servings.

Braised Leg of Hare

1 cup water	2/3 cup red-wine vinegar
2 carrots, sliced	4 legs of hare
2 celery stalks, sliced	2 tablespoons vegetable oil
2 tomatoes, peeled, sliced	2/3 cup game stock or homemade
6 to 8 small white	or canned beef stock
boiling onions	1/4 cup dry red wine
2 black peppercorns, crushed	2/3 cup dairy sour cream
4 juniper berries, crushed	Salt and freshly ground pepper
Pinch of dried leaf thyme	to taste
1/2 bay leaf	

In a saucepan, combine water, carrots, celery, tomatoes, onions, peppercorns, juniper berries, thyme, bay leaf and vinegar. Bring to a boil; cool. Meanwhile, wash hare in cold water; pat dry. Place hare in a bowl; pour in cooled marinade and turn hare to coat. Cover and refrigerate 12 to 24 hours, turning occasionally. Remove hare; pat dry. Strain marinade into a saucepan; reserve vegetables; discard bay leaf. Heat marinade through. Heat oil in a large, heavy saucepan. Add hare; brown on all sides. Stir in 2/3 cup hot marinade. Reduce heat to low, cover and simmer 50 minutes, adding remaining stock and marinade. Stir in vegetables; simmer 10 minutes or until meat is tender.
To serve, place meat on a platter. Stir wine and sour cream into sauce and heat through, but do not boil. Season with salt and pepper; spoon over meat. Makes 4 servings.

Burgundy-Style Rabbit

4 (8-oz.) rabbit legs,	1/4 lb. fresh mushrooms, sliced
thighs attached	2/3 cup red Burgundy wine
1/4 cup vegetable oil	1 tablespoon all-purpose flour
2 shallots, peeled, finely diced	2 tablespoons butter or
About 3/4 cup chopped parsley	margarine, room temperature
2 thyme sprigs, chopped	Salt to taste
1 bay leaf, crushed	Pinch of sugar
1 to 2 cups game stock or	Pinch of red (cayenne) pepper
beef stock	

Wash rabbit in cold water; pat dry. Place in a single layer in a glass container. In a small bowl, mix oil, shallots, parsley, thyme and bay leaf. Spread mixture over rabbit, cover and refrigerate 12 hours. Drain oil from rabbit into a large saucepan. Heat oil; add rabbit and brown on all sides. Add any shallots and herbs left in marinating container, then stir in 1 cup stock. Bring to a boil. Reduce heat, cover and simmer 25 to 30 minutes or until meat is tender, adding remaining stock as necessary.
To serve, lift rabbit from pan, transfer to a warm platter and keep warm. Strain cooking liquid, return to saucepan and boil until slightly reduced. Stir in mushrooms and wine. Blend flour and butter or margarine; stir into sauce until dissolved. Simmer 10 minutes. Season sauce with salt, sugar and red pepper; pour over meat. Makes 4 servings.

Roast Wild Duck

1 (3-lb.) wild duck	6 bacon slices
Salt and freshly ground white	4 juniper berries, crushed
pepper to taste	1 cup game stock or beef stock
3 tablespoons vegetable oil	2/3 cup dry red wine
2 tart apples	1 teaspoon cornstarch
2 onions	2 tablespoons half and half

Preheat oven to 425F (220C). Wash duck inside and out with cold water; pat dry. Rub duck body cavity with salt and white pepper. Heat oil in a roasting pan on top of the range; add duck and brown on all sides. Meanwhile, peel apples. Cut each apple in about 8 wedges and remove cores. Cut each wedge in half again. Cut onions in wedges. Place duck on a rack in roasting pan; cover duck with bacon. Add apples, onions, crushed juniper berries and 2/3 cup stock to pan. Roast duck on lowest oven rack 1 hour or until duck is cooked rare, basting often and adding remaining stock as necessary.

To serve, lift duck from pan, transfer to a warm platter and let stand 10 minutes. Dilute pan juices with a little hot water, then strain into a small saucepan. Skim and discard fat. Stir in wine. In a small bowl, stir together cornstarch and half and half; stir into sauce. Heat, stirring, until sauce is thickened. Pass sauce at the table to accompany duck. Makes 6 servings.

Stuffed Partridge

2 (1-1/2-lb.) partridges	Salt and freshly ground white
1/3 cup raisins	pepper to taste
2 day-old dinner rolls	8 thin bacon slices
2 onions, diced	2/3 cup game stock or beef stock

Preheat oven to 450F (230C). Wash partridges inside and out with cold water; pat dry. Set aside. Soak raisins briefly in hot water; drain. Tear rolls in small pieces and soften in a little cold water, then squeeze out any excess moisture. In a bowl, mix softened rolls, onions and drained raisins. Rub partridge body cavities with salt and white pepper, then stuff partridges with raisin mixture. Sew cavities closed with strong thread. Tie legs and wings of each partridge to body with string. Lay 1 bacon slice on back, breast and each leg of each partridge; tie in place. Place partridges, breast down, on a rack in a large roasting pan. Roast 30 to 35 minutes, turning birds breast up and pouring stock into pan after 15 minutes. After 30 minutes, meat will still be pink inside; after 35 minutes, it will be well-done.

To serve, remove bacon from partridges. Remove trussing string. Transfer partridges to a warm platter and let stand 10 minutes. Meanwhile, dilute pan juices with a little hot water. Skim and discard fat. Pass juices at the table to accompany meat. Makes 4 servings.

Roast Pheasant

2 (1-3/4-lb.) pheasants,
    with giblets and necks
    if possible
	2/3 cup game stock or beef stock
	1/2 lb. carrots, peeled,
	    thinly sliced

Salt and freshly ground white pepper to taste	2/3 cup dairy sour cream 2/3 cup dry white wine
Juice of 1 lemon	Cranberry sauce
8 thin bacon slices	
1/4 lb. leeks	

Preheat oven to 425F (220C). Wash pheasants inside and out with cold water; pat dry. Rub body cavities with salt and white pepper. Sprinkle skin with lemon juice. Then truss pheasants: Thread a trussing needle or large embroidery needle with strong thread. Run thread through both wings of each pheasant, then through both legs. Tie firmly so legs and wings lie close to body. Lay 1 bacon slice on back, breast and each leg of each pheasant; tie in place. Place pheasants on their sides on a rack in a large roasting pan. Arrange pheasant hearts and necks (if you have them) in pan around birds. Wash livers (if you have them) in cold water and set aside. Roast pheasants on next-to-lowest oven rack 10 minutes. Meanwhile, trim roots and green tops of leeks; split leeks lengthwise and wash thoroughly to remove sand. Thinly slice leek halves crosswise. Pour stock into a small saucepan;

bring to a simmer. After pheasants have roasted 10 minutes, pour stock into roasting pan, then arrange leeks and carrots in pan. Every 10 minutes, add a little hot water to pan, turn pheasants over and baste with pan juices. Roast 30 to 35 minutes longer or until breast of each pheasant gives slightly under the pressure of a finger, then returns to its original shape. At this point, meat is cooked, but still pink and juicy. About 10 minutes before end of roasting time, remove and reserve bacon; turn pheasants breast up. Reserve 1 tablespoon sour cream; spread remainder over pheasants and let brown well.

To serve, lift pheasants from pan; transfer to a warm platter. Arrange bacon around pheasants. Remove trussing thread. Let pheasants stand in turned-off oven 15 minutes with oven door slightly ajar. Meanwhile, dilute pan juices with a little hot water; strain into a saucepan. Skim and discard fat. Stir in wine. Finely chop pheasant livers, crush with a fork and stir into juices with reserved 1 tablespoon sour cream. Heat, stirring, until livers are cooked; do not boil. Season with salt and white pepper. Pass sour-cream sauce and cranberry sauce at the table to accompany meat. Makes 4 servings.

Carrots in Cream

2 lbs. carrots
2 tablespoons butter or
   margarine
1 tablespoon sugar
1 cup chicken stock

2/3 cup half and half
Salt and freshly ground white
   pepper to taste
2 tablespoons finely
   chopped parsley

Peel carrots; cut in 3-inch-long strips about 1/2 inch thick. Melt butter or margarine in a large saucepan; sprinkle in sugar. Cook, stirring, until sugar dissolves and begins to caramelize. Add carrots and stir to coat with butter-sugar mixture. Stir in stock; bring to a simmer. Cover and simmer 15 minutes. Then uncover pan; simmer 10 to 15 minutes longer or until carrots are tender and almost all liquid has evaporated.

To serve, stir half and half into carrots, season with salt and white pepper. Sprinkle with parsley. Makes 4 servings.

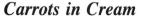

Cook's tip

For a reduced calorie count, omit the sugar; instead, fry diced onion in the butter or margarine. Substitute 1/2 teaspoon ground dried mushrooms for the half and half.

Dill Cucumbers

2 lbs. cucumbers
Salt
2-1/2 to 3 tablespoons
   lemon juice
1/2 teaspoon vegetable or
   chicken bouillon granules
2/3 cup plain low-fat yogurt

About 1/2 teaspoon sugar
3 tablespoons butter or
   margarine, melted
1 teaspoon cornstarch mixed
   with 2 teaspoons cold water
1/4 cup chopped fresh dill

Peel cucumbers, halve lengthwise and scoop out seeds with a spoon. Then cut cucumber halves in about 1-inch chunks. In a saucepan, combine cucumbers, a pinch of salt, 2 tablespoons lemon juice, bouillon, yogurt and 1/2 teaspoon sugar. Bring to a simmer over low heat, stirring; then cover and simmer 10 minutes, stirring frequently. Stir in melted butter or margarine; simmer 10 minutes longer. Stir in cornstarch-water mixture; bring to a boil, stirring constantly.

To serve, adjust sweet-sour flavor with sugar, remaining lemon juice and salt. Sprinkle with dill and serve at once. Makes 4 servings.

Green Beans

1-3/4 lbs. fresh green beans
2 tablespoons butter or
  margarine
1 large onion, finely diced
1/2 pint half and half (1 cup)

Salt and freshly ground white
  pepper to taste
2 tablespoons chopped fresh dill
2 tablespoons chopped parsley

Wash beans in cold water. Trim ends from beans; remove any strings. Cut larger beans in half; leave smaller ones whole. Cook beans in boiling lightly salted water until beans are tender. Meanwhile, melt butter or margarine in a large skillet. Add onion and cook, stirring, until soft. Drain cooked beans; add to onion and stir well.

To serve, stir in half and half; heat through. Season beans with salt and white pepper. Sprinkle with dill and parsley. Makes 4 servings.

Cauliflower in Herb Sauce

1 (about 1-3/4-lb.) cauliflower

Juice of 1 lemon

Herb Sauce:
1 vegetable or chicken
  bouillon cube
2 tablespoons butter or
  margarine
2 tablespoons all-purpose flour
1/4 cup half and half
Salt to taste

1/4 cup chopped parsley
1 tablespoon chopped fresh basil
1 tablespoon chopped
  fresh borage (optional)
1 tablespoon chopped fresh
  lemon balm (optional)

Trim thick stalk and outer leaves from cauliflower. Soak cauliflower, upside down, in cold salted water 30 minutes to drive out any insects. Then, in a saucepan, bring about 1 quart water to a boil. Add lemon juice and cauliflower. Reduce heat, cover and simmer 25 to 30 minutes or until cauliflower is tender. Lift cauliflower from cooking water, transfer to a warm serving dish and keep hot.

To make sauce, measure 1-3/4 cups of the cauliflower-cooking water; dissolve bouillon cube in cooking water. Melt butter or margarine in a saucepan, sprinkle in flour and cook over low heat, stirring about 1 minute. Gradually stir in hot bouillon; cook, stirring, until sauce is slightly thickened. Stir in half and half; heat through. Season with salt. Stir in parsley, basil, borage and lemon balm.

To serve, pour sauce over cauliflower. Makes 4 servings.

Spinach with Pistachios

2 tablespoons raisins	Salt and freshly ground white
1/4 cup apple-flavored liqueur	pepper to taste
or apple juice	Pinch of ground nutmeg
2-1/4 lbs. fresh spinach	2 tablespoons coarsely chopped
2 tablespoons plus 1 teaspoon	pistachio nuts or
butter or margarine	sliced almonds
1 small onion, finely diced	

In a small bowl, stir together raisins and apple-flavored liqueur or apple juice. Set aside to soak. Remove stems and any tough leaves from spinach, then wash spinach thoroughly in cold water. Cook spinach in boiling lightly salted water 3 minutes. Drain well in a colander; press out excess water. Set spinach aside. Melt 2 tablespoons butter or margarine in a large skillet. Add onion and cook, stirring, until soft. Then add spinach, loosening it with 2 forks. Add raisins and any unabsorbed liqueur or apple juice. Stir well; cover and cook over low heat 5 minutes. Season with salt, white pepper and nutmeg.

To serve, melt remaining 1 teaspoon butter or margarine in a small skillet. Add pistachios or almonds and cook, stirring, until nuts are lightly toasted. Sprinkle toasted nuts over spinach. Makes 4 servings.

Spinach with Garlic Cream

2-1/4 lbs. fresh spinach	Salt and freshly ground white
2 tablespoons vegetable oil	pepper to taste
1 tablespoon plus 1 teaspoon	Pinch of garlic powder
butter or margarine	1 tablespoon slivered almonds
1 onion, finely chopped	

Garlic Cream:

1/4 cup whipping cream	3 garlic cloves

Remove stems and any tough leaves from spinach, then wash spinach thoroughly in cold water. Cook spinach in boiling lightly salted water 3 minutes. Drain well in a colander; press out excess water. Coarsely chop drained spinach; set aside. Heat oil and 1 tablespoon butter or margarine in a large skillet. Add onion and cook until golden, stirring frequently. Stir in spinach, cover and cook over very low heat 10 minutes. Season with salt, white pepper and garlic powder. Keep warm.

To make Garlic Cream, in a bowl, beat cream until stiff. Press garlic cloves through a garlic press into cream; fold in gently but thoroughly.

To serve, melt remaining 1 teaspoon butter or margarine in a small skillet. Add almonds and cook, stirring, until lightly toasted. Spoon Garlic Cream over spinach and sprinkle with toasted almonds. Makes 4 servings.

Sweet-Sour Beets

**1-3/4 lbs. fresh beets,
   scrubbed**
1 tablespoon vegetable oil
1 medium onion, chopped
1 cup beef stock
Salt to taste
3 whole cloves
1 teaspoon sugar
1/2 teaspoon cornstarch
1 tablespoon red-wine vinegar
1/4 cup dry red wine
**3 small fresh dill pickles,
   cut in julienne strips**

Cook beets in water to cover in a 4- to 5-quart covered kettle until tender, 20 to 45 minutes. Let cool. Trim off root and stem and slip off skins. Cut into strips about 1/4-inch thick. Set aside. Heat oil in a saucepan; add onion and cook until golden, stirring constantly. Add stock; bring to a simmer. Stir in salt, cloves and 1 teaspoon sugar. Reduce heat to low, cover and simmer 15 to 20 minutes. Add beets and simmer until very tender. In a small bowl, mix cornstarch, 1 tablespoon vinegar and wine. Stir into beet mixture and cook, stirring, until sauce is slightly thickened. Stir in pickles. Cook over lowest possible heat 3 minutes longer.

To serve, adjust the sweet-sour flavor with sugar and vinegar. Makes 4 servings.

Broccoli with Hazelnut Butter

2-1/4 lbs. fresh broccoli	2 tablespoons lemon juice

Hazelnut Butter:

1/4 cup butter or margarine	1/2 cup hazelnuts, thinly sliced or chopped

Wash broccoli. Trim and discard bases of stalks, then cut broccoli into spears. Peel stalks of spears almost up to flowerets; cut a cross in end of each stalk. Cook broccoli in boiling lightly salted water mixed with 2 tablespoons lemon juice until tender. Meanwhile, prepare Hazelnut Butter.

To make Hazelnut Butter, heat butter or margarine in a small skillet until lightly browned. Add hazelnuts and cook, stirring, until nuts are golden. Keep warm.

To serve, drain cooked broccoli and arrange on a warm platter; spoon Hazelnut Butter over broccoli. Makes 4 servings.

Variation

Broccoli with Almond Sauce: In a small bowl, beat together 6 tablespoons milk and 1-1/2 (3-oz.) packages cream cheese (at room temperature). Stir in 1 egg yolk and about 1/2 cup ground almonds. Season with salt and freshly ground pepper. In another bowl, beat 2/3 cup whipping cream until it holds soft peaks; fold into cream-cheese mixture. Prepare broccoli as directed above and serve with almond sauce.

Fennel au Gratin

1-3/4 lbs. small fennel bulbs	2/3 cup dry white wine
3 tablespoons butter or margarine	1 teaspoon lemon juice
1 tablespoon sugar	2/3 cup shredded Emmentaler or Cheddar cheese
Salt to taste	(about 2-1/2 oz.)

Trim feathery leaves from fennel. Wash leaves in cold water, shake dry, chop and set aside. Trim and halve fennel bulbs. Melt butter or margarine in a large skillet or saucepan over medium heat; sprinkle in sugar. Cook, stirring, until sugar dissolves and begins to caramelize. Add fennel bulbs, sprinkle with salt and stir to coat with butter-sugar mixture. Then continue to cook until fennel is lightly browned. Stir in wine, reduce heat, cover and simmer 25 minutes or until fennel is tender; add a little hot water occasionally, if necessary. Preheat oven to 425F (220C). Drain fennel, reserving cooking liquid; add lemon juice and cheese to hot cooking liquid and stir until cheese is melted. Arrange fennel in a baking dish. Pour cheese sauce over fennel and bake 10 minutes or until sauce is lightly browned.

To serve, sprinkle with reserved chopped fennel leaves. Makes 4 servings.

Cauliflower with Cheese Sauce

1 (about 1-3/4-lb.) cauliflower	1 tablespoon lemon juice

Cheese Sauce:

2 tablespoons butter or margarine	Salt to taste
1 tablespoon all-purpose flour	1/8 teaspoon ground nutmeg
2/3 cup chicken stock	1 egg yolk
2/3 cup milk	2 tablespoons fine dry bread crumbs
1 cup shredded Gouda or Cheddar cheese (4 oz.)	1 tablespoon chopped parsley

Separate cauliflower into flowerets. Cook in boiling water mixed with lemon juice until tender. Meanwhile, prepare sauce.

To make sauce, melt 1 tablespoon butter or margarine in a saucepan. Sprinkle in flour; cook over low heat, stirring about 1 minute. Gradually stir in stock and milk; cook, stirring, until sauce is slightly thickened. Sprinkle in cheese and stir until melted. Season with salt and nutmeg. Remove from heat. In a bowl, beat egg yolk; stir in 2 to 3 tablespoons of the hot sauce, then stir egg-yolk mixture back into sauce. Return to heat and cook, stirring, about 1 minute. Keep warm over very low heat.

To serve, melt 1 tablespoon butter or margarine in a small skillet; add bread crumbs. Cook, stirring, until golden brown. Drain cooked cauliflower; arrange on a platter; sprinkle with bread crumbs and parsley. Serve sauce separately. Makes 4 servings.

Ratatouille

6 tablespoons olive oil	1 zucchini, sliced
2 onions, sliced	3 garlic cloves, finely chopped
1 red bell pepper, seeded, cut in strips	1/2 teaspoon dried leaf rosemary
1 green bell pepper, seeded, cut in strips	2/3 cup water
1 medium (1-lb.) eggplant, diced	1 small bunch mixed fresh thyme and basil
Salt to taste	2 large, firm tomatoes
	1 tablespoon chopped parsley

Heat oil in a large saucepan. Add onions and cook, stirring, until soft. Add bell peppers and cook a few minutes, then stir in eggplant and sprinkle with salt. Top evenly with zucchini; sprinkle with salt, garlic and rosemary. Add water and bunch of thyme and basil. Bring to a boil. Reduce heat, cover and simmer 15 minutes. Peel tomatoes, cut in wedges and remove seeds. Stir into ratatouille and simmer 15 minutes longer or until all vegetables are tender.

To serve, remove bunch of thyme and basil; sprinkle with parsley. Makes 4 servings.

Mixed Peppers

1-3/4 lbs. mixed yellow, green and red bell peppers	2/3 cup chicken stock
2 tablespoons vegetable oil	Salt to taste
2 onions, diced	1 tablespoon paprika
1 garlic clove, very finely chopped	2 tablespoons chopped parsley

Preheat oven to 475F (245C). Place bell peppers on a baking sheet; bake 8 to 10 minutes or until skins begin to darken. Remove peppers from oven, enclose in a damp cloth or paper bag and let stand 15 to 20 minutes. Peel off skin; remove stems. Halve and seed peppers. Rinse in cold water, pat dry and cut crosswise in thick strips. Set aside. Heat oil in a large skillet or saucepan; add onions and garlic; cook, stirring, until onions are soft. Add peppers and cook a few minutes, stirring constantly. Pour in stock, reduce heat to low, cover and simmer 5 to 10 minutes. Season with salt and stir in paprika.

To serve, sprinkle with parsley. Makes 4 servings.

Kohlrabi in Herb-Cream Sauce

2-1/4 lbs. kohlrabi	About 1/2 cup chicken stock
1 tablespoon lemon juice	5 tablespoons half and half
2 tablespoons butter or margarine	1 tablespoon chopped mixed fresh herbs (parsley, oregano, rosemary, tarragon, basil, etc.)
Salt to taste	
1/8 teaspoon sugar	

Discard any tough kohlrabi leaves; wash tender leaves in cold water, chop and set aside. Peel kohlrabi bulbs; remove any woody parts. Cut bulbs in quarters; cut each quarter in fairly thick strips. In a large saucepan, combine about 2 quarts water and lemon juice. Bring to a boil. Place kohlrabi in a wire strainer and suspend in boiling water and blanch 5 minutes. Then rinse kohlrabi under cold running water and drain well. Melt butter or margarine in a large saucepan; add kohlrabi and cook a few minutes, stirring frequently. Stir in salt, sugar and stock. Bring to a simmer; cover and simmer 15 to 20 minutes or until kohlrabi is tender.

To serve, in a small bowl, mix reserved chopped kohlrabi leaves, half and half, parsley, burnet and lovage. Stir into kohlrabi. Makes 4 servings.

Cabbage au Gratin

1 large (2-1/4-lb.) head cabbage	1/4 cup chicken stock
1 tablespoon clarified butter or lard	1/3 cup dairy sour cream
2 teaspoons caraway seeds	1 tablespoon butter or margarine

Trim base of cabbage stalk; remove any wilted outer leaves. Then cut cabbage in 8 wedges. Cook cabbage in boiling lightly salted water 15 minutes. Drain cabbage, rinse under cold running water and drain again. Set aside. Heat clarified butter or lard in a heavy saucepan with an ovenproof handle. Add cabbage and brown lightly on all sides. Sprinkle caraway seeds and stock over cabbage; reduce heat to low, cover and simmer 15 minutes. Add a little hot water occasionally, if necessary. Preheat oven to 425F (220C). Spoon sour cream evenly over cabbage, dot with butter or margarine and bake 5 to 8 minutes or until lightly browned. Makes 4 servings

Mixed Spring Vegetables

1 lb. white or green asparagus	2 to 3 tablespoons water
	Salt to taste
1/4 lb. morels or other mushrooms	1/2 teaspoon sugar
3 tablespoons butter or margarine	1 lb. young green peas, shelled
3/4 lb. baby carrots, diced	1 egg yolk
	2 tablespoons half and half
	1 tablespoon chopped parsley

Snap off and discard woody ends of asparagus stalks. Peel bases of stalks; tie asparagus into a bundle. In a saucepan, bring 1-inch lightly salted water to a boil. Add asparagus, reduce heat, cover and simmer 8 to 12 minutes or until tender. Drain well; cut each stalk in half. Cover and keep warm. Cut ends off morel stalks, wash morels under running water and drain. Cut large morels in halves or quarters; leave smaller ones whole. Set aside. Melt butter or margarine in a large saucepan or skillet. Add carrots; cook, stirring, a few minutes. Stir in 2 to 3 tablespoons water, salt and sugar. Reduce heat, add morels and peas; cover and simmer 10 minutes or until peas and carrots are tender. Stir in cooked asparagus; heat through. In a small bowl, beat together egg yolk and half and half; stir into vegetables. Heat through, but do not boil.

To serve, sprinkle with parsley. Makes 4 servings.

Mixed Wild Greens

1 lb. mixed wild leafy greens, such as nettle leaves, dandelion leaves, burnet and sorrel	3/4 cup mixed strawberry and raspberry leaves Cooked crepes (optional)

Sauce:

1 vegetable-bouillon cube	1 tablespoon all-purpose flour
1 cup boiling water	1/2 pint half and half (1 cup)
3 tablespoons butter or margarine	2 egg yolks
5 shallots, peeled, diced	Salt and freshly ground white pepper to taste

Wash all leaves thoroughly in cold water; remove any withered leaves. In a saucepan, bring 1 cup lightly salted water to a boil. Add leaves, reduce heat, cover and simmer gently 3 minutes. Drain leaves well in a colander, then coarsely chop. Set aside. **To make sauce,** dissolve bouillon cube in boiling water; set aside. Melt butter or margarine in a medium saucepan; add shallots and cook, stirring, until soft. Sprinkle in flour and cook over low heat, stirring, about 1 minute. Gradually add bouillon. Cook, stirring constantly, until sauce is slightly thickened. Remove from heat. In a bowl, beat together half and half, egg yolks and 2 to 3 tablespoons of the hot sauce. Stir yolk mixture back into sauce; cook, stirring, until slightly thickened. Season with salt and white pepper. Stir cooked leaves into sauce; heat through. Spoon into crepes, if desired. Makes 4 servings.

Swiss Chard with Bread Crumbs

1 lb. Swiss chard	About 1/2 cup dairy sour cream
3 tablespoons butter or margarine	1/4 cup fine dry bread crumbs
Salt and freshly ground white pepper to taste	

Wash chard thoroughly in cold water; drain well. Cut leaves from stalks. Cut leaves crosswise in 1-1/2-inch-wide strips; cut stalks in 1-1/2-inch lengths. Cook chard leaves and stems, covered, in boiling lightly salted water 20 minutes. Drain chard well. Melt 2 tablespoons butter or margarine in a skillet; stir in chard, salt, white pepper and sour cream. Heat through, but do not boil. Keep warm, uncovered, over low heat.
To serve, melt remaining 1 tablespoon butter or margarine in a small skillet. Add bread crumbs; cook, stirring, until golden brown. Sprinkle over chard. Makes 4 servings.

French-Style Tomatoes

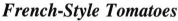

3-1/2 lbs. large, firm tomatoes
  (about 8 tomatoes)
Salt to taste
1 small onion, finely chopped
2 garlic cloves, finely chopped
1 tablespoon chopped parsley
1-1/2 teaspoons chopped fresh
  chervil
1-1/2 teaspoons chopped fresh
  tarragon
6 tablespoons fine dry
  bread crumbs
3 tablespoons butter or
  margarine

Preheat oven to 400F (205C). Lightly grease a baking dish. Cut a 1/4-inch slice from top of each of 6 tomatoes. Carefully remove centers of tomatoes with a small pointed spoon; discard seeds and dice flesh. Sprinkle insides of hollowed tomatoes with salt, then invert tomatoes on paper towels to drain. Peel, seed and dice remaining whole tomatoes. In a saucepan, combine all diced tomatoes, a pinch of salt, onion and garlic. Bring to a simmer, then cover and simmer over low heat 5 minutes. Stir in parsley, chervil and tarragon; season with salt. Spoon evenly into hollowed tomatoes. Arrange tomatoes in greased baking dish; sprinkle evenly with bread crumbs and dot with butter or margarine. Bake about 10 minutes or until browned. Makes 6 servings.

Dutch-Style Peas

1-1/4 lbs. young green peas
  in the pod
Chervil sprig
Tarragon sprig

Hollandaise Sauce:
1/2 cup butter
2 egg yolks
1 tablespoon water
1 teaspoon lemon juice
Salt and freshly ground white
  pepper to taste

Shell peas. Tie chervil sprig and tarragon sprig together. Cook peas in boiling lightly salted water with chervil and tarragon until tender. Drain peas; remove herbs. Keep peas hot.

To make sauce, melt butter in a small saucepan over low heat. Remove from heat and cool to room temperature. In the top of a double boiler, beat together egg yolks, 1 tablespoon water, lemon juice, salt and white pepper. Then place over simmering water and beat with a whisk until mixture is creamy. Remove from heat; add melted, cooled butter, a few drops at a time, whisking until sauce is thickened.

To serve, pour peas into a warm serving dish; mix in sauce. Makes 4 servings.

Stuffed Kohlrabi

4 medium kohlrabi	1 tablespoon chopped parsley
1 day-old dinner roll	1 egg, beaten
1 onion, finely chopped	Salt and freshly ground white
3/4 lb. mixed lean ground beef	pepper to taste
and pork	1/2 teaspoon paprika
	8 thin bacon slices

Discard any tough kohlrabi leaves; wash tender leaves in cold water, shake dry and chop. Set aside. Peel kohlrabi bulbs. Cook kohlrabi bulbs in boiling lightly salted water until tender throughout; drain, reserving about 6 tablespoons of the cooking water. Cool kohlrabi bulbs. Preheat oven to 400F (205C). Grease a baking dish. Cut a "lid" from top of each cooled kohlrabi; set lids aside. Carefully remove centers of bulbs with a small, pointed spoon. Finely dice removed kohlrabi flesh and set aside. Tear roll in small pieces and soften in a little cold water; squeeze out any excess moisture. In a bowl, mix reserved chopped kohlrabi leaves, chopped kohlrabi bulbs, softened roll, onion, beef, pork, parsley, egg, salt, white pepper and paprika. Fill hollowed kohlrabi bulbs evenly with meat mixture and arrange in greased baking dish. Cover stuffed kohlrabi with reserved "lids"; top each with 2 bacon slices. Pour reserved 6 tablespoons kohlrabi-cooking water around stuffed kohlrabi. Bake 25 minutes or until bacon is crisp and stuffing is cooked through. Makes 4 servings.

Belgian Endive with Ham

4 heads Belgian endive	2 tablespoons fine dry
1 tablespoon butter or margarine	bread crumbs
4 (4-oz.) slices lean cooked ham	1 tablespoon chopped parsley

Sauce:

1 tablespoon butter or margarine	2/3 cup half and half
1 tablespoon all-purpose flour	Salt and freshly ground white
2/3 cup dry white wine	pepper to taste

Remove any damaged outer leaves from each head of endive; trim root end. With a sharp knife, cut a small wedge out of root end; discard. Cook endive in boiling salted water 10 minutes; drain and cool completely. Preheat oven to 400F (205C). Butter a baking dish, using 1 tablespoon butter or margarine. Trim any excess fat from ham. Wrap each cooled endive head in 1 ham slice; arrange ham-wrapped endive in buttered baking dish.
To make sauce, melt 1 tablespoon butter or margarine in a saucepan. Sprinkle in flour; cook over low heat, stirring, about 1 minute. Gradually stir in wine; continue to cook, stirring constantly, until sauce is bubbly and thickened. Stir in half and half, then season with salt and white pepper.
To complete, pour sauce over endive and sprinkle with bread crumbs. Bake on center oven rack about 15 minutes or until browned. Sprinkle with parsley. Makes 4 servings.

Asparagus with Melted Butter

**2 lbs. fresh white or
  green asparagus
1 sugar cube**

**2 tablespoons lemon juice
1/2 cup butter or margarine**

Wash asparagus. Snap off and discard woody ends of stalks. Peel stalks. Tie asparagus into 4 equal-size bundles. In a very large saucepan, combine 1 cup salted water, sugar cube and lemon juice. Bring to a boil. Add asparagus. Reduce heat, cover and simmer briskly 10 to 15 minutes or until tender. Drain; place 1 bundle on each individual plate. Untie bundles; keep hot.
To serve, melt butter or margarine in a small pan. Drizzle over asparagus. Makes 4 servings.

Variations

Asparagus with Hollandaise Sauce: Prepare and cook 2 lbs. asparagus as directed above. Serve with Hollandaise Sauce, page 107, instead of melted butter or margarine.

Asparagus in Butter Sauce: Prepare and cook 4-1/2 lbs. asparagus as directed above; cook in batches, if necessary. Drain cooked asparagus; cut in 1-1/2-inch lengths. Preheat oven to 425F (220C). Butter a baking dish. Melt 2 tablespoons butter or margarine in a saucepan. Sprinkle in 2 tablespoons all-purpose flour; cook over low heat, stirring, about 1 minute. Gradually add 1 cup milk and 2/3 cup half and half; continue to cook, stirring constantly, until bubbly and slightly thickened. Season with salt, white pepper, ground nutmeg and lemon juice. Remove from heat. In a bowl, beat 2/3 cup whipping cream until stiff; fold whipped cream into sauce. Place asparagus in buttered baking dish; cover evenly with cream sauce. Dot with butter or margarine. Bake on center oven rack 10 to 15 minutes or until sauce is lightly browned. Garnish with parsley. Makes 8 servings.

Stuffed Onions

2 large (3/4-lb.) mild white onions	3 tomatoes, peeled, diced
1 tablespoon butter or margarine	1 tablespoon chopped parsley
1/2 cup plus 1 tablespoon uncooked long-grain white rice	Salt and white pepper
	About 1/4 teaspoon paprika
	1 cup shredded Cheddar cheese (4 oz.)
1-1/3 cups beef stock	3 tablespoons milk
1 tablespoon oil	2/3 cup dairy sour cream
1/4 lb. cooked ham, diced	1 tablespoon chopped mixed fresh herbs

Cut off top 1/4 to 1/3 of each onion. Scoop out onion centers. Chop onion centers and cut-off onion tops; set aside. Cook hollowed onions in boiling lightly salted water 20 minutes; drain and set aside. Melt 1 tablespoon butter or margarine in a saucepan; add rice and cook a few minutes, stirring. Stir in stock and bring to a boil; reduce heat, cover and simmer 20 minutes or until rice is tender. Preheat oven to 425F (220C). Lightly butter a baking dish. Heat oil in a skillet. Add chopped onions; cook, stirring, until soft. Stir in ham, tomatoes, cooked rice, parsley, salt, white pepper, 1/4 teaspoon paprika and cheddar cheese; mix well. Spoon mixture into drained onions; arrange stuffed onions in buttered baking dish. In a small bowl, stir together milk and sour cream. Season with paprika and mixed herbs. Spoon sauce over onions. Bake 15 minutes or until heated through. Makes 2 servings.

Tomatoes Stuffed with Feta Cheese

6 medium tomatoes	6 tablespoons fine dry bread crumbs
Salt and freshly ground white pepper to taste	1 tablespoon chopped parsley
2 garlic cloves, finely chopped	1 tablespoon chopped fresh basil
1 cup crumbled feta cheese (4 oz.)	1 tablespoon olive oil

Preheat oven to 400F (205C). Grease a baking dish. Cut a 1/4-inch slice from top of each tomato; set slices aside. Carefully remove centers of tomatoes with a small pointed spoon; reserve for other uses, if desired. Sprinkle insides of hollowed tomatoes with salt and white pepper; invert on paper towels to drain. Finely chop slices cut from tops of tomatoes. In a bowl, mix chopped tomatoes, garlic, cheese, bread crumbs, parsley and basil. Fill hollowed tomatoes evenly with cheese mixture; sprinkle with oil. Arrange stuffed tomatoes in greased baking dish. Bake on center oven rack 20 minutes or until heated through. Makes 6 servings.

Stuffed Green Peppers with Pepper Sauce

4 medium green bell peppers	1 teaspoon paprika
1 day-old dinner roll	2 tablespoons butter or
1 onion, finely chopped	margarine
3/4 lb. mixed lean ground beef	1-3/4 cups beef stock
and pork	2/3 cup half and half
2 eggs, beaten	1 teaspoon cornstarch
1 (about 8-oz.) can whole-kernel	1 tablespoon bottled green
corn, drained	peppercorns, drained
Salt and freshly ground white	
pepper to taste	

Halve bell peppers and remove seeds; do not remove stems. Tear roll in small pieces and soften in a little cold water; squeeze out any excess moisture. In a bowl, mix softened roll, onion, beef, pork, eggs, corn, salt, white pepper and paprika. Stuff bell pepper halves evenly with meat mixture. Melt butter or margarine in a saucepan; add peppers, stuffed-side up. Cover and cook 5 minutes. In another saucepan, bring stock to a boil; pour around peppers, cover and simmer 30 minutes longer.
To serve, lift peppers from pan, transfer to a warm platter and keep warm. Skim and discard fat from cooking juices. In a small bowl, stir together half and half and cornstarch; stir into cooking juices. Cook, stirring, until sauce is slightly thickened. Stir in peppercorns. Spoon sauce over peppers. Makes 4 servings.

Chinese Cabbage Rolls

8 large Chinese cabbage leaves	1/8 teaspoon red (cayenne)
1/2 lb. lean corned beef	pepper
2 onions	2 tablespoons vegetable oil
1 dill pickle, chopped	3 bacon slices, finely chopped
1/2 red bell pepper, chopped	1 garlic clove, finely chopped
1 egg, beaten	1 cup beef stock
3 tablespoons fine dry	2 tablespooons half and half
bread crumbs	1 teaspoon all-purpose flour
Salt and black pepper	3 tablespoons tomato paste

Blanch cabbage leaves 3 minutes in lightly salted boiling water. Drain leaves well; arrange in 4 stacks of 2 leaves each. Set aside. Chop beef and 1 onion. In a bowl, mix beef, chopped onion, pickle, bell pepper, egg, bread crumbs, salt, black pepper and red pepper. Spoon mixture evenly onto cabbage leaves. Roll leaves around filling; tie with string. Set aside. Finely chop remaining onion; set aside. Heat oil in a heavy saucepan. Add bacon; cook until crisp. Remove from pan. Add finely chopped onion and garlic to drippings; cook, stirring, until onion is soft. Add cabbage rolls; cook a few minutes. Add stock and bacon. Bring to a boil. Reduce heat; cover. Simmer 20 minutes.
To serve, arrange cabbage rolls on a platter. Skim and discard fat from cooking juices. Combine half and half, flour and tomato paste; stir into juices. Cook, stirring, until slightly thickened. Pour over cabbage rolls. Makes 4 servings.

Celery au Gratin

1 lb. celery	1/4 cup milk
Salt and freshly ground black pepper to taste	3 tablespoons freshly grated Parmesan cheese
1-1/2 lbs. marrow bones, if desired	2 tablespoons butter or margarine
1 tablespoon all-purpose flour	
1/2 cup plus 2 tablespoons Madeira	

Preheat oven to 400F (205C). Grease a baking dish. Separate celery into stalks; trim off base of each stalk. Wash stalks in cold water. Trim off leafy tops, finely chop and set aside. Peel off and discard any tough strings from celery stalks. Arrange celery stalks in greased baking dish; sprinkle with salt and pepper. If using marrow bones, cover bones with boiling water and let stand a few minutes. Then press marrow out of bones, using handle of a wooden spoon. Cut marrow in 1/2-inch-thick slices. Arrange marrow slices over celery. In a small bowl, stir together flour, Madeira and milk; pour mixture over celery. Sprinkle with reserved chopped celery leaves and cheese; dot with butter or margarine. Bake on center oven rack 40 minutes or until celery is tender. Makes 4 servings.

Leeks au Gratin

2 lbs. leeks	1 cup shredded Emmentaler cheese (4 oz.)
1/8 teaspoon ground nutmeg	
1 tablespoon chopped parsley	

Sauce:

1/4 cup butter or margarine	2 tablespoons half and half
2 tablespoons all-purpose flour	Salt and freshly ground white pepper
1 cup milk	

Use only white parts of leeks; cut off all green leaves and reserve for other uses, if desired. Trim root ends of leeks and split thicker leeks lengthwise, then wash leeks thoroughly to remove sand. Cook leeks in boiling lightly salted water seasoned with nutmeg 20 minutes or until tender. Drain leeks. Preheat oven to 425F (220C). Grease a baking dish. Arrange drained leeks in greased baking dish. Set aside.

To make sauce, melt butter or margarine in a saucepan, sprinkle in flour and cook over low heat, stirring, about 1 minute. Gradually stir in milk; continue to cook, stirring, until bubbly and thickened. Stir in half and half and season with salt and white pepper.

To complete, pour sauce over leeks; sprinkle with parsley and cheese. Bake about 10 minutes or until cheese begins to brown. Makes 4 servings.

Brussels Sprouts with Sausages

2 lbs. Brussels sprouts
1/2 lb. small smoked sausages
1 tablespoon chopped parsley

1/2 cup shredded Emmentaler
   cheese (2 oz.)
1 tablespoon butter or margarine

Sauce:

1 tablespoon butter or margarine
1 tablespoon all-purpose flour
2/3 cup milk
Pinch of sugar

Pinch of ground nutmeg
1 egg
Salt to taste

Remove any damaged leaves from sprouts. Cut off sprout stalks, then cut a cross in base of each sprout. In a large saucepan, bring 1 cup lightly salted water to a boil. Add sprouts; reduce heat, cover and simmer gently 15 minutes. Drain sprouts, reserving 2/3 cup of the cooking water. Slice sausages; set aside. Preheat oven to 425F (220C). Grease a baking dish.

To make sauce, melt butter or margarine in a saucepan. Sprinkle in flour; cook over low heat, stirring, about 1 minute. Gradually stir in reserved 2/3 cup hot sprout-cooking water and milk; cook, stirring constantly, until bubbly and slightly thickened. Remove from heat. In a bowl, beat together sugar, nutmeg and egg. Beat in 4 to 5 tablespoons of the hot sauce; stir egg mixture back into sauce. Cook, stirring, until thickened. Season with salt.

To complete, arrange sprouts and sausage in baking dish; cover with sauce. Top with parsley, cheese and butter or margarine. Bake 15 minutes or until browned. Makes 4 servings.

Pepper & Ham Rolls

2 lbs. green bell peppers,
   seeded, cut in 1-inch-wide
   strips
2 tablespoons vegetable oil
1/2 teaspoon dried leaf thyme
1/2 teaspoon dried leaf oregano
1/2 teaspoon dried leaf basil

Salt and freshly ground
   white pepper
3/4 lb. lean cooked ham, sliced
1 cup hot water
2 slices pasteurized process
   cheese
1 tablespoon chopped chives

Arrange bell peppers in a shallow dish. In a small bowl, beat together oil, thyme, oregano, basil, salt and white pepper; sprinkle over peppers. Cover and let stand at room temperature 1 hour. Trim any excess fat from ham slices, then cut ham in 2-inch-wide strips. Preheat oven to 425F (220C). Grease a baking dish with some of the seasoned oil from peppers. Wrap a few pepper strips in a ham strip; place in greased baking dish. Repeat with remaining pepper strips and ham strips. Sprinkle with remaining seasoned oil. Pour hot water around pepper-ham rolls; cover dish with foil. Bake on next-to-lowest oven rack 25 minutes. Cut cheese slices in strips and arrange strips in a crisscross pattern over rolls. Continue to bake, uncovered, until cheese is melted. Sprinkle with chives. Makes 4 servings.

Stuffed Turnips

8 (3- to 4-oz.) round turnips	2 tablespoons butter or
1/2 lb. bulk pork sausage	margarine
2 tablespoons half and half	2/3 cup dairy sour cream
2 tablespoons shredded Gouda	1 teaspoon paprika
cheese	

Cut tops from turnips. Peel turnips. Cook turnips in boiling salted water until tender throughout. Drain turnips and cool slightly. Cut a slice off top of each turnip; remove about 2/3 of center with a sharp knife; chop finely. Preheat oven to 425F (220C). Grease a baking dish. In a bowl, mix sausage, half and half and chopped turnips. Fill hollowed turnips evenly with sausage mixture; arrange in greased baking dish. Sprinkle with cheese, dot with butter or margarine and surround with sour cream. Sprinkle with paprika. Bake 10 to 12 minutes or until browned. Makes 4 servings.

Burgundy-Style Beans

3/4 lb. dried red kidney beans	Salt to taste
About 12 bacon slices, diced	Pinch of hot paprika
2 onions, diced	1 tablespoon all-purpose flour
1/2 lb. carrots, peeled, sliced	1 tablespoon butter or margarine
2/3 cup dry red wine	2 thyme sprigs

Rinse and sort beans; soak 12 hours in water to cover. Drain beans. Place in a large saucepan and add about 4-1/2 cups water. Bring to a boil; reduce heat, cover and simmer about 1-1/2 hours or until beans are tender, adding more water as necessary. Drain beans and set aside. In another large saucepan, cook bacon until crisp. Remove from pan; add onions and carrots to drippings and cook about 3 minutes, stirring constantly. Stir in cooked bacon, drained beans, wine, salt and paprika. Reduce heat to low, cover and simmer about 20 minutes. In a small bowl, blend flour and butter or margarine; add to beans and stir until dissolved. Simmer 10 minutes longer.
To serve, chop thyme sprigs and sprinkle over beans. Makes 4 servings.

Eggplant Lyons-Style

4 medium (1-lb.) eggplants
Salt
3 to 5 tablespoons olive oil
2 teaspoons Dijon-style mustard
3 onions, finely chopped
2 garlic cloves, chopped
1/2 cup fine dry bread crumbs
2 tablespoons butter or
  margarine
1 teaspoon chopped fresh
  rosemary
Rosemary sprigs

Halve eggplants lengthwise, sprinkle generously with salt and let stand 15 minutes. Rinse off salt; pat eggplants very dry. Using a sharp knife, hollow each eggplant half, removing 2/3 of flesh. Finely chop removed flesh; set aside. Heat 2 tablespoons oil in a large skillet. Add as many hollowed eggplant halves as will fit and cook, turning frequently, until eggplants begin to soften. Remove from pan. Repeat with remaining eggplant halves, adding more oil as necessary. Cool eggplants, then lightly spread inside of each cooked eggplant half with mustard. Preheat oven to 400F (205C). Grease a large baking dish. Heat 1 tablespoon oil in skillet; add chopped eggplant, onions, and garlic. Cook, stirring, until onions and eggplant are soft. Season with salt. Spoon mixture evenly into eggplant halves, then arrange stuffed eggplants in greased baking dish. Sprinkle eggplants evenly with bread crumbs; dot with butter or margarine and sprinkle with chopped rosemary. Place rosemary sprigs between eggplant halves in dish. Bake on center oven rack 15 minutes or until eggplant shells are soft and bread crumbs are browned and crisp. Makes about 8 servings.

Cook's tip

If you prefer a main course that contains meat, you may include 3/4 lb. chopped cooked meat in the filling.

Curly Kale with Sausage

2 lbs. curly kale	Pinch of sugar
3 tablespoons lard or vegetable shortening	1 cup beef stock
1 onion, chopped	1 lb. pinkelwurst (North German specialty) or other boiling sausage
Salt and freshly ground white pepper to taste	
Pinch of ground nutmeg	

Wash kale thoroughly in cold water. Strip leaves from stalks; discard stalks. Place leaves, with water that clings to them, in a saucepan. Cover and cook over medium heat until kale begins to wilt. Drain kale thoroughly in a colander, then coarsely chop. Set aside. Heat lard or shortening in a skillet; add onion and cook until golden, stirring frequently. Add kale and cook a few minutes, stirring constantly. Season with salt, white pepper, nutmeg and sugar. Stir in stock. Bring to a boil. Reduce heat, cover and simmer 45 minutes, adding a little hot water if necessary. Wash sausage in hot water, place on top of kale, cover and simmer 15 minutes longer.

To serve, cut sausage in serving-size portions. Accompany portions of sausage with kale. Makes 4 servings.

Stuffed Zucchini in Batter

Beer Batter:

1/4 cup all-purpose flour	1/2 teaspoon sugar
6 tablespoons beer	1/2 teaspoon garlic salt
1 egg	1 tablespoon vegetable oil

Stuffed Zucchini:

1-3/4 lbs. medium zucchini	1/4 lb. liverwurst
Salt and white pepper	3 tablespoons butter or margarine
2 tablespoons chopped parsley	
3 tablespoons freshly grated Parmesan cheese	

To make batter, in a bowl, beat together flour, beer, egg, sugar, garlic salt and oil. Cover and let stand 15 minutes.

To make stuffed zucchini, cut zucchini crosswise in 1/4-inch-thick slices. Arrange zucchini slices on a platter or flat surface; sprinkle with salt and white pepper. Let stand 5 minutes. In a small bowl, beat together parsley, cheese and liverwurst. Pat zucchini slices dry with paper towels. Sandwich slices together, 2 at a time, with liverwurst mixture.

To complete, melt butter or margarine, a little at a time, in a large skillet. Dip zucchini "sandwiches" in batter. Immediately place in skillet; cook in batches, turning once, until golden brown on both sides. Drain on paper towels. Makes 4 servings.

Stuffed Artichokes

4 artichokes
2 tablespoons butter or
  margarine
2 onions, finely chopped
1 garlic clove, finely chopped
3/4 lb. cooked, shelled
  small shrimp
1/4 cup fine dry bread crumbs

Salt to taste
1 tablespoon chopped fresh dill
5 tablespoons half and half
2 tablespoons freshly grated
  Parmesan cheese
1 tablespoon vegetable oil
2/3 cup dry white wine

Cut stalk and top 1/3 of leaves from each artichoke. Then snip off any remaining thorny leaf tips. In a large saucepan, bring about 2-1/2 quarts lightly salted water to a boil. Add artichokes. Cover and simmer briskly 30 to 45 minutes, until tender. Drain; let cool briefly. Push open leaves of each artichoke; remove and discard small inner leaves. Scrape out choke with a spoon. Set artichokes aside. Preheat oven to 400F (205C). Grease a baking dish. Melt butter or margarine in a large skillet. Add onions and garlic; cook, stirring, until onions are soft. Stir in shrimp, bread crumbs, salt and dill; warm through, stirring constantly. Stir in half and half and cheese. Spoon mixture evenly into artichokes. Arrange stuffed artichokes in greased baking dish; sprinkle with oil. Pour wine around artichokes. Cover and bake 15 minutes or until leaves pull easily from artichokes. Makes 4 servings.

Corn-on-the-Cob with Bacon

4 fresh corn ears
1/4 cup butter or margarine

Salt to taste
8 bacon slices

Remove husks and silk from corn. Trim stalks, if necessary. In a large saucepan, bring about 4 quarts lightly salted water to a boil. Add corn; cover and boil 3 to 5 minutes or until kernels are tender. Drain. Melt butter or margarine in a large skillet. Add corn; cook until lightly browned on all sides, turning frequently and sprinkling with salt. Meanwhile, in another skillet, cook bacon until crisp.
To serve, drain bacon on paper towels. Garnish each ear of corn with 2 bacon slices. Makes 4 servings.

Cook's tip

Very young, tender ears of corn need not be boiled before frying. Simply cook them in oil over low heat, turning often, about 10 minutes or until browned all over.

Cepes in Cream Sauce

2 lbs. cepes or other
  mushrooms
1/2 vegetable bouillon cube
2/3 cup boiling water
2 tablespoons butter or
  margarine

2 medium onions, diced
Salt and freshly ground white
  pepper to taste
3 egg yolks
2/3 cup half and half
2 tablespoons chopped parsley

Carefully trim cepes, removing any damaged parts. If caps are slightly slimy, scrape with a sharp knife and remove gills beneath caps. Scrape stalks and trim ends. Wash cepes in cold water and drain well. Cut larger cepes in halves or quarters; leave smaller ones whole. Dissolve bouillon cube in boiling water; set aside. Melt butter or margarine in a large skillet. Add onions and cook until golden, stirring frequently. Add cepes and cook a few minutes, stirring constantly. Gradually pour in bouillon, cover and simmer 10 to 15 minutes. Season with salt and white pepper. In a small bowl, beat together egg yolks and half and half. Remove cepe mixture from heat and stir in egg-yolk mixture. Return to heat; heat through, stirring constantly, but do not boil.
To serve, sprinkle with parsley. Makes 4 servings.

Chanterelles in Toast Cases

Toast Cases:
8 thick (about 2-inch)
  slices white bread

3 tablespoons butter or
  margarine

Chanterelle Filling:
1-3/4 lbs. chanterelles
1 tablespoon butter or margarine
2 shallots, peeled,
  finely chopped

Salt to taste
1 tablespoon chopped parsley

To make cases, cut bread slices in 2-inch squares. With a knife, hollow out each bread square by removing some of center. Heat butter or margarine in a large skillet; cook bread squares, turning as needed, until crisp and golden brown all over. Remove from pan and keep warm in a 200F (95C) oven.
To make filling, carefully trim chanterelles, removing any damaged parts. Gently scrape caps and stalks with a sharp knife; trim ends of stalks. Wash chanterelles thoroughly in cold water and drain well. Cut larger chanterelles in halves or quarters; leave smaller ones whole. Set aside. Melt 1 tablespoon butter or margarine in a large skillet; add shallots and cook, stirring, until soft. Add chanterelles, cover and cook over low heat 10 minutes, stirring frequently. Season with salt and sprinkle with parsley.
To serve, fill toast cases with chanterelle filling; spoon remaining filling between filled cases. Makes 4 servings.

Braised Mushrooms

1/3 vegetable bouillon cube	1/8 teaspoon garlic powder
1/3 cup boiling water	2 large, firm tomatoes, peeled,
1-3/4 lbs. small Hallimash	seeded, diced
or other mushrooms	1 teaspoon all-purpose flour
6 bacon slices, finely chopped	2 tablespoons butter or
2 medium onions, finely chopped	margarine, room temperature
Salt and freshly ground pepper	2/3 cup half and half
to taste	2 teaspoons chopped fresh thyme

Dissolve bouillon cube in boiling water; set aside. Carefully trim mushrooms, removing any damaged parts. Gently scrape caps with a sharp knife, if necessary; trim ends of stalks. Wash mushrooms thoroughly in lukewarm water and drain well. Cut larger mushrooms in quarters; leave smaller ones whole. Set aside. In a large skillet, cook bacon until crisp. Remove bacon from pan; add onions to drippings and cook, stirring, until soft. Add mushrooms; cook a few minutes, stirring constantly. Stir in bouillon and cooked bacon. Season with salt, pepper and garlic powder, reduce heat to low, cover and simmer 8 minutes. Stir in tomatoes and cook 5 minutes longer. In a small bowl, blend flour and butter or margarine; add to mushroom mixture. Stir until dissolved, then simmer a few minutes.

To serve, stir in half and half; heat through, but do not boil. Sprinkle mushrooms with thyme. Makes 4 servings.

Mushroom Risotto

Risotto:

1 cup short-grain rice	2-1/4 cups water
1 tablespoon vegetable oil	1/8 teaspoon salt
1 large onion, diced	

Mushroom Mixture:

1 lb. chanterelles or	2/3 cup water
other mushrooms	1/4 cup shredded Gruyere cheese
1/2 vegetable-bouillon cube	(1 oz.)

To make risotto, wash rice well in cold water; drain. Set aside. Heat oil in a medium saucepan; add onion and cook until golden, stirring frequently. Add rice and cook 5 minutes, stirring constantly. Stir in 2-1/4 cups water and salt; bring to a boil. Reduce heat, cover and simmer about 25 minutes or until rice is tender. While rice is cooking, prepare mushrooms.

To make mushroom mixture, trim mushrooms, removing any damaged parts. Remove large gills, if necessary. Gently scrape caps and stalks with a sharp knife; trim ends of stalks. Wash mushrooms in cold water, drain well and thinly slice. In a large saucepan, combine bouillon cube and 2/3 cup water. Bring to a boil, stirring until bouillon cube is dissolved. Stir in mushrooms, reduce heat, cover and simmer 10 minutes.

To serve, drain cooked rice, if necessary. Stir rice into mushroom mixture. Sprinkle with cheese. Makes 4 servings.

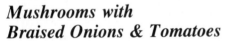

Mushrooms with Braised Onions & Tomatoes

3 tablespoons olive oil
2 large onions, cut in
  thin wedges
1-3/4 lbs. fresh mushrooms,
  halved or thickly sliced
4 large, firm tomatoes, peeled,
  cut in wedges
10 pitted ripe olives
1 teaspoon chopped fresh
  rosemary
Salt and freshly ground white
  pepper to taste
1 tablespoon chopped mixed
  fresh herbs, such as parsley,
  chervil and tarragon

Heat oil in a large skillet. Add onions and cook, stirring, until tender. Add mushrooms and cook, stirring, a few minutes. Then stir in tomatoes, olives and rosemary. Reduce heat, cover and simmer about 10 minutes. Season with salt and white pepper. **To serve,** sprinkle with mixed herbs. Makes 4 to 6 servings.

Mushroom & Potato Dish

2-1/2 tablespoons butter or
  margarine
1 lb. small fresh mushrooms
Salt to taste
Juice of 1 lemon
About 3 cups hot mashed potatoes,
  homemade or instant
Pinch of ground nutmeg
1/4 cup shredded Emmentaler
  cheese (1 oz.)
2/3 cup dairy sour cream
2 tablespoons fine dry
  bread crumbs

Melt 1 tablespoon butter or margarine in a skillet. Add mushrooms and cook 5 minutes, stirring frequently. Season mushrooms with salt and sprinkle with lemon juice. Set aside. Preheat oven to 425F (220C). Butter a baking dish, using 1/2 tablespoon butter or margarine. Season mashed potatoes with salt and nutmeg; spread 2/3 of potatoes in buttered baking dish. Arrange mushrooms in center of potatoes. Spoon remaining potatoes into a pastry bag fitted with a large fluted tip; pipe potatoes around edge of dish. In a small bowl, beat together cheese and sour cream; spoon mixture over mushrooms. Sprinkle with bread crumbs; dot with remaining 1 tablespoon butter or margarine. Bake about 20 minutes or until potatoes are lightly browned. Makes 4 servings.

Deep-Fried Oyster Mushrooms

8 oyster mushrooms
Salt
3/4 cup all-purpose flour
2 eggs
2 tablespoons half and half
Freshly ground white pepper
  to taste
1 cup fine dry bread crumbs
2 tablespoons freshly grated
  Parmesan cheese
Vegetable oil for deep-frying

Cut off tough stalk of each mushroom just below cap. Remove any broken edges and dirt from mushrooms but do not wash them. Sprinkle mushrooms with salt. Set aside. Spread flour on a plate. In a shallow bowl, beat together eggs, half and half, white pepper and salt to taste. In another shallow bowl, mix bread crumbs and cheese. Dip mushrooms in flour to coat, then in egg mixture, and finally in crumb mixture. Press crumbs gently onto mushrooms. In a deep, heavy saucepan, heat about 2 inches of oil to 350F (175C) or until a 1-inch bread cube turns golden brown in about 65 seconds. Add mushrooms, without crowding, and cook 2 to 3 minutes on each side or until browned and crisp. Drain cooked mushrooms on paper towels; keep hot until all mushrooms have been cooked. Makes 4 servings.

Cook's Tip

When picking or buying oyster mushrooms, choose young mushrooms with shiny, white, dry gills.

Potato Dumplings with Marjoram

3 lbs. russet potatoes	1 to 2 tablespoons all-purpose
Salt to taste	flour
1 teaspoon dried leaf marjoram	

Peel 1 pound potatoes, cut in quarters and cook in boiling salted water until soft. Drain, heat to evaporate excess moisture and mash thoroughly. While potatoes are cooking, peel remaining 2 pounds potatoes and grate into a bowl of cold water; stir to mix. Drain grated potatoes, then place on a clean dishcloth. Bring cloth up around potatoes; hold wrapped potatoes over a large bowl and squeeze firmly to extract as much water as possible. Let water that drains into bowl stand until potato starch has settled to the bottom. Pour off and reserve water, leaving potato starch in bowl. In another bowl, mix mashed cooked potatoes and drained grated uncooked potatoes; blend in potato starch. Season with salt and marjoram. Work ingredients together into a pliable dough, adding 1 to 2 tablespoons flour or a little reserved potato water as needed for the correct consistency.

To cook dumplings, in a large saucepan, bring 3 quarts salted water to a boil. With wet hands, shape dough into equal-size dumplings. Drop dumplings into boiling salted water. Immediately reduce heat and simmer dumplings, uncovered, 20 minutes. Drain well. Makes 4 servings.

Fried Potato Fingers

1-1/2 to 2 lbs. russet potatoes, scrubbed	1 tablespoon all-purpose flour
	Salt to taste
1/4 cup butter or margarine, melted, cooled	About 1/4 teaspoon ground nutmeg
2 egg yolks	1/4 cup vegetable oil

Cook unpeeled potatoes in boiling salted water until soft. Drain potatoes. Cool, peel and cut potatoes in chunks. Place potatoes in a bowl and mash thoroughly. Pour melted butter or margarine over potatoes. Add egg yolks, flour, salt and nutmeg. Work ingredients together into a smooth dough. With floured hands, shape dough into a long rope about the thickness of your thumb. Cut rope in 2-inch lengths.

To cook dumplings, heat oil, about 1 tablespoon at a time, in a large skillet. Add potato fingers, a portion at a time, without crowding; cook, turning frequently, until browned and crisp. Keep cooked dumplings hot until all dumplings have been cooked. Makes 4 servings.

Potato & Bacon Dumplings

3 lbs. russet potatoes	6 bacon slices, finely chopped
1 to 3 tablespoons all-purpose flour	2 onions, finely chopped
	1 tablespoon chopped parsley
1 egg	1 tablespoon chopped chives
Salt to taste	1 tablespoon chopped fresh dill
Pinch of ground nutmeg	

Peel 1 pound potatoes, cut in quarters and cook in boiling salted water until soft. Drain, heat to evaporate excess moisture and mash thoroughly. While potatoes are cooking, peel remaining 2 pounds potatoes and grate into a bowl of cold water; stir to mix. Drain grated potatoes, then place on a clean dishcloth. Bring cloth up around potatoes; hold wrapped potatoes over a large bowl and squeeze firmly to extract as much water as possible. Let water that drains into bowl stand until potato starch has settled to the bottom. Pour off and reserve water, leaving potato starch in bowl. In another bowl, mix mashed cooked poatoes and drained grated uncooked potatoes; blend in potato starch. Work in 1 to 2 tablespoons flour, egg, salt and nutmeg; add a little reserved potato water, if necessary, to make a pliable dough. Set aside. In a large skillet, cook bacon until crisp. Remove from pan; add onions to drippings and cook until golden, stirring frequently. Mix cooked bacon, onions, parsley, chives and dill into dumpling dough.

To cook dumplings, in a large saucepan, bring about 4 quarts salted water to a boil. With wet hands, shape some of the dough into a tennis-ball-size dumpling. Drop this dumpling into boiling salted water, reduce heat and simmer, uncovered, about 25 minutes. If dumpling begins to fall apart during cooking, work about 1 tablespoon flour into dumpling dough. Shape and cook remaining dumplings as directed for test dumpling. Drain. Makes 6 servings.

Variation

Boiled Potato Dumplings: Scrub about 2 lbs. russet potatoes. Cook unpeeled potatoes in boiling salted water until soft. Drain potatoes and peel while still hot. Cut in chunks, heat to evaporate excess moisture and mash thoroughly. Spead mashed potatoes on a board. Cool. Sprinkle 4 to 5 tablespoons all-purpose flour over cooled potatoes; rub in to form crumbs. Beat 2 eggs with a generous pinch of salt; mix into potato "crumbs" to make a light, dry dough. Form dough into equal-size dumplings. Drop dumplings into boiling salted water, return to a boil and cook 15 to 20 minutes. Drain. Makes 4 servings.

Potato Cake

1-1/2 lbs. cold boiled potatoes, peeled	6 tablespoons butter or margarine
1 onion	
Salt and freshly ground white pepper to taste	

Coarsely grate potatoes into a bowl. Grate onion into bowl. Gently mix potatoes and onion, then season with salt and white pepper. Melt 3 tablespoons butter or margarine in a large skillet. Spoon potato mixture evenly into pan; flatten into a cake. Cook until bottom of potato cake is browned and crisp. Place a flat plate over pan; carefully invert potato cake onto plate. Melt remaining 3 tablespoons butter or margarine in pan; slide potato cake back into pan, browned-side up. Continue to cook until second side is browned and crisp. Makes 4 servings.

Cook's tip

For a more filling main course, add crisp-cooked bacon to the potato cake. Serve with a green salad.

Potatoes Dauphin

1 lb. russet potatoes	2 tablespoons butter or margarine
Salt to taste	Vegetable oil for deep-frying
1/8 teaspoon ground nutmeg	

Choux Pastry:

1 cup water	1 cup all-purpose flour
1/4 cup butter or margarine	4 eggs
Pinch of salt	

Peel potatoes. Cut in quarters; cook in boiling salted water until soft. Drain, heat to evaporate excess moisture and mash thoroughly. Mix in salt, nutmeg and butter or margarine; set aside.
To make pastry, combine water and 1/4 cup butter or margarine in a saucepan. Bring to a boil, stirring until butter or margarine is melted. Stir in a pinch of salt. Add flour all at once; beat with a wooden spoon until mixture leaves sides of pan and forms a ball. Remove from heat. Beat in eggs, 1 at a time, beating until smooth after each addition.
To complete, mix potato mixture into pastry. With floured hands, shape mixture into walnut-size balls. In a deep, heavy saucepan, heat about 2 inches of oil to 350F (175C) or until a 1-inch bread cube turns golden brown in about 60 seconds. Add potato balls, a portion at a time, without crowding; cook until golden brown. Keep cooked potato balls hot until all have been cooked. Makes 6 servings.

Viennese Potatoes

1-1/2 lbs. cold boiled potatoes, peeled	Salt and freshly ground white pepper to taste
1/4 lb. leeks	1 teaspoon dried leaf marjoram
1/2 lb. veal cutlets	2/3 cup milk
2 tablespoons butter or margarine	2/3 cup beef stock

Preheat oven to 425F (220C). Grease a baking dish. Dice potatoes and set aside. Trim roots and green tops of leeks, then split leeks lengthwise and wash thoroughly to remove sand. Thinly slice leek halves crosswise; set aside. Trim any membrane from veal, then cut meat in small cubes. Melt 1 tablespoon butter or margarine in a large skillet; add veal and cook, stirring, until browned. Set veal aside. Melt remaining 1 tablespoon butter or margarine in skillet; add leeks and cook, stirring, until soft. In a large bowl, mix veal, leeks, potatoes, salt, white pepper and marjoram. Turn into greased baking dish. In a small saucepan, combine milk and stock; bring to a simmer and pour over potato mixture. Bake 15 minutes or until heated through. Makes 2 or 3 servings.

Potato Cake with Sour Cream

2 lbs. russet potatoes	2/3 cup dairy sour cream
5 eggs, beaten	1-1/4 cups all-purpose flour
Salt to taste	1 piece salt pork

Peel potatoes and grate into a bowl of cold water; stir to mix. Drain grated potatoes, then place on a clean dishcloth. Bring cloth up around potatoes; hold wrapped potatoes over a large bowl and squeeze firmly to extract as much water as possible. Let water that drains into bowl stand until potato starch has settled to the bottom. Pour off and discard water, leaving potato starch in bowl. Add drained grated potatoes to potato starch; mix well. Mix in eggs, salt, sour cream and flour. Work ingredients together into a smooth dough. Heat a large, heavy skillet and rub salt pork over bottom of skillet. Turn dough into skillet and flatten evenly. Cook until bottom of potato cake is browned and crisp. Place a flat plate over pan; carefully invert potato cake onto plate. Slide potato cake back into pan, browned-side up; continue to cook until second side is browned and crisp.
To serve, cut in wedges. Makes 4 servings.

Potato Omelet

1-3/4 lbs. potatoes, scrubbed
3 tablespoons vegetable oil
2 onions, chopped
1 garlic clove, finely chopped
4 eggs
Salt and freshly ground white
   pepper to taste

Pinch of ground nutmeg
1 to 2 tablespoons chopped mixed
   fresh herbs, such as parsley,
   chives and dill

Cook unpeeled potatoes in boiling salted water until tender. Drain potatoes; then cool, peel and slice. Set aside. Heat oil in a large skillet; add onions and garlic and cook until onions are golden, stirring frequently. Add sliced potatoes; cook until browned, turning slices frequently. In a bowl, beat together eggs, salt, white pepper and nutmeg. Pour egg mixture over potatoes; cook, lifting edges of omelet to let uncooked eggs flow underneath, until eggs are set but still moist.

To serve, sprinkle with herbs. Makes 4 servings.

Cook's tip

For a more filling omelet, add diced cooked beef, pork, chicken, sausage or ham.

Potato Pancakes

2 lbs. russet potatoes
2 tablespoons all-purpose flour
2 eggs
Salt to taste

1 large onion
About 1/4 cup clarified butter
   or lard

Peel potatoes and grate into a bowl of cold water; stir to mix. Drain grated potatoes, then place on a clean dishcloth. Bring cloth up around potatoes; hold wrapped potatoes over a large bowl and squeeze firmly to extract as much water as possible. Let water that drains into bowl stand until potato starch has settled to the bottom. Pour off and discard water, leaving potato starch in bowl. Add drained grated potatoes to potato starch; mix well. Beat flour, eggs and salt into potato mixture; then grate onion into mixture. Mix well. Heat about 1 tablespoon clarified butter or lard in a large skillet. Add potato mixture in 2-tablespoon portions; flatten each portion gently. Cook pancakes, turning once, until browned and crisp on both sides. Add more clarified butter or lard to pan as necessary. Keep cooked pancakes hot until all have been cooked. Makes 4 servings.

Cook's tip

In southern Germany, potato pancakes are eaten with cinnamon sugar or applesauce. If you're making your pancakes to eat with sugar or a fruit sauce, reduce the salt and omit the onion.

Béchamel Potatoes

1-3/4 lbs. potatoes, scrubbed	2 tablespoons chopped parsley

Béchamel Sauce:

2 tablespoons butter or margarine	Salt and freshly ground white pepper to taste
2 tablespoons all-purpose flour	Pinch of ground nutmeg
1-1/2 cups hot milk	1 teaspoon lemon juice
2/3 cup half and half	Pinch of sugar

Cook unpeeled potatoes in boiling salted water until tender. Drain potatoes; then cool, peel and cut in fairly thick slices. Set aside.

To make sauce, melt butter or margarine in a large saucepan. Sprinkle in flour and cook over low heat, stirring, about 1 minute. Gradually add hot milk; continue to cook, stirring constantly, until bubbly and thickened. Stir in half and half; heat through. Season with salt, white pepper, nutmeg, lemon juice and sugar.

To serve, mix potatoes into sauce; heat through, but do not allow sauce to boil. Sprinkle with parsley. Makes 4 servings.

Hot Potato Salad

1-3/4 lbs. potatoes, scrubbed	1/4 teaspoon dried leaf marjoram
6 bacon slices, finely chopped	1/4 teaspoon dried leaf thyme
2 onions, finely chopped	1 bay leaf
1 tablespoon all-purpose flour	Salt and freshly ground pepper to taste
1-1/2 cups beef stock	1 tablespoon white-wine vinegar
1 tablespoon capers	3 or 4 dill pickles, chopped
3/4 teaspoon grated lemon peel	3 tablespoons chopped parsley

Cook unpeeled potatoes in boiling salted water until tender. Drain potatoes. Cool, peel and cut in fairly thick slices. Set aside. In a large, deep skillet, cook bacon until crisp. Remove from pan. Add onions to drippings and cook until golden brown, stirring frequently. Sprinkle in flour; cook over low heat, about 1 minute, stirring constantly. Gradually stir in stock, bring to a boil and boil a few minutes, stirring constantly. Stir in cooked bacon, capers, lemon peel, marjoram, thyme, bay leaf, salt, pepper and vinegar. Then stir in pickles and potatoes; heat through.

To serve, sprinkle with parsley. Makes 4 servings.

Hearty Potato Omelet with Shrimp

1-1/2 lbs. potatoes, scrubbed
3 bacon slices, finely chopped
3 tablespoons butter or
  margarine
1 large onion, finely chopped
3/4 lb. cooked, shelled
  small shrimp

2 eggs
2 tablespoons water
1 teaspoon soy sauce
Salt to taste
1 tablespoon chopped fresh dill

Cook unpeeled potatoes in boiling salted water until tender. Drain potatoes. Cool, peel and cut in 1/2-inch-thick slices. Set aside. In a large skillet, cook bacon until crisp. Remove from pan. Add butter or margarine to drippings and let melt; add onion and cook until golden, stirring frequently. Gently stir in cooked bacon, shrimp and potatoes; heat through. In a small bowl, beat together eggs, water, soy sauce and salt; pour egg mixture over potato mixture. Reduce heat and cook, stirring gently, until eggs are set.

To serve, sprinkle with dill. Makes 4 servings.

Potatoes with Sausage Balls

1-3/4 lbs. potatoes, scrubbed
1/2 lb. bulk pork sausage
1 cup beef stock
3 tablespoons vegetable oil
3 bacon slices, diced
2 onions, diced

1 large red bell pepper, seeded,
  cut in strips
1/8 teaspoon hot paprika
Salt and freshly ground white
  pepper to taste
2 tablespoons chopped parsley

Cook unpeeled potatoes in boiling salted water until tender. Drain potatoes. Cool, peel and slice. Set aside. Shape sausage into small balls. Pour stock into a small saucepan; bring to a boil. Add sausage balls to boiling stock, reduce heat to very low, cover and simmer 10 minutes. Remove from heat; keep warm. Skim off fat. Heat oil in a skillet, add bacon and cook until crisp. Remove from pan. Add onions and bell pepper to drippings; brown quickly over high heat. Stir in potatoes and paprika. Cook, stirring, until potatoes are browned. Reduce heat. Stir in cooked bacon and sausage balls and any remaining stock; heat through. Season with salt and white pepper.

To serve, sprinkle with parsley. Makes 4 servings.

Sausage with Mashed Potatoes & Apples

2 lbs. russet potatoes	2 large onions, sliced,
1 lb. tart apples	separated into rings
1 cup water	Salt and freshly ground white
2 tablespoons sugar	pepper to taste
6 bacon slices, diced	8 brown-and-serve pork sausages

Peel potatoes, cut in quarters and cook in boiling salted water until soft. Drain, heat to evaporate excess moisture and mash thoroughly. Set aside. Peel, quarter, core and thinly slice apples. In a saucepan, combine apples, 1 cup water and sugar. Bring to a boil; then reduce heat, cover and boil gently 15 minutes or until apples are very soft. Coarsely mash apples and their cooking liquid; add to mashed potatoes and mix well. Set aside. In a large skillet, cook bacon until crisp. Remove from pan. Add onions to drippings and cook until golden brown, stirring frequently. Remove onions from pan; stir onions and cooked bacon into potato-apple mixture. Season with salt and white pepper. Heat mixture through; keep hot. Heat bacon drippings remaining in skillet; add sausages and cook until browned on all sides and hot throughout.

To serve, drain sausages on paper towels; arrange atop potato-apple mixture. Makes 4 servings.

Potato Stew

6 bacon slices, finely chopped	2 teaspoons caraway seeds
1/2 lb. onions, chopped	Salt and red (cayenne) pepper
1-3/4 lbs. potatoes	to taste
1 tablespoon paprika	2/3 cup dairy sour cream
1 cup beef stock	

In a large skillet, cook bacon until crisp. Remove from pan. Add onions to drippings; cook until golden, stirring frequently. Peel and dice potatoes. Stir potatoes, cooked bacon and paprika into onions; cook a few minutes, stirring constantly. Stir in stock and caraway seeds. Bring to a simmer, then reduce heat to low, cover and simmer 20 to 25 minutes or until potatoes are tender. Season with salt and red pepper.

To serve, stir in sour cream; heat through, but do not boil. Adjust seasoning, if necessary. Makes 4 servings.

Pepper Risotto

2 tablespoons olive oil
1-2/3 cups long-grain white rice
1 onion, finely chopped
1 red bell pepper, seeded,
  cut in squares
1 green bell pepper, seeded,
  cut in squares

2-1/4 cups dry white wine
2-1/4 cups chicken stock
Pinch of ground nutmeg
Salt and freshly ground white
  pepper to taste
1 cup shredded Emmentaler
  cheese (4 oz.)

Heat oil in a large saucepan. Add rice and onion; cook until rice is
pale golden, stirring constantly. Stir in bell peppers and cook a
few minutes longer, then stir in wine, stock and nutmeg. Bring to
a boil. Reduce heat, cover and simmer gently 20 to 25 minutes or
until rice is tender. Season with salt and white pepper.
To serve, stir 3/4 cup cheese into rice mixture; sprinkle remaining 1/4 cup cheese on top. Makes 4 servings.

Mushroom Rice

2 tablespoons butter or
  margarine
1 lb. small fresh mushrooms,
  very thinly sliced
1 teaspoon lemon juice
1/2 teaspoon grated lemon peel
About 1 teaspoon salt

Freshly ground white pepper
  to taste
1-1/2 cups long-grain white rice
3-3/4 cups water
1/4 cup shredded Emmentaler
  cheese (1 oz.)
2 tablepoons chopped parsley

Melt butter or margarine in a large saucepan. Add mushrooms;
cook until soft, stirring frequently. Stir in lemon juice, lemon
peel, salt, white pepper and rice. Cook, stirring, a few minutes.
Stir in water and bring to a boil. Reduce heat, cover and simmer
20 to 25 minutes or until rice is tender.
To serve, stir cheese into rice mixture; sprinkle with parsley.
Makes 4 servings.

Cook's tip

If you wish, you may use fresh mixed wild mushrooms in this dish.

Vegetable Rice with Ham

2 lbs. leeks
1 tablespoon butter or margarine
3/4 cup plus 1 tablespoon
   long-grain white rice
1-3/4 cups beef stock
Pinch of dried leaf thyme

1/2 lb. lean cooked ham, trimmed
   of any excess fat, diced
1/2 lb. tomatoes, peeled,
   seeded, chopped
Salt and freshly ground white
   pepper to taste
2 tablespoons chopped parsley

Trim roots and green tops of leeks, then split leeks lengthwise and wash thoroughly to remove sand. Slice leek halves crosswise. Set aside. Melt butter or margarine in a large saucepan, add rice and cook until pale golden, stirring constantly. Stir in leeks and cook a few minutes, then stir in stock and thyme. Bring to a boil. Reduce heat, cover and simmer 15 minutes, adding a little hot water as necessary. Stir in ham and tomatoes; simmer about 10 minutes longer or until rice is tender. Season with salt and white pepper.
To serve, sprinkle with parsley. Makes 4 servings.

Curried Rice with Bananas in Ham

Curried Rice:
1/3 cup raisins
6 tablespoons orange juice
2-1/2 cups chicken stock
1 cup plus 2 tablespoons
   long-grain white rice

1 to 2 teaspoons curry powder
Salt and white pepper
1 tablespoon chopped parsley

Bananas in Ham:
2 bananas
1 tablespoon butter or
   margarine

4 thin slices cooked ham,
   trimmed

To make rice, in a small bowl, combine raisins and orange juice; set aside. In a saucepan, bring stock to a boil; stir in rice and 1 teaspoon curry powder. Reduce heat, cover and simmer 20 to 25 minutes or until rice is tender. Drain, if necessary. Stir in raisins and orange juice, salt, white pepper and additional curry powder, if desired. Cover and keep warm.
To make bananas in ham, peel bananas; cut in half lengthwise. Melt butter or margarine in a skillet; add banana halves and cook, turning, until lightly browned on all sides. Wrap each banana half in 1 ham slice; secure with wooden picks. Return ham-wrapped bananas to pan; cook over low heat 5 minutes, turning frequently.
To serve, spoon rice into a bowl; top with ham-wrapped bananas and sprinkle with parsley. Makes 4 servings.

Dutch Rice Specialty

1 leek
2 tablespoons olive oil
3/4 lb. lean boneless pork
    (shoulder or leg), diced
1/4 small celeriac
1/4 lb. cabbage, coarsely
    shredded
1-1/4 cups beef stock
2-3/4 cups water
1 cup plus 2 tablespoons
    long-grain white rice
About 1 teaspoon salt
1 tablespoon cornstarch
1 tablespoon cold water
1-1/2 teaspoons superfine sugar
1/2 teaspoon ground ginger
Dash of wine vinegar
1/2 cup sliced almonds

Trim roots and green top of leek, then split leek lengthwise and wash thoroughly to remove sand. Slice leek halves crosswise; set aside. Heat oil in a large saucepan. Add pork and cook until browned, stirring frequently. Peel and dice celeriac; stir celeriac, leek, cabbage and stock into browned pork. Reduce heat, cover and simmer 30 minutes. Meanwhile, in another saucepan, bring 2-3/4 cups water to a boil. Stir in rice and 1 teaspoon salt. Reduce heat, cover and simmer 20 to 25 minutes or until rice is tender. Keep warm.

To complete, in a small bowl, stir together cornstarch, water, sugar, ginger and vinegar. Stir into meat mixture; heat, stirring, until sauce is thickened. Season to taste with salt. Transfer rice to a warm serving dish or platter; spoon meat mixture on top and sprinkle with almonds. Makes 4 servings.

Cook's tip

If desired, you may add peeled, diced tomatoes to the sauce 10 minutes before the end of cooking time.

Wild Rice with Chicken

1 cup wild rice	2 tablespoons vegetable oil
2-1/2 cups water	1 (10-oz.) pkg. frozen
About 1 teaspoon salt	green peas
1-1/4 lbs. cooked, boned,	2/3 cup chicken stock
skinned chicken	Freshly ground white pepper
1 small fennel bulb	1 tablespoon chopped fresh dill

Wash wild rice under cold running water; drain. In a saucepan, bring 2-1/2 cups water to a boil; stir in wild rice and 1 teaspoon salt. Reduce heat, cover and simmer about 40 minutes or until rice is tender. Drain, if necessary; set aside. Cut chicken in bite-size pieces and set aside. Trim feathery leaves from fennel; chop and set aside. Trim and chop fennel bulb. Heat oil in a large saucepan; add chopped fennel bulb and cook about 5 minutes, stirring frequently. Stir in peas and stock; bring to a boil. Stir in chicken and cooked wild rice. Reduce heat, cover and simmer about 10 minutes or until peas are tender and chicken is heated through. Season with salt and white pepper.

To serve, sprinkle with dill and fennel leaves. Makes 4 servings.

Cook's tip

In place of chicken, you may use another cooked meat of your choice. Substitute other herbs for the dill, depending on the meat used.

Tomato Rice with Garlic

1 cup wild rice	About 1/3 cup tomato paste
2-1/2 cups water	2/3 cup chicken stock
1/2 teaspoon salt	4 large, firm tomatoes, peeled,
1 small leek	seeded, diced
2 tablespoons vegetable oil	1 teaspoon paprika
2 onions, finely chopped	2 tablespoons chopped parsley
2 garlic cloves, finely chopped	

Wash wild rice under cold running water; drain. In a saucepan, bring 2-1/2 cups water to a boil. Stir in wild rice and 1 teaspoon salt, reduce heat, cover and simmer about 40 minutes or until rice is tender. Drain, if necessary; set aside. Trim roots and green top of leek; then split leek lengthwise and wash thoroughly to remove sand. Slice leek halves crosswise. Set aside. Heat oil in a large saucepan. Add onions and garlic; cook until onions are golden, stirring frequently. Stir in leek; cook a few minutes. Stir in tomato paste. Stir in stock, tomatoes, cooked wild rice and paprika. Reduce heat, cover and simmer gently 10 minutes. Season with salt.

To serve, sprinkle with parsley. Makes 4 servings.

Spaghetti with Vegetable Sauce

2 bunches green onions
2 tablespoons olive oil
1 garlic clove, finely chopped
1/2 lb. carrots, peeled, chopped
1 cup beef stock
3/4 lb. fresh mushrooms, sliced

4 tomatoes, peeled, chopped
Salt and freshly ground white
   pepper to taste
8 oz. uncooked spaghetti
2 tablespoons chopped parsley

To make sauce, trim roots and any wilted leaves from green onions, then chop green onions. Heat oil in a large skillet; add green onions and garlic. Cook, stirring, until onions are soft. Stir in carrots and cook a few minutes, then stir in stock. Reduce heat, cover and simmer gently 10 minutes. Stir in mushrooms and tomatoes; cook until mushrooms are soft, stirring occasionally. Season with salt and white pepper. Keep hot.
To cook spaghetti, in a large saucepan, bring 3 quarts salted water to a boil. Add spaghetti; boil about 12 minutes or until spaghetti is tender but still firm to the bite. Drain well.
To serve, arrange drained spaghetti in a warm serving dish. Pour hot sauce over spaghetti; sprinkle with parsley. Makes 4 servings.

Fusilli with Bolognese Sauce

2 tablespoons vegetable oil
1 large onion, finely chopped
2 garlic cloves, finely chopped
1 lb. lean ground beef
1 (16-oz.) can tomatoes
2 tablespoons tomato paste
2 bay leaves, crumbled
1/4 teaspoon dried leaf rosemary
1/2 teaspoon dried leaf basil

1/2 teaspoon dried leaf oregano
1/2 teaspoon dried leaf thyme
Salt and white pepper
8 oz. fusilli or spaghetti
2/3 cup freshly grated Parmesan
   cheese (2 oz.)
2 tablespoons butter or
   margarine
1 tablespoon chopped parsley

Heat oil in a large skillet. Add onion and garlic; cook, stirring, until onion is soft. Crumble in beef and cook until lightly browned, stirring frequently. Drain tomatoes, reserving liquid. Cut tomatoes in quarters and stir into beef mixture with tomato paste, bay leaves, rosemary, basil, oregano and thyme. Reduce heat, cover and simmer 15 minutes. Season with salt and white pepper. If sauce is too thick, stir in some reserved tomato liquid. In a large saucepan, bring 3 quarts salted water to a boil. Add fusilli and boil about 12 minutes or until tender but still firm to the bite. Drain well. Preheat oven to 425F (220C). Lightly grease a baking dish. Arrange cooked pasta and sauce in alternate layers in greased baking dish, finishing with a layer of sauce. Sprinkle with cheese; dot with butter or margarine. Bake about 10 minutes or until cheese begins to brown. Sprinkle with parsley. Makes 4 servings.

Macaroni with Basil Sauce

1 large bunch fresh basil	Salt and red (cayenne) pepper
1 tablespoon pine nuts	to taste
1 garlic clove, quartered	2-1/4 cups uncooked macaroni
1-1/3 cups freshly grated	1/4 cup hot chicken stock
Parmesan cheese (4 oz.)	
6 tablespoons olive oil	

To make sauce, trim basil stems, then wash basil in cold water and shake dry. Coarsely chop basil. In a food processor fitted with a metal blade, combine chopped basil, pine nuts, garlic, cheese and oil. Process until pureed. Season with salt and red pepper.
To cook macaroni, in a large saucepan, bring 3-1/2 quarts salted water to a boil. Sprinkle in macaroni; cook about 12 minutes or until tender but still firm to the bite. Drain well.
To serve, pour macaroni into a warm serving bowl. Stir hot stock into sauce, then pour sauce over macaroni and toss gently to mix. Makes 4 servings.

Italian Tomato & Garlic Sauce

1 (16-oz.) can tomatoes	1 teaspoon dried leaf oregano
1 (about 8-oz.) can tomatoes	1 tablespoon chopped fresh basil
3 tablespoons olive oil	1 bay leaf
2 onions, finely chopped	2 teaspoons sugar
2 garlic cloves, finely chopped	Salt and freshly ground pepper
1/2 cup plus 2 tablespoons	to taste
tomato paste	

Drain tomatoes, reserving liquid. Chop tomatoes and set aside. Heat oil in a large skillet or saucepan; add onions and cook, stirring, until soft. Stir in garlic and cook 2 minutes longer. Stir in chopped tomatoes, reserved tomato liquid, tomato paste, oregano, basil, bay leaf and sugar. Bring to a boil; then reduce heat and simmer, uncovered, 1 hour or until sauce has the consistency of a thick puree. Stir sauce frequently during cooking. When sauce is done, remove bay leaf and season with salt and pepper. Makes 4 servings.

Cook's tip

This sauce will keep in the freezer up to 4 months.

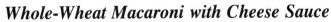

Whole-Wheat Macaroni with Cheese Sauce

2-1/4 cups whole-wheat macaroni | 1 tablespoon finely chopped
fresh sage, dill or parsley

Cheese Sauce:
3/4 lb. leeks | 2/3 cup half and half
3 tablespoons vegetable oil | 1/8 teaspoon ground ginger
8 oz. low-fat cottage cheese | Salt and white pepper
 (1 cup)
1-1/3 cups freshly grated
 Parmesan cheese (4 oz.)

To cook macaroni, in a large saucepan, bring 3-1/2 quarts salted water to a boil. Add macaroni; boil about 15 minutes or until tender but still firm to the bite. Drain well, rinse and set aside.

To make sauce, trim roots and green tops of leeks, then split leeks lengthwise and wash thoroughly to remove sand. Thinly slice leek halves crosswise. Heat 1 tablespoon oil in a skillet; add leeks. Cook, stirring, a few minutes. Pour in a little hot water, reduce heat, cover and simmer until leeks are soft. Remove from heat. In a saucepan, combine cottage cheese, Parmesan cheese and half and half; heat through over low heat, stirring constantly. Stir cheese mixture into cooked leeks; heat through. Season with ginger, salt and white pepper. Keep hot.

To serve, heat 2 tablespoons oil in a large skillet; add cooked macaroni. Heat through, stirring. Spoon into a warm serving dish; top with cheese sauce. Sprinkle with herbs. Makes 4 servings.

Whole-Wheat Macaroni with Tomato Sauce

2-1/4 cups whole-wheat macaroni | 1 tablespoon chopped fresh basil

Tomato Sauce:
2 lbs. tomatoes, chopped | 1 garlic clove, minced
1 cup water | Salt and white pepper
2 tablespoons vegetable oil | Few drops of maple syrup
2 onions, very finely chopped | 1/4 cup half and half

To cook macaroni, in a large saucepan, bring 3-1/2 quarts salted water to a boil. Add macaroni and boil 15 minutes or until tender but still firm to the bite. Drain well, rinse and set aside.

To make sauce, in a large saucepan, combine tomatoes and 1 cup water. Bring to a boil; reduce heat, cover and simmer 10 minutes. Meanwhile, heat oil in another large saucepan. Add onions and garlic; cook, stirring, until onions are soft. Remove from heat; place a wire strainer over saucepan. Pour simmered tomatoes and their juice into strainer. Stir tomatoes to strain juice and pulp into onion mixture. Season with salt and white pepper. Bring to a boil; boil a few minutes, stirring. Stir in maple syrup and half and half. Heat through, but do not boil.

To serve, stir cooked macaroni into sauce and warm through over very low heat. Season with salt, then sprinkle with basil. Makes 4 servings.

Crusty Corn Cakes with Creamed Carrots

Crusty Corn Cakes:
1 egg, beaten
1/2 cup yellow cornmeal
**1 (12-oz.) can whole-kernel
  corn, drained**
**Salt and red (cayenne) pepper
  to taste**

Creamed Carrots:
1-3/4 lbs. baby carrots
**2 tablespoons butter or
  margarine**
2 teaspoons sugar
2/3 cup chicken stock
2/3 cup half and half
Salt to taste
Vegetable oil for deep-frying

To make batter for corn cakes, in a bowl, combine egg and corn-meal; cover and let stand at room temperature 30 minutes. Stir in corn; season with salt and red pepper. Set aside.

To make carrots, peel carrots. Cut larger carrots in half length-wise; leave smaller ones whole. Melt butter or margarine in a saucepan; sprinkle in sugar and cook, stirring, until sugar dis-solves and begins to caramelize. Add carrots and stir to coat with butter-sugar mixture. Stir in stock; bring to a boil. Then re-duce heat, cover and simmer about 25 minutes or until carrots are tender, adding a little hot water occasionally, if necessary. Stir in half and half; season with salt. Keep hot.

To cook corn cakes, in a deep, heavy saucepan, heat about 1-1/2 inches of oil to 375F (190C) or until a 1-inch bread cube turns golden brown in about 50 seconds. Drop corn-cake mix-ture, 1 tablespoon at a time, into hot oil; do not crowd cakes in oil. Cook cakes 4 to 5 minutes on each side or until golden brown and crisp. Drain on paper towels. Keep cooked corn cakes hot until all have been cooked.

To serve, arrange corn cakes on a warm platter. Spoon carrots into a warm serving dish. Serve with corn cakes. Makes 4 servings.

Rye Rissoles with Tomato Salad

Tomato Salad:

4 large firm tomatoes, sliced	2 tablespoons vegetable oil
1 onion, finely chopped	Salt and white pepper
1 tablespoon white-wine vinegar	3 tablespoons chopped chives

Rye Rissoles:

1 cup plus 6 tablespoons light rye flour	2 tablespoons chopped parsley
2/3 cup chicken stock	1-1/3 cups freshly grated Parmesan cheese (4 oz.)
4 shallots, minced	Salt to taste
2 eggs, beaten	2 tablespoons vegetable oil

To make tomato salad, arrange tomatoes on a serving plate. Sprinkle with onion. In a small bowl, beat together vinegar, oil, salt and white pepper; pour over tomatoes. Sprinkle with chives. Cover and refrigerate.

To make rissoles, in a saucepan, combine rye flour and stock. Bring to a boil, stirring constantly. Reduce heat to very low; simmer, uncovered, 30 minutes, stirring frequently. Cool. Stir shallots, eggs, parsley and cheese into cooled rye mixture; season with salt. Shape mixture into flat cakes. Heat oil in a large skillet over low heat; add rissoles and cook, turning as needed, 12 to 15 minutes or until browned on both sides.

To serve, arrange a portion of rissoles and tomato salad on each individual plate. Makes 4 servings.

Buckwheat Cakes with Carrot Salad

Carrot Salad:

1 lb. carrots	3 tablespoons half and half
1 large tart apple	Salt to taste
1 teaspoon maple syrup	1/2 cup chopped hazelnuts
1 tablespoon lemon juice	

Herbed Buckwheat Cakes:

2 cups plus 2 tablespoons buckwheat flour	Salt to taste
2 eggs, beaten	2 tablespoons chopped chives
1/2 teaspoon dried leaf marjoram	1 cup sparkling water
	About 1/4 cup vegetable oil

To make salad, peel and grate carrots. Peel, core and grate apple. In a serving bowl, combine carrots, apple, maple syrup, lemon juice, half and half and salt. Cover and refrigerate.

To make buckwheat cakes, in a bowl, mix buckwheat flour, eggs, marjoram, salt, chives and sparkling water. Cover and let stand at room temperature 30 minutes. Heat about 1 tablespoon oil in a large skillet. Add buckwheat batter in 2-tablespoon portions; spread each portion to make about a 4-inch pancake. Cook pancakes, turning once, until browned on both sides. Add more oil to skillet as needed. Transfer cooked pancakes to a warm platter and keep warm.

To serve, stir salad; sprinkle with hazelnuts. Serve salad alongside buckwheat cakes. Makes 4 servings.

Rye & Egg Pancakes with Radish Salad

Radish Salad:
1 large white radish, grated
1 tablespoon lemon juice
2 teaspoons honey

2/3 cup dairy sour cream
Salt to taste
1 tablespoon chopped fresh mint

Rye & Egg Pancakes:
2 cups plus 2 tablespoons
   rye flour
1 onion
2/3 cup sparkling water
3 eggs, beaten
Salt to taste

1 cup grated Pamesan
   cheese (3 oz.) or 1 cup
   shredded Swiss cheese (4 oz.)
About 3 tablespoons
   vegetable oil

To make salad, place radish in a serving bowl; stir in lemon juice, honey, sour cream and salt. Cover and refrigerate.
To make pancakes, place rye flour in a bowl. Grate onion into flour. Mix in sparkling water, eggs and salt; cover and let stand at room temperature 30 minutes. Stir in cheese. Shape mixture into 4 flat cakes. Heat some of the oil in a large skillet; add as many rye cakes as will fit without crowding. Cook, turning once, until browned on both sides. Transfer to a warm platter; keep warm. Repeat with remaining rye cakes, adding more oil as needed.
To serve, stir salad; sprinkle with mint. Serve salad alongside rye cakes. Makes 4 servings.

Polenta with Bacon

1 qt. water (4 cups)
4 vegetable-bouillon cubes
2-3/4 cups yellow cornmeal

Salt to taste
8 thin bacon slices
2 tablespoons vegetable oil

Combine water and bouillon cubes in a large saucepan. Bring to a boil, stirring until bouillon cubes are dissolved. Sprinkle in cornmeal, reduce heat and simmer gently 10 minutes, stirring frequently. Then reduce heat to very low; cook 20 minutes longer, stirring frequently. Season with salt. Spread polenta in a 2-inch-thick layer on a flat surface; let stand until completely cooled. Cut polenta in 2'' x 1-1/2'' strips; set aside. In a large skillet, cook bacon until crisp. Remove from pan, transfer to a warm platter and keep hot. Add oil to bacon drippings; heat. Add polenta strips; cook, turning as needed, until browned on all sides.
To serve, arrange browned polenta on platter with bacon. Makes 4 servings.

Cook's tip

Fried polenta strips are an excellent accompaniment for stews or Ratatouille, page 103.

Sauerkraut Whirls

2-2/3 cups all-purpose flour	1 onion
1/2 teaspoon salt	1 whole clove
2 eggs, beaten	3 juniper berries, crushed
2 tablespoons clarified butter	1 (8-oz.) can sauerkraut,
3 tablespoons water	drained
10 bacon slices, diced	About 6 tablespoons water

In a bowl, mix flour, salt, eggs, clarified butter and 3 tablespoons water to make a smooth dough. Cover and let stand at room temperature 30 minutes. Meanwhile, in a heavy saucepan, cook bacon until crisp. Pour off and discard drippings. Peel onion; stick clove into onion. Add clove-studded onion, crushed juniper berries, sauerkraut and 6 tablespoons water to bacon in saucepan. Stir to mix. Cover and cook over low heat 20 minutes. Remove from heat; remove and discard clove-studded onion. Preheat oven to 400F (205C). Grease a deep baking pan. On a floured pastry cloth, roll out dough to a thin rectangle. Spread evenly with sauerkraut mixture. Using pastry cloth to help you, roll up dough jelly-roll style, starting with a long side. Using a sharp knife, cut rolled-up dough crosswise in 12 equal slices. Place slices, cut-side up and close together, in greased baking pan. Pour in water to a depth of about 1-1/2 inches, cover pan with foil and bake 15 minutes. Remove foil; bake about 10 minutes longer. Makes 6 servings.

Gnocchi alla Romana (Roman Semolina Slices)

2-1/4 cups milk	1-1/3 cups freshly grated
2 cups water	Parmesan cheese (4 oz.)
3/4 teaspoon salt	2 tablespoons grated pecorino
1-1/2 cups coarse semolina	cheese
2 egg yolks, beaten	

In a large saucepan, combine milk, water and salt. Bring to a boil. Sprinkle in semolina, reduce heat and cook, stirring constantly, until mixture has the consistency of a thick oatmeal. Then cook a few minutes longer over lowest possible heat. Remove from heat; mix in egg yolks and 2/3 of Parmesan cheese. Dampen a baking sheet or other flat surface with cold water; spread semolina mixture on dampened surface in a 1/2-inch-thick layer. Let stand until completely cooled. Preheat oven to 400F (205C). Butter a baking dish. Using a 2-1/2-inch-diameter cookie cutter or drinking glass, cut cooled semolina mixture into rounds. Arrange rounds in overlapping layers in buttered baking dish. Sprinkle with pecorino cheese and remaining 1/3 of Parmesan cheese. Bake on center oven rack about 15 minutes, just until semolina slices begin to brown. Makes 4 servings.

Spinach Triangles

Dough:
2-3/4 cups all-purpose flour	1 tablespoon white-wine vinegar
1/2 teaspoon salt	5 tablespoons vegetable oil
2/3 cup lukewarm water	

Filling:
3/4 lb. fresh spinach	2 eggs, beaten
1-1/2 day-old dinner rolls	Salt and freshly ground white
1 onion, finely chopped	pepper to taste
1/2 lb. lean ground beef	1-1/2 qts. beef stock (6 cups)
1/2 lb. bulk pork sausage	Chopped chives
1 tablespoon chopped parsley	

To make dough, in a bowl, mix flour, salt, lukewarm water, vinegar and oil to make a smooth, glossy dough. Cover and let stand in a warm place 20 minutes. Meanwhile, prepare filling.
To make filling, remove stems and any tough leaves from spinach, then wash spinach thoroughly in cold water. Cook spinach in boiling lightly salted water 3 minutes; drain well in a colander and press out excess water. Finely chop and set aside. Tear rolls in small pieces and soften in a little cold water, then squeeze out any excess moisture. In a large bowl, mix softened rolls, spinach, onion, beef, sausage, parsley and eggs. Season with salt and white pepper.
To complete, on a lightly floured board, roll out dough to a thickness of about 1/8 inch. Cut rolled-out dough in 6-inch squares. Place a spoonful of filling on each square; fold each square in half diagonally to make a triangle. Press edges firmly

with a fork to seal. In a large saucepan, bring stock to a boil. Drop in triangles; cook about 10 minutes or until they rise to the surface. Serve triangles in stock; sprinkle each serving with chives. Makes 6 servings.

Cook's tip

Spinach Triangles need not be served in stock. If you wish, drain them after cooking in stock, then dip in beaten egg and fry in oil until golden brown. Sprinkle with chopped chives; serve with a green salad and plenty of crisp-fried onion rings.

Cassoulet

1 lb. dried small white beans	1/2 teaspoon dried leaf thyme
1/4 lb. leeks, washed	2 parsley sprigs
3 onions, finely chopped	1 bay leaf
2 qts. chicken stock (8 cups)	2 tablespoons vegetable oil
1/2 lb. unsliced bacon	1 lb. tomatoes, peeled, diced
1/4 lb. garlic sausage	3 tablespoons diced celery
1 turkey leg	2/3 cup dry white wine
1/2 teaspoon garlic salt	Salt and freshly ground pepper

Soak beans 12 hours in water to cover. Drain; set aside. Finely chop white part of leeks. Reserve 3 tablespoons onion; place remaining onions in a large, heavy saucepan. Stir in ingredients through bay leaf. Bring to a boil. Reduce heat, cover and simmer 45 minutes. Cut sausage in slices; cut bacon in cubes. Discard bay leaf and skin and bone from turkey leg; cut meat in cubes. Drain bean mixture remaining in pan; reserve stock. Preheat oven to 425F (220C). Heat oil in a skillet. Add reserved 3 tablespoons onion, tomatoes and celery. Cook about 5 minutes, stirring often; stir in wine. Stir tomato mixture into drained bean mixture. In a large baking dish, arrange bean mixture and meats in alternate layers. Skim and discard fat from reserved stock, then pour stock into baking dish. Cover and bake 1-1/4 hours or until beans are very soft. Season with salt and pepper. Makes 8 servings.

Hunter's Stew

1 lb. game meat, such as venison	1/2 lb. onions, finely chopped
1 lb. chanterelles	1 lb. potatoes
1 tablespoon butter or margarine	1/2 lb. carrots
3 bacon slices, finely chopped	1 cup beef stock
	Salt and white pepper

Trim meat well, then cut in fairly large cubes. Set aside. Carefully trim chanterelles, removing any damaged parts. Gently scrape caps and stalks with a sharp knife; trim ends of stalks. Wash chanterelles in cold water; drain well. Cut larger chanterelles in half; leave smaller ones whole. Set aside. Melt butter or margarine in a large, heavy saucepan; add bacon; cook until crisp. Remove bacon from pan. Add meat and onions to drippings and cook until meat is browned, stirring frequently. Peel and slice potatoes and carrots. Stir cooked bacon, chanterelles, potatoes, carrots and stock into meat-onion mixture; bring to a boil. Reduce heat, cover and simmer 1 hour or until meat is tender, stirring occasionally and adding a little hot water as necessary. **To serve,** season with salt and white pepper. Makes 4 servings.

Cook's tip

If chanterelles are out of season or too expensive, replace them with regular mushrooms or mixed wild mushrooms.

Polish Cabbage Stew

2 tablespoons vegetable oil
1 lb. lean boneless pork
    (shoulder or leg), cut in
    fairly large cubes
3 cups beef stock
1 (1-1/4 lb.) head cabbage
1/4 lb. leeks
1/4 small celeriac

1/4 lb. carrots, peeled, sliced
1/2 lb. onions, thinly sliced,
    separated into rings
1/2 teaspoon hot paprika
1 teaspoon caraway seeds
1/2 lb. Polish sausage
Salt and freshly ground white
    pepper to taste

Heat oil in a large, heavy saucepan; add pork and cook until browned, stirring frequently. Pour in 1 cup stock; bring to a simmer. Cover and simmer 20 minutes. Meanwhile, remove any damaged outer leaves from cabbage. Then quarter cabbage; core each quarter and thickly slice crosswise. Trim roots and green tops of leeks, then split leeks lengthwise and wash thoroughly to remove sand. Slice leek halves crosswise. Peel and dice celeriac. Stir cabbage, leeks, celeriac, carrots, onions, paprika, caraway seeds and remaining 2 cups stock into simmering pork. Bring to a boil. Reduce heat to medium-low, cover and simmer 40 minutes longer or until meat is tender, stirring occasionally and adding a little hot water as necessary. Ten minutes before meat is done, cut sausage in fairly thick slices; stir into stew and heat through. Season with salt and white pepper. Makes 6 servings.

Variation
Drained sauerkraut can be substituted for cabbage.

Lentil Stew with Spätzle

1 lb. lentils	2 tablespoons tomato paste
1 onion	Salt and freshly ground pepper
2 whole cloves	1/2 teaspoon dried leaf marjoram
2 parsley sprigs, chopped	1/2 teaspoon dried leaf thyme
2 thyme sprigs, chopped	1/2 lb. smoked pork sausage,
1 bay leaf	sliced
4 soup bones	

Spätzle:

1-1/2 cups plus 2 tablespoons milk	1/2 teaspoon salt
3/4 cup plus 1 tablespoon semolina	Pinch of ground nutmeg
	2 eggs

To cook lentils, place in a large saucepan. Peel onion; stick cloves into it. Add chopped herbs, bay leaf, clove-studded onion and soup bones to lentils. Add enough water to cover. Bring to a boil. Reduce heat, cover and simmer about 1 hour or until lentils are soft. Remove bay leaf, onion and bones. Stir remaining ingredients into lentils.
To make spatzle, bring milk to a simmer in a heavy saucepan. Sprinkle in semolina, 1/2 teaspoon salt and nutmeg, stirring constantly. Continue to cook, stirring, until mixture comes away from base of pan. Remove from heat; beat in eggs, 1 at a time. Press dough through a special spatzle maker into boiling water. Cook until spätzle rise to top; stir drained spatzle into lentils. Makes 4 to 6 servings.

Rice & Pork Stew

1 lb. lean boneless pork (shoulder or leg), cut in fairly large cubes	2/3 cup long-grain white rice
	2 tart apples
	1 (10-oz.) pkg. frozen green peas
All-purpose flour	Salt and freshly ground pepper to taste
2 tablespoons vegetable oil	
3 cups beef stock	2 tablespoons chopped chives
1 onion, finely chopped	

Dip pork cubes in flour to coat; shake off excess. Heat oil in a large, heavy saucepan. Add pork and cook until browned on all sides, stirring frequently. Stir in 1 cup stock; bring to a simmer. Cover and simmer 20 minutes. Stir in onion, rice and remaining 2 cups stock. Bring to a boil. Reduce heat, cover and simmer about 30 minutes or until rice is tender, adding a little hot water occasionally if necessary. Peel, quarter, core and dice apples. Stir apples and peas into stew; simmer 10 minutes longer or until apples, peas and meat are tender.
To serve, season stew with salt and pepper; sprinkle with chives. Makes 6 servings.

Cook's tip

If you wish, you may substitute diced tomatoes and bell peppers for the apples and peas.

Chicken & Vegetable Stew

1 (2-lb.) chicken	1/2 lb. Brussels sprouts,
4 black peppercorns	trimmed
1 onion, quartered	1/2 lb. carrots, sliced
1 small bunch mixed herbs,	4 oz. vermicelli
such as parsley, thyme	Few drops of soy sauce
and sage	Salt and white pepper
1 (1-lb.) cauliflower	2 tablespoons chopped parsley
1/4 lb. leeks, washed	

In a large, heavy saucepan, bring 2 quarts salted water to a boil. Add chicken, peppercorns and onion; reduce heat and simmer, uncovered, 20 minutes, skimming scum that forms. Add herbs. Cover and simmer about 20 minutes or until chicken is tender. Remove chicken; strain stock into large pan. Cool chicken; remove skin and bones. Cut meat in bite-size pieces. Separate cauliflower into flowerets. Slice leeks crosswise. Skim and discard fat from chicken stock; bring stock to a boil. Add cauliflowerets, leeks, Brussels sprouts and carrots; reduce heat, cover and simmer briskly 20 minutes or until vegetables are tender. In another saucepan, bring about 1 quart salted water to a boil. Add vermicelli; boil about 8 minutes or until tender but still firm to the bite. Drain. Stir vermicelli and chicken into vegetables; heat through. Season with soy sauce, salt and white pepper. Sprinkle with parsley. Makes 6 servings.

Lamb & Vegetable Hotpot

2 tablespoons vegetable oil	1 lb. fresh green beans
1-1/2 lbs. lean boneless lamb	1 green bell pepper, seeded,
(leg or shoulder), cut in	cut in strips
1-1/2 inch cubes	1 red bell pepper, seeded,
2 onions, finely chopped	cut in strips
2 garlic cloves, finely chopped	1/2 lb. eggplant, cut in cubes
1 teaspoon curry powder	1 or 2 savory sprigs
2 cups chicken stock	1 lb. tomatoes
1/8 teaspoon ground caraway	Salt and freshly ground black
seeds	pepper to taste
Pinch of red (cayenne) pepper	2 tablespoons chopped parsley

Heat oil in a large, heavy saucepan. Add lamb, onions and garlic; cook, stirring frequently, until meat is lightly browned on all sides. Stir in curry powder, then gradually stir in stock. Stir in ground caraway seeds and red pepper. Bring to a boil. Reduce heat, cover and simmer 30 minutes. Trim ends from beans; remove any strings. Break beans in pieces; add to simmering meat with bell peppers, eggplant and savory sprigs. Simmer 20 minutes longer, adding hot water to pan as necessary. Peel tomatoes, cut in wedges and stir into stew; simmer 10 minutes longer or until meat is tender.

To serve, season with salt and black pepper. Sprinkle with parsley. Makes 6 servings.

Simmered Apples & Bacon

1/2 lb. dried apple slices or rings (preferably unpeeled)	2 tablespoons sugar
2 tablespoons butter or margarine	1 lb. bacon slices
	1 lb. potatoes
	Salt to taste

Soak dried apples 12 hours in water to cover. Melt butter or margarine in a large, heavy saucepan with a tight-fitting lid. Sprinkle in sugar; cook, stirring, until sugar dissolves and begins to caramelize. Stir in apples and their soaking water; then stir in bacon. Bring back to a simmer; cover and simmer gently 1 hour. Check liquid in pan occasionally and add a little hot water as necessary. Peel potatoes and cut in cubes. Stir potatoes and 6 tablespoons water into apple mixture; then cover and simmer 25 to 30 minutes longer or until potatoes are tender. Season with salt. Serve straight from pan. Makes 6 servings.

Irish Stew

1/2 lb. potatoes	Salt to taste
1 lb. lean boneless lamb (leg or shoulder), cut in cubes	1/4 teaspoon dried leaf thyme
3/4 lb. onions, sliced, separated into rings	2-1/4 cups hot chicken stock
1/2 lb. carrots, peeled, sliced	2 tablespoons chopped parsley

Preheat oven to 350F (175C). Lightly grease a large, deep baking dish. Peel and thickly slice potatoes, then cover bottom of greased baking dish evenly with sliced potatoes. Top with 1/2 of lamb cubes, then 1/2 of onions and 1/2 of carrots. Sprinkle with salt and thyme. Repeat layers of vegetables and meat to fill dish. Pour in hot stock. Cover and bake about 1-1/2 hours or until meat is tender. About halfway through cooking time, check liquid in baking dish and add a little hot water if necessary. Potatoes should fall apart slightly during cooking, mixing with stock to make a thick gravy.

To serve, sprinkle with parsley. Makes 4 servings.

Djuveč

3 tablespoons vegetable oil
1/2 lb. onions, sliced,
　separated into rings
1-1/2 lbs. lean boneless lamb
　(leg or shoulder), cut in
　3/4-inch cubes
1 eggplant, diced
3/4 lb. pumpkin, peeled, diced
2 green bell peppers, seeded,
　cut in strips

2/3 cup long-grain white rice
3 cups boiling water
1 tablespoon paprika
2 tomatoes
Salt and freshly ground black
　pepper to taste

Heat oil in a large, heavy saucepan. Add onions and cook, stirring, until soft. Then add lamb; cook until lightly browned, stirring frequently. Stir in eggplant, pumpkin, bell peppers, rice, boiling water and paprika. Reduce heat to low, cover and simmer 30 minutes. Peel tomatoes, cut in wedges and stir into stew. Simmer 10 minutes longer or until meat is tender.
To serve, season with salt and black pepper. Makes 4 servings.

Chili con Carne

1/2 lb. dried red kidney beans
1 tablespoon lard or
　vegetable oil
1-1/4 lbs. round steak,
　cut in cubes
1 onion, finely chopped
2 garlic cloves, finely chopped

1 small dried red hot pepper,
　seeded, finely chopped
Salt and freshly ground black
　pepper to taste
1/8 teaspoon hot paprika
1 lb. tomatoes
2 tablespoons chopped parsley

Rinse and sort beans, then soak 12 hours in water to cover. Drain beans; place in a large, heavy saucepan and add about 3 cups water. Bring to a boil; reduce heat, cover and simmer gently 1 hour. Heat lard or oil in another large, heavy saucepan. Add steak, onion and garlic; cook until meat is lightly browned, stirring frequently. Stir meat mixture into beans with hot pepper, salt, black pepper and paprika. Cover and simmer 50 minutes longer, stirring occasionally and adding a little hot water as necessary. Peel and coarsely chop tomatoes; stir into chili and simmer about 10 minutes longer or until beans are soft and meat is very tender.
To serve, sprinkle with chopped parsley. Makes 4 servings.

Hungarian Pepper Stew

1 tablespoon lard or vegetable oil	1 lb. tomatoes, peeled, cut in wedges
6 bacon slices, diced	1 tablespoon paprika
1 large onion, diced	4 cooked smoked sausages
1 lb. mixed yellow, green and red bell peppers, seeded, cut in strips	Salt and freshly ground white pepper

Heat lard or oil in a large skillet; add bacon and cook until crisp. Remove from pan. Add onion to drippings; cook until golden, stirring frequently. Stir in bell peppers and cooked bacon; reduce heat to low and simmer 10 minutes. Then stir in tomatoes and paprika and arrange sausages over vegetables. Reduce heat to very low, cover and simmer 15 minutes longer or until sausages are heated through.

To serve, season with salt and white pepper. Makes 4 servings.

Italian Mixed Stew

1 small bunch mixed fresh herbs, such as thyme, basil, oregano and parsley	Salt
	3/4 lb. beef brisket
	3/4 lb. pork tongue
1 onion, coarsely chopped	1/2 lb. carrots
1 garlic clove, coarsely chopped	1/4 lb. leeks
1 bay leaf	2 whole chicken legs, thighs attached
2 whole allspice	

Trim herb stems. Wash herbs in cold water, shake dry and chop. In a large, heavy saucepan, bring 3 quarts water to a boil. Add chopped herbs, onion, garlic, bay leaf, allspice and a generous sprinkling of salt; return to a boil. Add beef to boiling water and boil 15 minutes, skimming and discarding any scum that forms on surface of water. Then reduce heat, cover and simmer 1 hour. Add tongue; simmer 30 minutes longer. Meanwhile, peel carrots and cut lengthwise in quarters. Trim roots and all dark green leaves from leeks; split leeks lengthwise and wash thoroughly to remove sand. Then cut leeks in about 2-inch lengths. Stir carrots, leeks and chicken into stew; simmer 30 minutes longer or until vegetables and all meats are tender. Lift meats from pan. Skin and slice tongue; slice beef.

To serve, arrange tongue, beef, chicken, carrots and leeks on a warm platter. Strain stock, skim and discard fat and season with salt. Serve stock as a clear soup to accompany meat and vegetables. Makes 6 servings.

Paella

Pinch of saffron threads
1 (2-lb.) chicken, cut up
Salt and white pepper
1/4 cup olive oil
1 onion, finely chopped
2 garlic cloves, finely chopped
1 cup plus 2 tablespoons
   uncooked long-grain
   white rice
1 green bell pepper,
   cut in strips

3 tomatoes, seeded,
   cut in wedges
About 1 qt. chicken stock
   (about 4 cups)
1/2 lb. redfish fillets
1/2 lb. cooked, shelled,
   deveined large shrimp
About 3/4 cup frozen green peas
2/3 cup dry white wine
10 pimento-stuffed green olives

In a small bowl, combine saffron and a little cold water. Set aside to soak. Wash chicken in cold water, pat dry and sprinkle with salt and white pepper. Heat oil in a large, heavy saucepan or paella pan. Add chicken pieces; cook, turning as needed, until lightly browned on all sides. Remove from pan. Add onion, garlic and rice to drippings in pan; cook, stirring, until onion is soft. Stir in browned chicken, bell pepper, tomatoes, 1 quart stock and saffron. Bring to a boil. Reduce heat, cover and simmer 25 minutes, stirring occasionally and adding a little stock if necessary. Dice fish, sprinkle with salt and stir into chicken mixture with shrimp, peas and wine. Cover and simmer 10 minutes or until chicken meat is no longer pink near bone and fish turns from transparent to opaque. Garnish with olives. Makes 8 servings.

Polish Stew

3/4 lb. chanterelles or
   mixed fresh mushrooms
6 bacon slices, diced
1 lb. round steak, cut in
   small cubes
2 onions, finely chopped
1 lb. cabbage, cut in 2-inch
   chunks

1 bay leaf
1 teaspoon caraway seeds
Pinch of dried leaf thyme
3 tablespoons tomato paste
1 cup dry white wine
2 garlic cloves
Salt, freshly ground white
   pepper and sugar to taste

Carefully trim chanterelles, removing any damaged parts. Gently scrape caps and stalks with a sharp knife; trim ends of stalks. Wash chanterelles thoroughly in cold water and drain well. Cut larger chanterelles in half; leave smaller ones whole. Set aside. In a large, heavy saucepan, cook bacon until crisp. Remove from pan. Add steak and onions to drippings; cook until meat is browned, stirring frequently. Stir in cooked bacon, chanterelles, cabbage, bay leaf, caraway seeds, thyme, tomato paste and wine. Press garlic into pan through a garlic press. Add enough water to cover; stir well. Bring to a boil. Reduce heat, cover and simmer 1 to 1-1/4 hours or until meat is tender.

To serve, skim and discard fat from stew. Remove bay leaf; season stew with salt, white pepper and sugar. Makes 8 servings.

Lasagna

1 (8-oz.) pkg. lasagna noodles
2 tablespoons olive oil
2 onions, finely chopped
1-1/4 lbs. mixed lean ground
   beef and pork
1/2 teaspoon dried leaf oregano
1 teaspoon paprika
Salt to taste
2 tablespoons butter or
   margarine

2 tablespoons all-purpose flour
2 cups milk
1 cup dry white wine
Freshly ground white pepper
1 cup shredded Emmentaler
   cheese (4 oz.)
2/3 cup freshly grated Parmesan
   cheese (2 oz.)
1/4 cup half and half

To cook noodles, following package directions, cook until tender but still firm to the bite; drain. Rinse with cold water; drain. **To complete,** preheat oven to 400F (205C). Heat oil in a large skillet. Add onions; crumble in beef and pork. Cook until meat is browned, stirring. Discard excess fat. Season with oregano, paprika and salt. Melt butter or margarine in a saucepan. Add flour; cook over low heat, stirring, about 1 minute. Gradually add milk and wine, stirring; simmer 5 minutes, stirring frequently. Season with salt and white pepper. Spread a thin layer of white sauce over bottom of a baking dish. Fill dish with alternate layers of cooked noodles and meat mixture, spooning a little white sauce over each meat layer. Finish with a layer of sauce; sprinkle with cheeses. Drizzle with half and half. Bake 40 minutes or until hot and bubbly. Makes 6 servings.

Manicotti

1 (8-oz.) pkg. manicotti
   (12 manicotti shells)
1 tablespoon olive oil
1/4 lb. prosciutto, chopped
1/4 lb. mushrooms, chopped
1 onion, chopped
1 lb. ground veal
Salt to taste

1 (16-oz.) can tomatoes
2 garlic cloves, chopped
2/3 cup half and half
1/2 teaspoon dried leaf basil
Freshly ground white pepper
1-1/2 cups grated Emmentaler,
   Mozzarella or jack
   cheese (6 oz.)
2 tablespoons butter or
   margarine

To cook manicotti, in a large saucepan, bring about 4 quarts salted water to a boil. Add manicotti; boil about 12 minutes. Drain, rinse under cold running water and drain again. Set aside. **To complete,** preheat oven to 425F (220C). Heat oil in a large skillet. Add prosciutto, mushrooms and onion; then crumble in veal. Cook until meat is lightly browned, stirring frequently. Season with salt; set aside. In a food processor fitted with a metal blade, puree tomatoes and their liquid. Add garlic, half and half and basil; process until blended. Season with salt and white pepper. Fill manicotti with meat mixture. Spread about 1/3 of tomato sauce in a large baking dish; arrange stuffed manicotti atop sauce. Cover evenly with remaining tomato sauce. Sprinkle with cheese; dot with butter or margarine. Bake about 30 minutes or until manicotti shells are tender. Makes 6 servings.

Pasta Casserole with Spinach

8 oz. tagliatelle or fettuccine
1 lb. fresh spinach
1/8 teaspoon garlic powder
6 bacon slices, diced
2 eggs
2/3 cup half and half
Pinch of ground nutmeg
Salt and freshly ground white
  pepper
1/2 cup shredded Emmentaler
  cheese (2 oz.)

To cook tagliatelle or fettuccine, in a large saucepan, bring 3 quarts salted water to a boil. Add pasta; boil about 10 minutes or until tender but still firm to the bite. Drain, rinse under cold running water and drain again. Set aside.

To complete, remove stems and any tough leaves from spinach, then wash spinach thoroughly in cold water. Place spinach with water that clings to leaves in a saucepan; cover and cook until spinach begins to wilt. Drain well, coarsely chop and mix with garlic powder. Set aside. Preheat oven to 400F (205C). In a large skillet, cook bacon until crisp. Drain; grease a baking dish with some of the bacon drippings. Discard remaining drippings. Set bacon aside. In a bowl, beat together eggs, half and half, nutmeg, salt and white pepper. Set aside. Cover bottom of greased baking dish with a layer of cooked tagliatelle, then top evenly with spinach and cooked bacon. Spread remaining tagliatelle on top; pour egg mixture evenly over tagliatelle. Bake 20 minutes. Sprinkle with cheese and bake about 10 minutes or until cheese is melted and casserole is heated through. Makes 4 servings.

Cook's tip

If you wish, you may substitute diced sausage or ham for the bacon; grease the baking dish with butter or margarine.

Ham & Noodle Casserole

2-3/4 cups all-purpose flour
1/2 teaspoon salt
3 eggs, beaten
5 tablespoons butter or
   margarine
1/2 lb. lean cooked ham

2 eggs, separated
2/3 cup dairy sour cream
Salt and freshly ground white
   pepper to taste
2 tablespoons fine dry
   bread crumbs

To make noodles, in a bowl, stir together flour and 1/2 teaspoon salt. Mix in 3 beaten eggs and a little water to make a smooth, firm dough. Cover and let stand at room temperature 1 hour. On a lightly floured board, roll out dough very thinly. Let dough dry slightly, then cut in 3/4-inch squares. In a large saucepan, bring 3 quarts lightly salted water to a boil. Sprinkle in noodles; boil about 5 minutes or until tender but still fairly firm to the bite. Drain, rinse under cold running water and drain again. Set aside. Preheat oven to 400F (205C). Butter a baking dish. Melt 4 tablespoons butter or margarine in a skillet; add cooked noodles and stir gently to coat. Set aside. Trim any excess fat from ham, then dice ham. In a bowl, beat together egg yolks, sour cream and salt and white pepper to taste. Stir in ham. In another bowl, beat egg whites until stiff; fold into ham mixture. Then carefully fold together egg mixture and noodles; turn into buttered baking dish. Sprinkle with bread crumbs; dot with remaining 1 tablespoon butter or margarine. Bake about 30 minutes or until firm and lightly browned. Makes 6 servings.

Macaroni Casserole

1-1/2 cups macaroni
3 tablespoons vegetable oil
1 onion, finely chopped
1 garlic clove, finely chopped
1 lb. lean boneless pork,
   finely chopped
1 cup beef stock
1 tablespoon chopped mixed fresh
   herbs, such as basil,
   sage and thyme

Salt to taste
1/2 lb. zucchini, sliced
1/8 teaspoon dried leaf thyme
4 tomatoes, peeled, diced
1 cup shredded Emmentaler
   cheese (4 oz.)
1 tablespoon chopped parsley

To cook macaroni, in a large saucepan, bring 3 quarts salted water to a boil. Sprinkle in macaroni; boil about 12 minutes or until macaroni is tender but still firm to the bite. Drain, rinse under cold running water and drain again. Set aside.

To complete, preheat oven to 400F (205C). Grease a baking dish. Heat 2 tablespoons oil in a large skillet; add onion and garlic. Cook, stirring, until onion is soft. Add pork; cook until lightly browned, stirring frequently. Stir in stock. Simmer 10 minutes. Stir in mixed herbs and salt. Heat remaining 1 tablespoon oil in another skillet. Add zucchini; cook a few minutes, turning frequently. Season with salt and thyme. Fill greased baking dish with alternate layers of cooked macaroni, meat mixture, tomatoes and cooked zucchini; finish with a layer of macaroni. Sprinkle with cheese. Bake about 20 minutes or until hot and bubbly. Sprinkle with parsley. Makes 6 servings.

Pastizio

Tomato-Meat Sauce:

1 tablespoon butter or margarine	2/3 cup beef stock
1 small onion, chopped	1-1/2 tablespoons fine dry
1 lb. mixed lean ground beef	bread crumbs
and pork	2 tablespoons freshly grated
1/2 (3-inch) cinnamon stick	Parmesan cheese
2/3 cup dry white wine	Salt and white pepper
2 tablespoons tomato paste	

Macaroni Layer:

1 egg white	1-1/2 cups macaroni, cooked
2 tablespoons freshly grated	
Parmesan cheese	

White Sauce:

2 tablespoons butter or	Salt and white pepper
margarine	2 tablespoons butter or
3 tablespoons all-purpose flour	margarine
1-1/2 cups milk	3-1/2 tablespoons fine dry
3 tablespoons freshly grated	bread crumbs
Parmesan cheese	2 tablespoons freshly grated
1 egg yolk	Parmesan cheese
1 tablespoon half and half	

To make meat sauce, melt butter or margarine in a skillet. Add onion; cook until golden, stirring frequently. Crumble in beef and pork; cook until lightly browned, stirring frequently. Discard excess fat. Stir in cinnamon stick, wine, tomato paste and stock. Simmer, uncovered, until sauce is thickened. Remove cinnamon stick; stir in bread crumbs and 2 tablespoons cheese.

Season with salt and white pepper and set aside.
To make macaroni layer, in a bowl, beat egg white until stiff; fold in cheese. Fold egg-white mixture into macaroni. Set aside.
To make white sauce, melt 2 tablespoons butter or margarine in a saucepan. Sprinkle in flour and cook over low heat, stirring, about 1 minute. Gradually add milk; continue to cook, stirring constantly, until sauce is bubbly and thickened. Stir in 3 tablespoons cheese. Remove sauce from heat. In a small bowl, beat together egg yolk and half and half. Beat in 2 tablespoons of the hot sauce; then beat egg-yolk mixture back into sauce. Return to heat; cook a few minutes over low heat, stirring constantly. Season with salt and white pepper.
To complete, preheat oven to 400F (205C). Butter a baking dish with 1 tablespoon of the butter. Sprinkle bottom of dish with 1-1/2 tablespoons bread crumbs, then spread with 1/2 of macaroni mixture. Spread meat sauce over macaroni; cover with remaining macaroni, then pour white sauce over all. Stir together remaining 2 tablespoons breadcrumbs and 2 tablespoons cheese; sprinkle over sauce. Dot with remaining 1 tablespoon butter or margarine. Bake about 40 minutes or until hot and bubbly. Makes 6 servings.

Potato Casserole

2 lbs. potatoes
1/2 lb. lean cooked ham
2/3 cup milk
1-1/3 cups freshly grated
   Parmesan cheese (4 oz.)
Salt and freshly ground pepper
Pinch of ground nutmeg
2/3 cup dairy sour cream
2 eggs
1/4 cup chopped mixed fresh
   herbs, such as parsley,
   chives and basil
1 tablespoon fine dry
   bread crumbs
1 tablespoon butter or margarine

Peel potatoes, cut in quarters and cook in boiling salted water until soft. Drain, heat to evaporate excess moisture and mash thoroughly. Set aside. Preheat oven to 425F (220C). Grease a baking dish. Trim any excess fat from ham; cut ham in cubes. In a large bowl, mix mashed potatoes, ham, milk, cheese, salt, pepper and nutmeg. Spread potato mixture evenly in greased baking dish. In a bowl, beat together sour cream, eggs and herbs; pour over potato mixture. Sprinkle with bread crumbs; dot with butter or margarine. Bake on center oven rack about 20 minutes or until lightly browned and heated through. Makes 4 servings.

Cook's tip

For a dish with more texture, boil the potatoes whole; peel and slice. Mix the sliced potatoes with ham, milk and cheese; complete casserole as directed above.

Belgian Endive & Cheese Casserole

1 lb. Belgian endive, trimmed	2 tablespoons fine dry
1/2 to 2/3 lb. lean cooked ham	bread crumbs
1 tablespoon vegetable oil	1 tablespoon chopped parsley
Salt and white pepper	1 tablespoon butter or margarine

Cheese Sauce:

2 tablespoons butter or	2/3 cup dry white wine
margarine	1 cup shredded Swiss cheese
2 tablespoons all-purpose flour	(4 oz.)
1 cup milk	2 egg yolks

Cut endive crosswise in 1/2-inch-wide strips. Trim ham; cut in 2'' x 1/4'' strips. Heat oil in a skillet. Add endive and ham; cook, stirring, until endive wilts. Season with salt and pepper.
To make sauce, melt butter or margarine in a saucepan. Sprinkle in flour; cook over low heat, stirring, about 1 minute. Gradually add milk; cook, stirring constantly, until sauce is bubbly and thickened. Stir in wine; heat through. Gradually stir in cheese, stirring until cheese is melted. Remove sauce from heat. Beat 2 tablespoons of the hot sauce into egg yolks, then beat egg-yolk mixture back into sauce. Cook about 1 minute, stirring.
To complete, preheat oven to 400F (205C). Butter a baking dish. Spread ham-endive mixture in buttered baking dish. Cover with cheese sauce, sprinkle with bread crumbs and parsley and dot with butter or margarine. Bake about 25 minutes or until hot and bubbly. Makes 4 servings.

Moussaka

2 medium (1-lb.) eggplants	Freshly ground black pepper
Salt	5 tablespoons fine dry
Vegetable oil	bread crumbs
2 onions, grated	2 tablespoons butter
1-1/4 lbs. ground lamb	2 tablespoons all-purpose flour
5 tablespoons dry vermouth	1 cup milk
6 tablespoons water	3 eggs, beaten
1 teaspoon sugar	1 cup Parmesan cheese (3 oz.)
1 teaspoon dried leaf oregano	1 lb. tomatoes, thickly sliced

Peel and thickly slice eggplants, sprinkle with salt and let stand at room temperature 1 hour. Rinse slices; pat very dry. Heat about 2 tablespoons oil in a large skillet; add as many eggplant slices as will fit. Cook, turning frequently, until soft; set aside. Repeat until all slices are cooked, adding oil as necessary. Wipe skillet clean. Heat 2 tablespoons oil in skillet. Add onions and lamb. Cook, stirring, until meat is browned. Stir in vermouth, water, sugar, oregano, salt, pepper and bread crumbs. Cook, stirring, a few minutes; set aside. Melt butter in a saucepan. Sprinkle in flour; stir over low heat about 1 minute. Gradually add milk; cook, stirring constantly, until bubbly and thickened. Remove from heat. In a small bowl, beat eggs and 4 to 5 tablespoons of the hot sauce; stir egg mixture back into sauce. Cook a few minutes, stirring. Preheat oven to 400F (205C). Cover bottom of a baking dish with eggplant slices. Sprinkle with some of cheese, then some of meat sauce. Continue layering until all casgredients are used. Arrange tomatoes over top; pour sauce over tomatoes. Bake 45 minutes or until bubbly. Makes 6 servings.

Potato & Tomato Casserole

1-1/2 lbs. potatoes, scrubbed	2 onions, sliced
About 1-1/2 tablespoons vegetable oil	1 lb. tomatoes, sliced
	1/2 teaspoon dried leaf thyme
3/4 lb. beef tenderloin, thinly sliced	1/2 cup shredded Gouda cheese (2 oz.)
Salt and freshly ground pepper to taste	2/3 cup dairy sour cream

Cook unpeeled potatoes in boiling lightly salted water until tender. Drain potatoes; cool, peel, slice and set aside. Preheat oven to 400F (205C). Lightly grease a baking dish. Heat about 1 tablespoon oil in a skillet, add beef slices and cook about 2 minutes on each side. Remove meat from pan and sprinkle with salt and pepper. Set aside. Arrange a layer of potato slices over bottom of greased baking dish; arrange meat over potatoes and sprinkle with remaining oil. Cover with alternate layers of potato slices, onion slices and tomato slices. Sprinkle with salt, pepper and thyme. In a small bowl, stir together cheese and sour cream; pour over vegetables in baking dish. Bake about 15 minutes or until heated through. Makes 4 servings.

Sauerkraut Casserole

1 (28-oz.) can sauerkraut, drained	1 large red bell pepper, seeded, cut in strips
2/3 cup beef stock	2/3 cup dry white wine
2/3 cup apple juice	1 lb. potatoes
2 whole cloves	2 tablespoons chopped parsley
2 juniper berries	2 tablespoons whipping cream
6 bacon slices, diced	1 tablespoon butter or margarine

In a saucepan, combine sauerkraut, stock, apple juice, cloves and juniper berries. Bring to a simmer over low heat, then cover and simmer about 40 minutes. Remove cloves and juniper berries. Preheat oven to 425F (220C). In a skillet, cook bacon until crisp. Remove from pan; add bell pepper to drippings and cook a few minutes, stirring frequently. Stir cooked bacon and bell pepper into sauerkraut mixture; stir in wine. Pour mixture into a large baking dish. Peel potatoes and slice very thinly. Top sauerkraut mixture with potatoes; sprinkle with parsley. Drizzle cream over top; dot with butter or margarine. Bake on center oven rack 20 minutes or until potatoes are tender. Makes 4 servings.

Potato-Dumpling Casserole

2 lbs. potatoes	About 2/3 cup buttermilk
Salt to taste	1 tablespoon butter or margarine
1/8 teaspoon ground nutmeg	1/4 cup clarified butter or lard
6 to 8 tablespoons all-purpose	3 eggs
flour	2/3 cup half and half

Peel 1 pound potatoes, cut in quarters and cook in boiling salted water until soft. Drain, heat to evaporate excess moisture and mash thoroughly. While potatoes are cooking, peel remaining 1 pound potatoes and grate into a bowl of cold water; stir to mix. Drain grated potatoes, then place on a clean cloth. Bring cloth up around potatoes; hold wrapped potatoes over a large bowl and squeeze firmly to extract as much water as possible. Let water that drains into bowl stand until potato starch has settled to the bottom. Pour off and discard water, leaving potato starch in bowl. Add grated uncooked potatoes and mashed cooked potatoes to potato starch; mix well. Stir in salt, nutmeg, flour and buttermilk to make a soft dough. Preheat oven to 400F (205C). Butter a baking dish. Heat clarified butter or lard in a skillet. Using a large spoon dipped in cold water, shape dough into ovals; as each is shaped, place in hot fat. Cook until golden brown on bottom. Place browned-side down in buttered baking dish. In a bowl, beat eggs and half and half; pour over dumplings. Bake 20 to 30 minutes or until golden brown. Makes 4 servings.

Potato & Herring Casserole

3/4 lb. salted herring fillets	2/3 cup water
2 lbs. potatoes, scrubbed	1/4 cup half and half
5 tablespoons butter or	1/4 lb. lean cooked ham
margarine	2 tablespoons shredded
1 onion, chopped	Emmentaler cheese
3 tablespoons all-purpose flour	

Soak herring in cold water overnight. Drain, pat dry and cut in 1-inch-squares. Set aside. Cook unpeeled potatoes in boiling salted water until tender; drain, cool, peel and cut in thick slices. Set aside. Preheat oven to 400F (205C). Lightly grease a baking dish. Melt 3 tablespoons butter or margarine in a saucepan. Add onion and cook, stirring, until soft. Sprinkle in flour and cook over low heat, stirring, about 1 minute. Gradually stir in 2/3 cup water and half and half; continue to cook, stirring, until sauce is bubbly and thickened. Remove sauce from heat. Trim any excess fat from ham; dice ham and stir into sauce. Layer potato slices and herring in greased baking dish, finishing with a layer of potatoes. Pour sauce over potatoes, sprinkle with cheese and dot with remaining 2 tablespoons butter or margarine. Bake 30 minutes or until bubbly and heated through. Makes 6 servings.

Cherry Pudding

1 qt. water (4 cups)	1/2 teaspoon vanilla extract
1/2 cup sugar	1 tablespoon cornstarch
1 lb. red tart cherries, pitted	6 tablespoons milk
16 oz. low-fat cottage cheese	4 egg whites
(2 cups)	Pinch of salt
2 egg yolks	1/3 cup raisins

Preheat oven to 350F (175C). Grease a baking dish. In a saucepan, combine water and 1/3 cup sugar. Bring to a boil, add cherries and boil 5 minutes. Drain and set aside. In a bowl, beat together cottage cheese, egg yolks, remaining sugar and vanilla. Dissolve cornstarch in milk; stir into cottage-cheese mixture. Set aside. In another bowl, beat egg whites and salt until stiff. Fold into cottage-cheese mixture, then fold in raisins and cherries. Turn mixture into greased baking dish; bake about 45 minutes or until pudding is firm. Makes 4 servings.

Cook's tip

If you wish, use another fruit in place of tart cherries—dark sweet cherries, raspberries, blackberries, or black currants. Adjust the amount of sugar according to the sweetness of the fruit.

Rum & Raisin Pancake Pudding

1 cup plus 6 tablespoons	3 tablespoons sugar
all-purpose flour	1/3 cup raisins
Pinch of salt	1 egg yolk
3 eggs	1 tablespoon rum
1-1/2 cups sparkling water	1/2 teaspoon vanilla extract
About 1/4 cup butter or	1/4 cup dairy sour cream
margarine	1/2 cup sliced almonds, toasted
1-1/2 cups cottage cheese	

In a bowl, stir together flour and salt. Beat in eggs and sparkling water to make a smooth batter. Cover and let stand at room temperature 20 to 30 minutes. Stir batter well. Melt about 1 tablespoon butter or margarine in a skillet. Add 1/4 of pancake batter; tilt skillet to coat bottom evenly. Cook until pancake is firm on top and lightly browned on bottom. Remove from pan. Repeat with remaining butter or margarine and remaining batter, making 3 more large pancakes. Cover and keep warm. In a bowl, beat together cottage cheese, sugar, raisins, egg yolk, rum and vanilla. Preheat oven to 400F (205C). Lightly grease a baking dish. Spread each pancake with 1/4 of cottage-cheese filling; roll up pancakes jelly-roll style and arrange in greased baking dish. Spread sour cream evenly over pancakes. Bake on center oven rack 20 minutes. Sprinkle with almonds; serve hot. Makes 8 servings.

Apple & Rice Pudding

3/4 cup short-grain rice	2 tablespoons granulated sugar
3 cups milk	1/2 to 1 teaspoon vanilla
Pinch of salt	extract
About 1 tablespoon butter or	1 lb. apples
margarine	1 tablespoon lemon juice
2 eggs, separated	2 tablespoons powdered sugar

Wash rice well in cold water; drain. In a saucepan, combine milk and salt. Bring to a boil, then sprinkle in rice. Reduce heat to low, cover and simmer about 25 minutes or until rice is tender. Remove from heat and cool. Preheat oven to 400F (205C). Butter a baking dish, using about 1 tablespoon butter or margarine. In a bowl, beat together egg yolks, granulated sugar and vanilla; fold into cooked rice. Set aside. Peel and core apples; cut in rings into bowl of cold water. Beat egg whites until stiff; fold into rice mixture. Fill buttered baking dish with alternate layers of rice mixture and apple slices, finishing with a layer of apple slices. Sprinkle with lemon juice and dust with powdered sugar. Bake on center oven rack about 20 minutes or until pudding is golden brown. Makes 4 servings.

Cherry Bread Pudding

6 day-old dinner rolls	3/4 cup chopped almonds
3 cups lukewarm milk	Pinch of salt
4 eggs, separated	2 tablespoons butter or
2/3 cup granulated sugar	margarine
1 teaspoon ground cinnamon	2 tablespoons powdered sugar
2 lbs. Bing cherries or other	
sweet cherries, pitted	

Preheat oven to 400F (205C). Grease a baking dish. Cut rolls in cubes. Place cubed rolls in a large bowl; pour milk over rolls and let stand until softened. In another bowl, beat together egg yolks, granulated sugar and cinnamon. Stir egg-yolk mixture into softened rolls, then stir in cherries and almonds. In a third bowl, beat egg whites with salt until stiff. Fold beaten egg whites into cherry mixture; then turn mixture into greased baking dish. Dot with butter or margarine. Bake on next-to-lowest oven rack 40 to 50 minutes or until firm and golden brown. Dust with powdered sugar. Makes 8 servings.

Plum Dumpling

2 cups plus 2 tablespoons milk	1/4 cup sugar
3/4 cup plus 1 tablespoon	1 teaspoon ground cinnamon
semolina	1/4 teaspoon vanilla extract
3 day-old dinner rolls	1 teaspoon grated lemon peel
1 tablespoon butter or margarine	1 lb. plums, pitted, diced
2 eggs	About 1/4 cup fine dry
Pinch of salt	bread crumbs

In a saucepan, bring milk to a simmer. Slowly sprinkle in semolina, stirring constantly. Cook a few minutes to allow semolina to swell; remove from heat and cool. Slice crusts from rolls, removing as little bread as possible. Discard crusts; dice remainder of rolls. Melt butter or margarine in a skillet; add diced rolls and cook until lightly browned, stirring frequently. Transfer browned rolls to a bowl. In another bowl, beat together eggs, salt, sugar, cinnamon, vanilla and lemon peel. Pour egg mixture over rolls. Mix well. Stir in plums and semolina; stir in 1/4 cup bread crumbs. Mixture should form a ball; add more bread crumbs, if necessary. In a large saucepan, bring a large amount of water to a boil. Shape plum mixture into an oblong dumpling; place on a cloth. Knot corners of cloth over dumpling. Suspend cloth from handle of a wooden spoon; lower dumpling into boiling water, resting spoon handle across top of pan. Make sure dumpling is above bottom of pan. Boil gently 40 minutes. Makes 6 servings. Serve with vanilla sauce.

Dutch Rice Cake

1 (16-oz.) can apricot	4 egg yolks
halves, drained	2/3 cup granulated sugar
1 vanilla bean	7 tablespoons all-purpose flour
1 cup short-grain rice, washed	1/2 cup ground almonds
1 qt. milk (4 cups)	3 egg whites
1 teaspoon grated lemon peel	Pinch of salt
1/2 cup butter or margarine,	2 tablespoons powdered sugar
room temperature	1/4 cup whipping cream

Cut 6 apricot halves in half; reserve. Dice remaining apricots; set aside. Slit vanilla bean lengthwise with a sharp knife. In a saucepan, combine rice, vanilla bean, milk and lemon peel. Bring to a boil; reduce heat. Cover and simmer 25 minutes or until rice is tender. Remove vanilla bean; cool. Preheat oven to 400F (205C). Grease and flour a round 9- or 10-inch baking pan. In a bowl, beat butter or margarine, egg yolks, granulated sugar, flour and almonds until fluffy. Fold butter mixture and diced apricots into rice mixture. In another bowl, beat egg whites and salt until stiff. Fold egg whites into rice mixture. Pour into prepared pan; bake about 1 hour. Let cool in pan on a wire rack 10 minutes. Turn cake out onto a serving plate; cool completely. Dust cake with powdered sugar. Whip cream; spoon into a pastry bag fitted with a fluted tip; pipe around edge of cake. Top cream with reserved apricots. Makes 12 servings.

Apricot Crepes

Filling:
1 lb. fresh apricots or
   1 lb. can peeled apricots
1 cup water
2/3 cup granulated sugar
Juice of 1/2 lemon
1 tablespoon apricot- or
   almond-flavored liqueur

Batter:
1/2 cup all-purpose flour
1/4 teaspoon salt
1 teaspoon sugar
2/3 cup sparkling water
2 eggs
2 tablespoons butter or
   margarine
Powdered sugar, if desired

To make filling, blanch fresh apricots in boiling water; drain, peel and thinly slice. If using canned apricots, drain well; reserve juice, if desired; thinly slice apricots. In a saucepan, combine 1 cup water (or reserved apricot juice plus enough water to equal 1 cup), 2/3 cup granulated sugar and lemon juice. Bring to a boil; boil 3 minutes. Stir sliced apricots into hot syrup; simmer 10 minutes. Stir in liqueur; remove from heat and cool.

To make batter, in a bowl, stir together flour, salt and sugar. Beat in sparkling water and eggs to make a smooth batter.

To cook crepes, melt butter or margarine in a small saucepan. Keep warm. Stir crepe batter thoroughly. Pour a little of the melted butter or margarine into a small 7-inch nonstick skillet with sloping sides. Tilt to coat inside of skillet; pour any excess back into saucepan. Heat until foamy. Pour about 3 tablespoons batter into skillet and tilt skillet quickly to coat bottom evenly. Cook until crepe is firm on top and light golden brown on bottom; flip over and cook a few seconds on other side. Remove from pan and keep hot. Repeat with remaining crepe batter, adding more butter or margarine to skillet as necessary.

To serve, drain filling. Fold crepes into small cones and fill with apricots. Dust with powdered sugar; serve with chocolate sauce, if desired. Makes 6 crepes.

Apricot Dumplings

1 lb. fresh apricots	1 cup fine dry bread crumbs
Sugar cubes (1 for each apricot)	3 tablespoons powdered sugar
1/3 cup butter or margarine	

Dough:

1 cup water	1-1/3 cups all-purpose flour
2 tablespoons butter or	2 eggs
margarine	

Cut each apricot in half and remove pit. Then put apricot halves back together with a sugar cube between each pair of halves.

To make dough, in a saucepan, combine water and butter or margarine. Bring to a boil; stir until butter or margarine melts. Add flour all at once; beat with a wooden spoon until mixture leaves side of pan and forms a ball. Remove from heat. Beat in eggs, 1 at a time, beating dough until smooth after each addition. Shape warm dough into a long roll; cut in as many slices as you have apricots.

To complete dumplings, wrap each dough slice around a sugar-cube-stuffed apricot. Let dry 5 minutes. In a large saucepan, bring 3 quarts salted water to a boil. Add dumplings, reduce heat and simmer gently about 10 minutes. Drain well; keep warm. Melt butter or margarine in a skillet; add bread crumbs. Cook, stirring, until golden brown. Roll dumplings in crumbs; dust with powdered sugar. Makes 6 servings.

Viennese Pancake

8 eggs, separated	2-1/4 cups all-purpose flour
1 tablespoon granulated sugar	1/4 teaspoon salt
(or more to taste up	1/2 cup raisins, packed
to 3 tablespoons)	4 tablespoons butter or mar-
1 cup milk	garine
	Sifted powdered sugar

In large bowl, beat egg yolks with granulated sugar, milk, flour and salt to make a smooth batter. Cover and let stand 10 minutes. Pour boiling water over raisins and let stand 5 minutes, then drain well. Beat egg whites until stiff; fold into batter. Melt 1 tablespoon butter or margarine in a large (10- to 12-inch) skillet. Pour in 1/4 of batter and sprinkle with 1/4 of raisins. Cook until bottom of pancake is golden brown, about 3 minutes. Turn pancake and cook until browned on other side, about 3 more minutes. Using 2 forks, tear pancake in small, irregular pieces. Cook 1 minute longer, stirring frequently. Make sure pieces are cooked throughout, then turn out onto a warm platter, cover and keep warm. Repeat with remaining butter, batter and raisins, making 3 more pancakes.

To serve, sprinkle hot pancake pieces with powdered sugar; serve immediately. Makes 6 servings.

Elderflowers in Batter

16 elderflower heads **1/4 cup sugar**
2 teaspoons ground cinnamon

Batter:
3/4 cup plus 1 tablespoon **1 egg, separated**
 all-purpose flour **About 2/3 cup beer**
Pinch of salt **Vegetable oil for deep-frying**

Wash elderflowers under cold, slowly running water, then drain thoroughly on a clean towel. Set aside.
To make batter, in a bowl, stir together flour and salt. Beat in egg yolk and enough beer to make a smooth, thick batter. Cover and let stand at room temperature 30 minutes. In another bowl, beat egg white until stiff. Stir batter thoroughly, then fold egg white into batter.
To cook, in a deep, heavy saucepan, heat about 2 inches of oil to 350F (175C) or until a 1-inch bread cube turns golden brown in about 60 seconds. Dip elderflower heads, 1 at a time, in batter; lower into hot oil. Cook 4 to 6 minutes or until golden brown. Drain on paper towels. Keep cooked blossoms hot until all have been cooked.
To serve, in a small bowl, stir together cinnamon and sugar; sprinkle over blossoms. Makes 4 servings.

Apple Fritters

2 eggs, separated **1/4 teaspoon salt**
1-1/3 cups all-purpose flour **2 tablespoons powdered sugar**
1 cup milk or dry white wine *or* **2 tablespoons granulated**
4 large cooking apples **sugar mixed with 1 tablespoon**
Vegetable oil for deep-frying **ground cinnamon**

Combine egg yolks, flour and milk or wine; stir to make a thick batter. Let stand while you prepare apples and egg whites. Peel and core apples. Cut apples into rings about 1/2 inch thick. Heat 3 inches oil to 350F (175C) in a deep fryer or large saucepan. Beat egg whites with salt until stiff. Stir batter, then fold in egg whites until combined. Dip apple rings into batter, transfer to hot oil and fry until golden brown on both sides. Drain fritters on paper towels or absorbent paper and keep hot in the oven until all fritters are cooked. Before serving, dust with powdered sugar or cinnamon sugar. Makes 4 servings.

Cook's tip:

The same recipe can be used for pineapple fritters. Use two (20-oz.) cans of sliced pineapple. Drain well, then dry pineapple slices lightly with paper towels before dipping in batter. Wine batter is particularly delicious used with pineapple.

Plum Mold

1 cup water
1 lb. ripe plums, halved, pitted
4 teaspoons unflavored gelatin
1/4 cup cold water
1 cup plus 1 tablespoon sugar
7 tablespoons lemon juice
2 teaspoons grated lemon peel

1/4 cup slivovitz
1/8 teaspoon ground cinnamon
1/2 teaspoon vanilla extract
1/2 cup coarsely chopped
  almonds
2/3 cup whipping cream

In a saucepan, bring 1 cup water to a boil. Add plums, reduce heat, cover and simmer about 20 minutes or until plums are very soft. Meanwhile, in a small bowl, soften gelatin in 1/4 cup cold water. Set aside. Puree plums in a food processor fitted with a metal blade; return puree to pan. Stir in sugar, lemon juice and lemon peel. Heat plum mixture over low heat until sugar is dissolved, stirring constantly; stir in slivovitz, cinnamon, vanilla and softened gelatin. Heat, stirring, until gelatin is dissolved. Rinse a mold in cold water. Stir plum mixture well, pour into mold and cool. Then refrigerate about 4 hours or until set.

To serve, run tip of a knife around edge of mold, then invert mold onto a serving plate. Sprinkle plum mold with almonds. In a bowl, beat cream until stiff; spoon into a pastry bag fitted with a fluted tip and pipe around mold. Makes 8 servings.

Chocolate Sponge with Cream

4 oz. semisweet chocolate
1/4 cup butter or margarine,
  room temperature
2/3 cup granulated sugar
5 eggs, separated
1 cup ground almonds

1 to 2 tablespoons fine dry
  bread crumbs, if necessary
1/2 cup whipping cream
Powdered sugar to taste
Vanilla extract to taste

Grease a pudding mold. Break chocolate in pieces; place in the top of a double boiler over simmering water. Heat, stirring, until chocolate is melted and smooth. Remove from heat; cool. In a large bowl, beat butter or margarine, granulated sugar and egg yolks until smooth and creamy. Stir melted, cooled chocolate and almonds into butter mixture to make a soft batter that holds its shape when dropped from a spoon. If batter is too soft, stir in bread crumbs. In another large bowl, beat egg whites until stiff; fold into chocolate mixture. Turn batter into greased pudding mold. Cover mold tightly and place in a large saucepan; add boiling water to pan until water level reaches 2/3 of the way up sides of mold. Cover and cook about 50 minutes, keeping water at a gentle boil. Add more boiling water to pan as necessary.

To serve, in a bowl, beat cream until it holds soft peaks; sweeten with powdered sugar and flavor with vanilla. Turn out chocolate sponge onto a serving plate; serve hot, with whipped cream. Makes 6 servings.

Yeast Dumplings with Poppy Seeds

1 (1/4-oz.) pkg. active dry yeast (about 1 tablespoon)	1/2 teaspoon grated lemon peel
2 teaspoons granulated sugar	2 tablespoons rum
1/4 cup warm water (110F, 45C)	1/2 teaspoon ground cinnamon
1/4 cup warm milk (110F, 45C)	2/3 cup pureed cooked prunes
3-1/2 cups all-purpose flour	1 cup sifted powdered sugar
1/4 teaspoon salt	About 1 cup ground poppy seeds
2 eggs	1 cup butter or margarine, melted
1/2 cup butter or margarine, room temperature	

In a small bowl, dissolve yeast and granulated sugar in warm water. Stir in milk. Let stand until bubbly. In a large bowl, combine flour and salt. Mix in yeast mixture, eggs, 1/2 cup butter or margarine and lemon peel. Beat until light and glossy, about 5 minutes. Cover; let rise in a warm place 1 hour. Punch down dough, turn out onto a floured board and knead briefly. Divide into 30 portions; shape each portion into a 3-inch round. In a bowl, combine rum, cinnamon and prune puree. Place 1 teaspoon of prune mixture on each dough round; bring up dough around filling and pinch to seal. Shape into round dumplings. Cover; let rise in a warm place about 20 minutes. Fill a large saucepan about 2/3 full with salted water. Bring to a boil. Add dumplings in batches; reduce heat. Simmer 6 minutes; turn dumplings over. Simmer 6 minutes. Drain well. Sprinkle hot dumplings with powdered sugar and poppy seeds; serve with melted butter or margarine. Makes 30 dumplings.

Apricot Pancakes

1 cup all-purpose flour	About 2/3 cup apricot jam
1 teaspoon baking powder	3 tablespoons fine dry bread crumbs
1 tablespoon sugar	
1/8 teaspoon salt	2 tablespoons sugar
2 eggs	2 tablespoons chopped walnuts
1/4 cup milk	4 canned apricot halves, sliced
2/3 cup water	
6 tablespoons butter or margarine	

In a bowl, combine flour, baking powder, sugar and salt. Beat in eggs, milk and water to make a smooth batter. Cover and let stand at room temperature a few minutes. Melt 1/2 teaspoon butter or margarine in a skillet. Pour in 1/4 cup batter; tilt skillet to coat bottom evenly. Cook until bottom of pancake is golden brown, then turn pancake and cook until browned on other side. Remove from pan and keep hot. Repeat with up to 3 more tablespoons butter or margarine and batter. In a small saucepan, heat jam until melted, stirring constantly. Spread melted jam on each pancake. Fold in quarters; arrange on individual plates. Melt 3 tablespoons butter or margarine in a small skillet. Add bread crumbs, sugar and walnuts; cook, stirring, until crumbs are golden brown. Sprinkle mixture over pancakes; decorate with apricot slices. Makes 4 servings.

Poppy-Seed Pudding

1/3 cup raisins	2 tablespoons rum
6 day-old dinner rolls	1-1/2 cups ground poppy seeds
2 cups milk	1/2 cup chopped almonds
6 tablespoons granulated sugar	2 tablespoons powdered sugar

Place raisins in a small bowl; pour in enough hot water to cover. Set aside to soak. Slice rolls and place in a bowl. In a saucepan, combine milk and granulated sugar. Bring to a boil, stirring until sugar is dissolved. Then pour 1/2 of milk-sugar mixture over sliced rolls. Rolls should be moist, but not wet enough to fall apart. Pour remaining hot milk-sugar mixture into a bowl; stir in rum and poppy seeds. Drain raisins; add raisins and almonds to poppy-seed mixture. Stir thoroughly. Fill a serving dish with alternate layers of softened rolls and poppy-seed mixture, finishing with a layer of poppy-seed mixture. Cover and refrigerate pudding 2 hours.

To serve, dust with powdered sugar. Makes 8 servings.

Ducat Pudding

1 (1/4-oz.) pkg. active dry yeast (about 1 tablespoon)	3/4 cup plus 2 tablespoons warm milk (110F, 45C)
1 teaspoon sugar	2 tablespoons butter or margarine, melted
6 tablespoons warm water (110F, 45C)	1 cup milk
2-3/4 cups all-purpose flour	3 tablespoons butter or margarine
1/4 teaspoon salt	1/4 cup sugar
1 egg, beaten	
1 egg yolk	

In a small bowl, dissolve yeast and 1 teaspoon sugar in warm water. Let stand until bubbly. In a large bowl, combine flour and salt. In another bowl, combine egg, egg yolk and warm milk. Beat melted butter, yeast and milk mixture into flour. Beat until dough pulls away from side of bowl. Cover and let rise in a warm place 50 minutes or until doubled in bulk. Punch down dough; turn out onto a floured board. Knead briefly. Shape dough into 20 walnut-sized balls. Grease a 13'' x 9'' baking pan. Place balls of dough in greased pan, cover and let rise in a warm place about 20 minutes or until almost double in bulk. Preheat oven to 400F (205C). In a saucepan, combine 1 cup milk and 3 tablespoons butter or margarine. Heat until butter or margarine is melted, stirring constantly. Pour milk-butter mixture over dough in pan; sprinkle with 1/4 cup sugar; bake about 30 minutes or until golden brown. Serve hot or cold. Makes 30 rolls.

Cream Strudel

1-3/4 cups all-purpose flour	1/4 cup butter or margarine,
1/4 teaspoon salt	melted
1 egg	1/2 cup milk
2 teaspoons vegetable oil	2 tablespoons sugar
1/4 teaspoon white-wine vinegar	1 teaspoon vanilla extract
5 to 6 tablespoons water	

Filling:

4 day-old dinner rolls	1 teaspoon grated lemon peel
1 cup milk	3 eggs, separated
1/2 cup butter or margarine,	1/3 cup sugar
room temperature	1/2 cup raisins
1/2 cup sugar	

To make pastry, in a bowl, combine flour, salt, egg, 1 teaspoon oil, vinegar and water to make a firm, glossy dough. On a lightly floured board, shape dough into a ball, brush with remaining 1 teaspoon oil, cover with a warm bowl and let stand at room temperature 30 minutes.

To make filling, tear rolls in small pieces and soak in 1 cup milk until soft. Squeeze out any excess moisture and press softened rolls through a fine wire strainer. Set aside. In a bowl, beat 1/2 cup butter or margarine, 1/2 cup sugar and lemon peel until fluffy. Beat egg yolks into butter mixture, 1 at a time; beat in softened rolls. Set aside.

To assemble and bake strudel, dust a large towel with flour. On floured towel, roll out pastry to a 32'' x 28'' rectangle. Stretch pastry until paper-thin; cut off thick edges and use to patch any

tears. Let rolled-out pastry rest, uncovered, on towel. Preheat oven to 400F (205C). In a bowl, beat egg whites until stiff, gradually beating in 1/3 cup sugar to make a meringue. Fold meringue into filling. Spread filling over pastry to within 2 to 3 inches of edges. Sprinkle filling with raisins. Using cloth to help you, roll up pastry jelly-roll style, starting with a long side. Brush ends and seam with water; press to seal. Brush some of the melted butter or margarine over bottom of a large baking pan. Place strudel in buttered baking pan; drizzle with remaining melted butter or margarine. Bake about 1 hour. Meanwhile, in a saucepan, combine milk and 2 tablespoons sugar. Bring to a boil, then stir in vanilla. Remove from heat. As soon as strudel begins to brown, pour some of the milk mixture over strudel. Pour remaining milk mixture over strudel just before end of baking time. Serve hot. Makes 6 to 8 servings.

Plums in Red Wine

2/3 cup dry red wine
2/3 cup sugar
1/2 (3-inch) cinnamon stick
2 whole cloves
1 lb. plums, halved, pitted
2/3 cup whipping cream
2 teaspoons sugar
1 tablespoon sliced almonds,
 toasted

In a saucepan, combine wine, 2/3 cup sugar, cinnamon stick and cloves. Bring to a boil. Add plums, reduce heat, cover and simmer about 10 minutes. Remove from heat; cool. Cover and refrigerate until chilled. Remove cloves and cinnamon stick.
To serve, in a bowl, beat cream until it holds soft peaks. Sprinkle in 2 teaspoons sugar and continue to beat until stiff. Garnish plums with whipped cream and toasted almonds. Makes 4 servings.

Tart Cherry Dessert

2/3 cup dry white wine
2/3 cup water
2/3 cup sugar
1 lb. red tart cherries, pitted
1 teaspoon cornstarch mixed with
 2 teaspoons cold water
1-1/2 tablespoons kirsch
2/3 cup whipping cream
2 teaspoons sugar
1 tablespoon chopped
 pistachio nuts

In a saucepan, combine wine, water and 2/3 cup sugar. Bring to a boil. Add cherries, reduce heat, cover and simmer gently 8 minutes. Drain cherries; return cooking liquid to pan. Stir in cornstarch-water mixture. Heat, stirring, until sauce is thickened. Stir kirsch into cherries; pour sauce over top. Cool. Cover and chill.
To serve, beat cream until it holds soft peaks. Sprinkle in 2 teaspoons sugar and beat until stiff. Garnish cherries with whipped cream and pistachios. Makes 4 servings.

Peaches in Wine

2 large white or yellow peaches
2/3 cup dry white wine
2/3 cup water
2 teaspoons lemon juice
1/2 teaspoon grated lemon peel
1/2 teaspoon finely chopped
 fresh gingerroot
1/3 cup sugar
1/2 (3-inch) cinnamon stick
1 teaspoon cornstarch
2 teaspoons cold water
Semisweet chocolate curls

Blanch peaches in boiling water. Peel, halve and pit. In a saucepan, combine wine, water, lemon juice, lemon peel, gingerroot, sugar and cinnamon stick. Bring to a boil. Add peaches. Reduce heat, cover and simmer 10 minutes. Place peaches in a serving dish; let cool. Mix cornstarch and water; stir into cooking liquid; heat, stirring, until thickened. Remove cinnamon; pour syrup over peaches; let stand until cool. **To serve,** sprinkle with chocolate. Makes 4 servings.

Cherries with Wine

1 lb. stewed, pitted cherries
1 egg
2 egg yolks
1 tablespoon sugar
2 tablespoons mint-flavored
 liqueur
5 tablespoons Marsala

Spoon cherries into 4 dishes. Cover and refrigerate until chilled. In the top of a double boiler, beat remaining ingredients with a whisk. Place over simmering water and whisk until mixture is creamy. Set top of double boiler in a bowl of cracked ice; stir sauce until cold.
To serve, pour sauce over cherries. Makes 4 servings.

Flambéed Fruit Cocktail

3/4 lb. gooseberries	2 tablespoons sugar
1/2 lb. cherries	2 tablespoons butter or
3/4 lb. fresh pineapple (about	margarine
1/4 of a small pineapple)	3 tablespoons orange-flavored
1 large ripe peach	liqueur
2/3 cup apple juice	3 tablespoons kirsch

Clean gooseberries. Halve and pit cherries. Peel and dice pineapple. Blanch peach in boiling water, then peel, pit and cut in thin wedges. In a saucepan, combine apple juice and 1 tablespoon sugar. Bring to a boil; stir in gooseberries, cherries, pineapple and peach. Reduce heat, cover and simmer 10 minutes. Drain fruit, reserving 1/4 cup juice. Melt butter or margarine in a skillet; sprinkle in remaining 1 tablespoon sugar and cook, stirring, until sugar dissolves and begins to caramelize. Add drained fruit and stir to coat with butter mixture; keep hot over low heat. Pour liqueur and kirsch into a small saucepan; warm over low heat. Pour over fruit; carefully ignite. After a few seconds, extinguish flames with reserved 1/4 cup fruit juice. Makes 4 servings.

Flambéed Peaches with Vanilla Ice Cream

6 ripe peaches	1 tablespoon sugar
2 teaspoons honey	4-1/2 tablespoons
2/3 cup dry white wine	orange-flavored liqueur
2 tablespoons butter or	3 tablespoons raspberry brandy
margarine	6 scoops vanilla ice cream

Blanch peaches in boiling water, peel, halve and pit. In a large saucepan, combine honey and wine. Add peaches. Bring to a boil. Reduce heat, cover and simmer 10 minutes. Drain peaches, reserving juice. Melt butter or margarine in a skillet; sprinkle in sugar and cook, stirring, until sugar dissolves and begins to caramelize. Add peaches; turn to coat with butter-sugar mixture. Heat through over low heat, turning occasionally and gradually adding 6 tablespoons of the reserved peach juice. Pour liqueur and raspberry brandy into a small saucepan; warm over low heat. Pour over hot peaches; carefully ignite. Let flames die down. Serve peaches hot with vanilla ice cream. Makes 6 servings.

Apples in Red Wine

Custard Sauce:

2-1/2 tablespoons sugar	3/4 cup milk
1 tablespoon cornstarch	1 teaspoon vanilla extract
1 egg yolk	2/3 cup whipping cream

Poached Apples:

1 cup dry red wine	2 teaspoons unflavored gelatin
1 (1-inch) square lemon peel	1/3 cup cold water
1/4 (3-inch) cinnamon stick	1 tablespoon sugar
4 apples, peeled, cored	1 tablespoon chopped pistachio
1/4 cup red-currant jelly	nuts

To make sauce, in a saucepan, stir sugar and cornstarch. In a bowl, beat egg yolk and milk until blended; gradually stir into sugar mixture. Cook over medium heat, stirring constantly, until mixture thickens and boils. Boil 1 minute, stirring constantly. Pour into a bowl; stir in vanilla. Cover with plastic wrap, pressing wrap on surface of custard. Refrigerate until cold. Just before serving, beat cream until stiff; fold into cold custard.

In a saucepan, combine wine, lemon peel and cinnamon; bring to a boil. Add apples, reduce heat, cover and simmer until apples are fork-tender. Place apples in serving dishes. Remove lemon peel and cinnamon from wine. Cool apples; fill centers with jelly. In a small bowl, soften gelatin in cold water. Reheat wine; stir in gelatin and sugar. Heat, stirring, until gelatin dissolves. Pour over apples; refrigerate until set. Spoon sauce over apples; top with pistachios. Makes 4 servings.

Honey Bananas with Chocolate Cream

1 tablespoon raisins	2 tablespoons honey
1 tablespoon rum	2/3 cup whipping cream
2 bananas	1 oz. semisweet chocolate,
2 teaspoons lemon juice	grated
1 tablespoon orange juice	1 tablespoon chopped walnuts

In a small bowl, combine raisins and rum. Let soak 15 minutes. Cut bananas in diagonal slices; arrange on 4 individual plates. Stir together lemon juice, orange juice and honey; drizzle over bananas. Beat cream until stiff; fold in grated chocolate.

To serve, sprinkle rum-soaked raisins and walnuts over bananas; top each serving with 1/4 of chocolate-cream mixture. Makes 4 servings.

Cook's tip

For a fresh-tasting dessert, mix sliced orange with the bananas. Use up to 1 more tablespoon honey, depending on the sweetness of the orange.

Stewed Rhubarb

2 lbs. rhubarb
1 lemon
1-1/2 cups dry white wine
3/4 cup sugar
1/2 (3-inch) cinnamon stick
2 tablespoons cornstarch
3 tablespoons raspberry or
 other berry syrup

Trim and discard ends of rhubarb stalks; peel off thin outer skin. Then cut stalks in 1-inch lengths. Cut colored outer layer of peel from lemon in a thin spiral; halve and juice lemon. In a saucepan, combine wine, sugar, lemon juice, lemon peel and cinnamon stick. Bring to a boil. Add rhubarb, reduce heat to very low, cover and simmer 10 minutes. Drain rhubarb, reserving liquid. Discard cinnamon stick and lemon peel. Return liquid to pan. In a small bowl, stir together cornstarch and raspberry syrup; stir into cooking liquid. Bring to a boil, stirring until thickened. Return rhubarb to pan; heat through. Spoon stewed rhubarb evenly into 4 individual dessert dishes. Refrigerate until cold. Makes 4 servings.

Cook's tip

You can also use this recipe to make stewed berries, cherries or apricots. Increase or decrease the amount of sugar depending on the sweetness of the fruit.

Strawberry Charlotte

8 egg yolks, divided
1/2 cup plus 2 tablespoons
    granulated sugar
3 egg whites
1/2 cup all-purpose flour
About 2/3 cup strawberry jam
1 pint box fresh strawberries
2 tablespoons cognac
1 cup milk
1 teaspoon vanilla extract
1 (1/4-oz.) envelope unflavored
    gelatin (about 1 tablespoon)
1/4 cup cold water
1/2 pint whipping cream (1 cup)
2 tablespoons powdered sugar

Preheat oven to 475F (245C). Cover a jelly roll pan with parchment paper. In a medium bowl beat 4 egg yolks with 3 tablespoons sugar until thick and lemon colored. In a large bowl, beat egg whites with 1 tablespoon sugar until stiff. Gently fold egg whites into yolks. Fold in the flour, being careful to retain as much volume as possible. Spread batter in prepared pan; bake 5 to 7 minutes or until golden brown. Turn out of pan onto a dampened towel, peel off paper and trim any crisp edges with a serrated knife. Spread jam lightly over cake; roll up, jelly-roll style. Wrap in foil; let stand 12 hours. Halve strawberries; sprinkle with 1 tablespoon sugar and cognac. Marinate 2 hours, stirring occasionally. Beat remaining 4 egg yolks with 5 tablespoons sugar until thick and lemon-colored. Bring milk to a boil; add vanilla. Stirring constantly, slowly add to yolk mixture. Soften gelatin in water in a small bowl; set in a pan of hot water until dissolved. Stir into milk mixture. Refrigerate until syrupy. Beat cream with powdered sugar until stiff; fold into thickened custard. Cover and chill. Line a rounded 6- to 8-cup loaf pan with plastic wrap. Cut cake into 20 to 24 thin slices; line pan with 2/3 to 3/4 of the slices. Fill pan 2/3 full with custard mixture. Drain strawberries; arrange over custard. Cover with remaining custard. Top with remaining slices of cake. Refrigerate several hours. Turn out onto a platter before serving. Makes 8 to 12 servings.

Lemon Cream Dessert

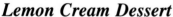

6 eggs, separated	1/4 cup cold water
1 cup sugar	1 cup fresh lemon juice
2 tablespoons cognac	1 tablespoon butter or margarine
1/2 pint half and half (1 cup)	2/3 cup flaked or grated coconut
About 1 tablespoon grated lemon peel	2/3 cup whipping cream
3-1/2 teaspoons unflavored gelatin	2 tablespoons powdered sugar

In the top of a double boiler, whisk egg yolks and sugar until thick and lemon-colored. Whisk in cognac, half and half and lemon peel. Place over simmering water; whisk until mixture begins to thicken and coats the back of a metal spoon. Pour into a large bowl. In a small bowl, soften gelatin in cold water. In a small saucepan, heat lemon juice over low heat; add softened gelatin. Heat, stirring, until gelatin is dissolved. Stir lemon-juice mixture into egg-yolk mixture. To serve, beat egg whites until stiff; fold into lemon mixture. Rinse a mold with cold water, fill with lemon mixture and refrigerate until set. Melt butter or margarine in a small skillet; add coconut and cook, stirring, until toasted. Cool. To serve, beat cream and powdered sugar until stiff; spoon into a pastry bag fitted with a fluted tip. Run tip of a sharp knife around edge of mold; invert lemon cream onto a serving plate. Decorate top with whipped cream; sprinkle cream with toasted coconut. Makes 8 to 12 servings.

Orange & Wine Cream

4 teaspoons unflavored gelatin	1 teaspoon finely grated orange peel
1/4 cup cold water	2 egg whites
4 egg yolks	1/2 pint whipping cream (1 cup)
1/2 cup sugar	2 tablespoons mixed candied
1 cup dry white wine	fruit and/or 1 tablespoon
1/3 cup fresh lemon juice	orange peel cut into
1/3 cup orange juice, fresh or frozen	fine strips

In a small bowl, soften gelatin in cold water. Set aside. In the top of a double boiler, beat egg yolks and sugar with a whisk until frothy. Beat in wine, lemon juice, orange juice and grated orange peel. Place over simmering water and beat until mixture is creamy. Stir softened gelatin into hot yolk mixture, stirring until it is completely dissolved; beat mixture until smooth. Pour into a large bowl, cover and refrigerate just until orange mixture begins to set. In a bowl, beat egg whites until stiff; fold into orange mixture. Cover and refrigerate. In another bowl, beat cream until stiff; fold in. Spoon orange cream evenly into 4 stemmed glasses or individual dessert dishes. Refrigerate until set.

To serve, garnish orange cream with candied fruit and/or slivered orange peel. Makes 4 servings.

Crème Caramel

2 eggs	1-1/2 cups whipping cream
5 tablespoons granulated sugar	7 tablespoons granulated sugar
1 teaspoon grated lemon peel	1 teaspoon powdered sugar
2 teaspoons grated orange peel	Milk chocolate curls

In a bowl, beat eggs and 5 tablespoons sugar until thick and frothy. Stir in lemon peel, orange peel and 1 cup cream. Set aside. Refrigerate remaining 1/2 cup cream. Place remaining granulated sugar in a heavy skillet over medium heat. Cook just until sugar is amber-colored and completely melted, shaking pan often to mix sugar as it melts. Pour caramelized sugar into a pudding mold with a tight-fitting lid; tilt mold to coat bottom and sides with caramel. Carefully pour in cream mixture. Cover mold tightly; set in a large saucepan. Add boiling water to pan until water level reaches 2/3 of the way up sides of mold. Cover pan; cook custard 1-1/4 hours, keeping water at a gentle simmer and adding more boiling water as necessary. Lift mold from pan; cool. Refrigerate until chilled.

To serve, run tip of a knife around edge of mold, then invert custard onto a serving plate. Beat remaining 1/2 cup cream with powdered sugar until stiff; spoon into a pastry bag fitted with a fluted tip. Pipe cream in center of top and around bottom of custard; garnish with chocolate curls. Makes 6 servings.

Lemon Wine Jelly

2 lemons	1 cup dry white wine
1 cup sugar	1 (1/4-oz.) envelope plus
2 tablespoons butter or	1 teaspoon unflavored gelatin
margarine	(about 3-1/2 teaspoons)
1 cup warm water	1/4 cup cold water

Preheat oven to 350F (175C). Line a jelly roll pan with foil. Cut colored outer layer of peel from 1 lemon in a thin spiral; set aside. Then cut off all white membrane. Cut peel and all white membrane from remaining lemon; thinly slice both lemons crosswise. Arrange lemon slices on foil-lined pan; sprinkle with about 1/4 cup sugar and dot with butter or margarine. Bake lemon slices on center oven rack 40 minutes or until lemon edges are golden brown. Remove candied lemons from pan; cool slightly. Arrange in 4 stemmed glasses or individual dessert dishes. Set aside. Dilute sugar and lemon juice left on foil with 1 cup warm water; pour into a saucepan and stir in wine, reserved spiral-cut lemon peel and remaining sugar. In a small bowl, soften gelatin in cold water. Place wine mixture over low heat; heat, stirring until sugar is dissolved. Add softened gelatin; stir until dissolved. Remove lemon peel. Remove from heat and let jelly cool to lukewarm. Pour jelly over lemon slices and refrigerate until set. Makes 4 servings.

Fig Dessert

1 lb. dried figs, trimmed	**2/3 cup fresh lemon juice**
4 teaspoons unflavored gelatin	**3 tablespoons cognac**
1/4 cup cold water	**1/2 pint whipping cream (1 cup)**
2 cups dry white wine	**2 tablespoons powered sugar**
1/4 cup sugar	**Milk chocolate curls**

Place figs in a saucepan, pour in enough water to cover and let soak 12 hours at room temperature. Then simmer figs in their soaking water about 40 minutes or until very soft, adding more water to pan as necessary. Drain and cool figs. Dice; set aside. In a small bowl, soften gelatin in cold water; set aside. In a medium saucepan, combine wine, sugar, lemon juice and cognac. Stir over low heat until sugar is dissolved; add softened gelatin. Stir until dissolved. Cool; refrigerate until egg-white consistency. Stir in diced figs. Refrigerate until mixture is almost set. In a bowl, beat cream and powdered sugar until stiff; fold 1/2 of whipped cream into fig mixture. Cover and refrigerate remaining whipped cream. Spoon fig cream evenly into 6 stemmed glasses or individual dessert dishes and refrigerate until set.
To serve, spoon reserved whipped cream into a pastry bag fitted with a fluted tip. Pipe cream in center of each serving of fig cream. Garnish with chocolate curls. Makes 6 servings.

Vanilla Cream with Cherries

**1 to 1-1/2 cups maraschino
  cherries or sweet cherries,
  cooked, pitted**

Vanilla Cream:

1 (1/4-oz.) envelope	**1/2 cup sugar**
unflavored gelatin	**1 teaspoon vanilla extract**
(about 1 tablespoon)	**2/3 cup whipping cream**
1/4 cup cold water	**2 tablespoons powdered sugar**
1 cup milk	**Milk chocolate curls**
3 eggs, separated	

Remove stems from cherries, if necessary. Drain well; set aside.
To make Vanilla Cream, in a small bowl, soften gelatin in cold water. In small saucepan, bring milk to a boil. Remove from heat; stir in softened gelatin until dissolved. In a bowl, beat egg yolks and sugar until thick and lemon-colored. Gradually add milk mixture, beating constantly. Stir in vanilla. Cool; refrigerate until it begins to set. In a bowl, beat egg whites until stiff; fold into gelatin mixture. Beat cream and powdered sugar until stiff. Fold about 3/4 into vanilla cream; cover and refrigerate remaining cream.
To complete, reserve 6 cherries for garnish; layer vanilla cream and remaining cherries in 6 stemmed glasses, finishing with a layer of Vanilla Cream. Refrigerate until set. Garnish with reserved whipped cream and cherries; sprinkle with chocolate curls. Makes 6 servings.

Cranberry Cream

1 (12-oz.) bag fresh cranberries	1 (1/4-oz.) envelope unflavored
1 cup water	gelatin (about 1 tablespoon)
1 cup sugar	1/4 cup cold water
Juice of 1 lemon	2/3 cup whipping cream
	2 tablespoons powdered sugar

Sort cranberries, removing any stems or soft berries. Wash under cold water; drain. In a large saucepan, combine berries, water, sugar and lemon juice. Bring to a boil, stirring until sugar is dissolved. Reduce heat, cover and simmer 15 minutes or until berries are soft. Reserve 12 or 16 berries for garnish. Pour cooked berries and their juice into a wire strainer set over a bowl. Press berries to get as much juice as possible. Discard seeds and skins. In a small saucepan, soften gelatin in 1/4 cup cold water. Then stir over low heat until gelatin is dissolved. Stir dissolved gelatin into cranberry mixture; cool slightly. Refrigerate until it starts to set. In a bowl, beat cream and powdered sugar until stiff. Cover and refrigerate about 1/4 cup whipped cream; fold remaining cream into cooled cranberry mixture. Spoon cranberry cream into 4 stemmed glasses or individual dessert dishes. Refrigerate until set.

To serve, garnish each serving with a spoonful of reserved 1/4 cup whipped cream and 3 or 4 cranberries. Makes 4 servings.

Passion-Fruit Cream with Raspberries

7 tablespoons sugar	3 passion fruits
3 tablespoons cornstarch	2/3 cup whipping cream
3 egg yolks	1 tablespoon butter or margarine
2-1/4 cups milk	2 tablespoons sliced almonds
1-1/2 to 2 teaspoons vanilla	About 2 cups raspberries
extract	

In a saucepan, stir together sugar and cornstarch. In a bowl, beat egg yolks and milk until blended; gradually stir into sugar mixture in pan. Cook over medium heat, stirring constantly, until mixture thickens and boils. Boil 1 minute, stirring constantly. Remove from heat; stir in vanilla. Pour into a bowl; cover with plastic wrap, pressing wrap directly onto surface of custard. Cool completely. Halve passion fruits, scoop out flesh and seeds with a spoon and stir into cooled custard. In a bowl, beat cream until stiff; fold into custard. Spoon passion-fruit cream evenly into 4 stemmed glasses or individual dessert dishes; refrigerate until chilled.

To serve, melt butter or margarine in a small skillet. Add almonds and cook, stirring, until lightly toasted. Remove from pan; cool. Garnish each serving of passion-fruit cream with raspberries and toasted almonds. Makes 4 servings.

Chocolate Mousse

4 oz. semisweet chocolate
1 tablespoon butter or margarine
2 eggs, separated
1 tablespoon granulated sugar
Pinch of salt

1/2 pint whipping cream (1 cup)
1 tablespoon powdered sugar
1 tablespoon chopped
  pistachio nuts
4 coffee beans

Break chocolate in pieces. Place chocolate pieces and butter or margarine in a small saucepan. Heat over very low heat until melted and smooth, stirring constantly. Remove from heat. In a bowl, beat egg yolks and granulated sugar until frothy. In another bowl, beat egg whites with salt until stiff. In a third bowl, beat cream with powdered sugar until stiff. Stir melted chocolate into egg-yolk mixture, then fold in 2 tablespoons beaten egg whites. Let mixture cool slightly, then fold in remaining egg whites and 1/2 of whipped cream. Cover and refrigerate remaining whipped cream. Spoon mousse evenly into 4 stemmed glasses or individual dessert dishes. Refrigerate until set.
To serve, spoon reserved whipped cream into a pastry bag fitted with a plain tip. Decorate each serving of mousse with small mounds of cream; sprinkle with pistachios and top with 1 coffee bean. Makes 4 servings.

Crème Russe

4 egg yolks
1/4 cup granulated sugar
3 tablespoons rum

1/2 pint whipping cream (1 cup)
4 grapes
Powdered sugar

In a bowl, beat egg yolks and granulated sugar until thick and lemon-colored. Gradually beat in rum. In another bowl, beat cream until stiff. Reserve about 1/4 cup whipped cream for garnish; fold remaining cream into egg-yolk mixture. Spoon into 4 stemmed glasses or dessert dishes. Spoon reserved whipped cream into a pastry bag fitted with a fluted tip; pipe a swirl of cream atop each serving. Dip grapes in powdered sugar; place 1 grape atop each serving. Makes 4 servings.

Cook's tip

There are many recipes for Creme Russe, each differing slightly from the other and each claiming authenticity. Often, the whipped cream is served over the egg-yolk mixture and the two are stirred together at the table. In another variation, each serving is garnished with small macaroons soaked in half the rum.

Vanilla Ice Cream with Candied Fruit

**About 1 cup mixed candied
  or glacéed fruit**
1 tablespoon hot water
1-1/2 tablespoons rum
2/3 cup whipping cream
1 pint vanilla ice cream
**2 tablespoons chopped
  pistachio nuts**

Chop fruit, if desired. In a small bowl, combine fruit, hot water and rum. Cover and let stand at room temperature 30 minutes. In a bowl, beat cream until stiff; spoon into a pastry bag fitted with a fluted tip.
To serve, scoop ice cream into 4 individual dessert dishes. Top with candied fruit and its juice. Pipe whipped cream atop ice cream; sprinkle with pistachios. Makes 4 servings.

Variations
Vanilla Ice Cream with Hot Raspberries: Melt 1 to 2 tablespoons butter or margarine in a small skillet over low heat. Add about 1 cup raspberries; warm through, stirring gently. Sweeten with powdered sugar, then spoon over ice cream.

Gingered Vanilla Ice Cream with Chocolate Sauce: In a small, heavy saucepan or in the top of a double boiler over simmering water, melt 4 ounces semisweet chocolate with 1 tablespoon butter or margarine. Stir until smooth. Scoop ice cream into 4 individual dessert dishes. Sprinkle each serving with 1 teaspoon chopped crystallized ginger, then top with hot chocolate sauce.

Pears Hélene

2 ripe pears
1 cup Moselle wine
5 teaspoons sugar
1/2 (3-inch) cinnamon stick
1/4 teaspoon vanilla extract

4 oz. semisweet chocolate
2/3 cup half and half
1 pint vanilla ice cream
12 candied cherries

Peel, halve and carefully core pears. In a saucepan, combine wine, sugar, and cinnamon stick. Bring to a boil. Add pears, reduce heat to low, cover and simmer 10 minutes. Remove from heat, stir in vanilla and cool. Remove cinnamon stick. Chill 4 individual dessert dishes in the freezer. Break chocolate in pieces; place in the top of a double boiler over simmering water. Stir until melted and smooth; stir in half and half, heat through and keep hot.

To serve, drain pears. Place 1/4 of ice cream in each chilled dish; top with a pear half and cover with hot chocolate sauce. Garnish each serving with 3 cherries and serve immediately. Makes 4 servings.

Peach Melba

About 2 cups raspberries
3/4 teaspoon vanilla extract
6 tablespoons water
1 cup powdered sugar
Juice of 1/2 lemon
1-1/4 tablespoons raspberry
brandy

2 ripe fresh peaches or
4 canned peach halves
2/3 cup whipping cream
2 teaspoons granulated sugar
1/2 pint vanilla ice cream
8 to 12 purchased chocolate
leaves, if desired

Place raspberries in a blender or food processor fitted with a metal blade; add 1/2 teaspoon vanilla, water, powdered sugar, lemon juice and raspberry brandy. Process until pureed. Press puree through a wire strainer; reserve strained raspberry puree. If using fresh peach halves, blanch in boiling water, drain, peel, halve and pit. If using canned peaches, drain well. In a bowl, beat cream until soft peaks form; sprinkle in granulated sugar and remaining 1/4 teaspoon vanilla. Beat until stiff. Spoon whipped cream into a pastry bag fitted with a fluted tip.

To serve, scoop ice cream into 4 individual dessert dishes. Top each serving of ice cream with 1 peach half. Cover 1 side of each peach half with raspberry puree. Pipe whipped cream around peach halves; garnish with chocolate leaves, if desired. Makes 4 servings.

Party Rounds

30 thin slices whole-wheat
  or pumpernickel bread
2 teaspoons butter or
  margarine, room temperature
1/4 lb. prosciutto
6 pimento-stuffed green olives
6 small parsley sprigs
4 hard-cooked egg yolks
1 tablespoon mayonnaise
1 teaspoon curry powder
Salt and freshly ground pepper
12 cooked, shelled, shrimp
6 small dill sprigs
1 (3-oz.) pkg. cream cheese,
  room temperature
2 tablespoons whipping cream
2 tablespoons diced avocado
  mixed with a few drops
  of lemon juice
4 teaspoons butter or
  margarine, room temperature
1 large chicory leaf
2 oz. Roquefort cheese
6 walnut halves
2 oz. Gouda cheese
3 maraschino cherries

Using a 2- to 2-1/2-inch-diameter cookie cutter, cut a neat round from center of each bread slice. Reserve unused portion of each bread slice for other uses, if desired. Cover bread rounds with toppings as directed below. Makes 30 rounds. Lightly butter 6 bread rounds. Cut prosciutto in 12 small slices; roll each into a cone. Cut olives in half. Top each buttered bread round with 2 prosciutto cones, 2 olive halves and 1 parsley sprig. In a small bowl, mash egg yolks; stir in mayonnaise. Season with curry powder, salt and pepper. Spoon mixture into a pastry bag fitted with a fluted tip; pipe onto 6 bread rounds. Top each with 2 shrimp and 1 dill sprig. In a small bowl, beat cream cheese and cream until smooth. Spoon into a pastry bag fitted with a fluted tip; pipe onto 6 bread rounds. Spoon avocado over cream-cheese mixture. Lightly butter remaining 12 bread rounds. Tear chicory leaf in 12 pieces; place 1 piece on each buttered bread round. Cut cheese in 6 equal slices. Top each of 6 bread rounds with 1 cheese slice and 1 walnut half. Using a small hors d'oeuvre cutter, cut Gouda cheese in 12 thick rounds. Cut cherries in half. Place 2 Gouda-cheese rounds and 1 cherry half on each remaining bread round. Makes 6 servings.

Ham Sandwich with Poached Egg

2 tablespoons distilled white vinegar	Butter or margarine
4 eggs	Mayonnaise
1/4 lb. lean cooked ham	Ketchup
4 slices firm-textured white bread	Sour cream
	Coarsely ground white pepper to taste

Lightly grease a deep skillet; pour in water to a depth of 1-1/2 inches. Bring to a gentle simmer; stir in vinegar. Break eggs, 1 at a time, into gently simmering water. Remove from heat; using a broad-blade knife, try to stop egg whites from spreading too much. Return to heat. When water again reaches a gentle simmer, remove pan from heat, cover and let eggs stand in hot water 4 minutes. Then carefully lift eggs from water, drain well and trim whites to make edges even. Cool eggs. Trim any excess fat from ham; cut ham in even strips. Set ham aside. Toast bread slices, cool slightly and spread 1 side of each slice with butter or margarine.

To assemble, place 1 toast slice, buttered-side up, on each individual plate. Top each slice with a cooled poached egg and surround with ham strips. Then top each egg with a stripe of mayonnaise, a stripe of ketchup and a dollop of dairy sour cream; sprinkle with white pepper. Makes 4 servings.

Scrambled-Egg & Tomato Sandwich

4 small tomatoes	2 tablespoons milk
1 teaspoon prepared mustard	Salt and freshly ground white pepper to taste
2 tablespoons butter or margarine, room temperature	4 slices firm-textured white bread
8 thin bacon slices	2 tablespoons chopped chives
4 eggs	

Core tomatoes and cut each in 4 equal slices; set aside. In a small bowl, blend mustard and 1 tablespoon butter or margarine. Set aside. In a skillet, cook bacon until crisp. Remove from pan, drain and keep hot. Pour off and discard all but 1 tablespoon drippings. In a bowl, beat eggs, milk, salt and white pepper until blended. Melt remaining 1 tablespoon butter or margarine in reserved bacon drippings in skillet; pour in egg mixture and cook, stirring gently, until eggs are set but still moist. While eggs are cooking, lightly toast bread.

To assemble, spread 1 side of each toast slice with mustard butter; top each slice with 4 tomato slices. Spoon scrambled eggs evenly over tomatoes; garnish each serving with 2 bacon slices and sprinkle with chives. Makes 4 servings.

Onion Flans

1 (1/4-oz.) pkg. active dry yeast (about 1 tablespoon)	6 tablespoons butter or margarine
1/2 teaspoon sugar	2 lbs. onions, thinly sliced, separated into rings
1/4 cup warm water (110F, 45C)	3-1/2 cups cottage cheese
4 cups all-purpose flour	1 egg
1/2 teaspoon salt	1 tablespoon all-purpose flour
3/4 cup warm milk (110F, 45C)	Salt to taste
5 tablespoons butter or margarine, melted	1 cup shredded Monterey jack cheese (4 oz.)
1 egg	

In a small bowl, dissolve yeast and sugar in warm water. Let stand until bubbly. In a large bowl, combine flour, salt, yeast mixture, milk, melted butter or margarine and egg. Beat until dough is light and elastic; cover and let rise in a warm place until doubled in bulk. Melt 3 tablespoons butter or margarine in a large skillet. Add onions; cook until soft, stirring. In a bowl, beat remaining 3 tablespoons butter or margarine until creamy; beat in cottage cheese, egg and flour. Stir in salt and onions. Punch down dough, turn out onto a floured board and knead briefly. Roll out dough to a thickness of 1/2 inch; cut into 4 (6-inch) rounds. Grease 2 baking sheets. Place rounds on greased baking sheets; turn up edges of each round slightly. Top with onion topping. Let rise in a warm place about 20 minutes. Preheat oven to 400F (205C). Bake 15 minutes or until crust is golden. Sprinkle with cheese; bake until cheese begins to brown. Makes 4 flans.

Artichoke Pizza

1-1/2 tablespoons active dry yeast	1 (15-oz.) can artichoke hearts, drained
1 teaspoon sugar	10 pitted ripe olives
2/3 cup warm water (110F, 45C)	8 oz. mozzarella cheese, thinly sliced
2-1/4 cups all-purpose flour	Pinch of dried leaf basil
1/2 teaspoon salt	Pinch of dried leaf oregano
1 tablespoon butter or margarine, room temperature	Pinch of dried leaf rosemary
3 small tomatoes, peeled, diced	2 tablespoons olive oil
1/4 lb. thinly sliced salami	

In a small bowl, dissolve yeast and sugar in 1/3 cup warm water. Let stand until bubbly. In a large bowl, stir together flour and salt. Mix in yeast mixture, remaining 1/3 cup warm water and butter or margarine to make a smooth dough. Turn out onto a floured board; knead 10 minutes. Clean and grease bowl. Return dough to bowl, turn to grease top, cover and let rise in a warm place 30 minutes. Grease 2 baking sheets. Punch down dough, turn out onto a lightly floured board and knead briefly. Divide in half; roll out each half to a 1/2-inch-thick circle. Place circles on greased baking sheets. Spread tomatoes and salami over dough. Cut up artichoke hearts; arrange artichoke hearts, olives and cheese over pizzas. Sprinkle with basil, oregano, rosemary and oil. Let rise in a warm place 15 minutes. Preheat oven to 425F (220C); bake pizzas about 25 minutes or until crusts are golden brown. Makes 2 pizzas.

Mushroom Piroshki

3 bacon slices, diced
2 tablespoons butter or
  margarine
1 large onion, diced
1/3 lb. mushrooms, sliced
1 tablespoon tomato paste

1/8 teaspoon freshly ground
  white pepper
Celery salt to taste
1 (10-oz.) pkg. frozen patty
  shells (6 patty shells),
  thawed
2 egg yolks

In a skillet, cook bacon until crisp. Remove from pan. Discard all but 1 tablespoon drippings. Melt butter or margarine in drippings; then add onion and cook, stirring, until soft. Stir in cooked bacon, mushrooms, tomato paste and white pepper. Cook, stirring frequently, until all liquid has evaporated. Season with celery salt; remove from heat and set aside. On a floured board, arrange thawed patty shells side by side. Roll out to a single sheet of pastry about 1/16 inch thick, then cut into 12 equal-size rounds. Spoon mushroom mixture evenly into center of each pastry round. Brush edges of pastry with water; fold each pastry round in half over filling. Press edges firmly with a fork to seal. Preheat oven to 350F (175C). Rinse a baking sheet in cold water. Arrange piroshki on wet baking sheet. Beat egg yolks; brush over pastry. Prick each piroshki several times with a fork to allow steam to escape during baking. Bake about 25 minutes or until golden brown. Serve hot. Makes 12 piroshki.

Bacon Pasties

1 (1/4-oz.) pkg. active dry
  yeast (about 1 tablespoon)
1/2 teaspoon sugar
1/4 cup warm water (110F, 45C)
2-2/3 cups all-purpose flour
1/8 teaspoon salt
About 1/4 cup warm milk
  (110F, 45C)

7 tablespoons butter or
  margarine, room temperature
2 eggs
10 bacon slices, diced
2 onions, diced
1/4 cup dairy sour cream
2 tablespoons chopped parsley

In a small bowl, dissolve yeast and sugar in warm water. Let stand until bubbly. In a large bowl, stir together flour and salt. Mix in yeast mixture, warm milk, 6 tablespoons butter or margarine and 1 egg to make a smooth dough. Beat dough until light and elastic. Cover and let dough rise in a warm place 1 hour. Melt 1 tablespoon butter or margarine in a skillet. Add bacon and onion; cook, stirring, until onion is soft and golden brown. Spoon off and discard excess fat. Remove from heat and cool slightly; stir in sour cream and parsley. Grease a baking sheet. Punch down dough, turn out onto a floured board and knead briefly. Roll out dough to a thickness of 3/4 inch; cut into 16 (3-1/2-inch) rounds. Spoon bacon filling into center of each round. Beat remaining egg. Brush edges of each round with beaten egg; fold in half over filling. Press edges firmly with a fork to seal. Arrange on greased baking sheet, cover and let rise in a warm place 20 minutes. Preheat oven to 350F (175C). Bake pasties about 25 minutes or until golden brown. Serve hot. Makes 16 pasties.

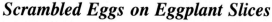

Scrambled Eggs on Eggplant Slices

1 medium (1-lb.) eggplant
Salt
3 tablespoons vegetable oil
2 tablespoons butter or
  margarine
1 onion, diced

1/4 lb. lean cooked ham, trimmed
  of any excess fat, diced
About 3/4 cup frozen green peas
4 eggs
Freshly ground white pepper
  to taste

Cut eggplant crosswise in about 1/2-inch-thick slices. Sprinkle slices with salt; let stand at room temperature 30 minutes. Rinse eggplant slices and pat very dry. Heat oil in a large skillet; add eggplant slices and cook, turning as necessary, until browned and soft. Remove from skillet and keep hot. Wipe skillet clean, then add butter or margarine and heat until melted. Add onion and cook, stirring, until soft. Stir in ham and peas; cook about 5 minutes, stirring frequently. In a bowl, beat eggs; season with salt and white pepper. Pour eggs over ham mixture in skillet and stir gently over low heat until eggs are set, but still moist.
To serve, spoon scrambled-egg mixture over eggplant slices. Makes 4 servings.

Egg & Ham Bake

1/3 lb. lean cooked ham
4 tablespoons butter or margarine
2 tablespoons all-purpose flour
1 cup milk
2/3 cup half and half
Salt and freshly ground white
  pepper to taste
Pinch of ground nutmeg

Pinch of garlic powder
6 hard-cooked eggs,
  thinly sliced
1-3/4 cups shredded Emmentaler
  cheese (7 oz.)
3 tablespoons fine dry
  bread crumbs

Preheat oven to 425F (220C). Grease a baking dish. Trim any excess fat from ham, then cut ham in thin strips. Set aside. Melt 2 tablespoons butter or margarine in a saucepan. Sprinkle in flour and cook over low heat, stirring, about 1 minute. Gradually add milk and half and half; continue to cook, stirring constantly, until sauce is bubbly and slightly thickened. Season with salt, white pepper, nutmeg and garlic powder. Remove from heat. Fill greased baking dish with alternate layers of hard-cooked-egg slices, ham strips and cheese, covering each layer with a layer of sauce. Sprinkle casserole with bread crumbs; dot with remaining 2 tablespoons butter or margarine. Bake about 30 minutes or until bubbly and heated through. Makes 4 to 6 servings.

Stuffed Crepes

16 cooked crepes
1 cup shredded Emmentaler
  cheese (4 oz.)

2 tablespoons butter or
  margarine

Filling:

3 bacon slices, finely chopped
1 onion, finely chopped
1 garlic clove, finely chopped
3/4 lb. Italian sausage,
  chopped
1 teaspoon paprika

1 tablespoon hot water
2 tablespoons tomato paste
Freshly ground black pepper
  to taste
Pinch of sugar
Pinch of red (cayenne) pepper

To make filling, cook bacon briefly in a skillet. Add onion and garlic; cook, stirring, until onion is soft. Add sausage and cook a few minutes, stirring. Spoon off and discard excess fat. In a small bowl, stir together paprika, hot water and tomato paste; stir into sausage mixture. Season with black pepper, sugar and red pepper.

To complete, preheat oven to 425F (220C). Grease a baking dish. Spread filling evenly over crepes; roll up and arrange in greased baking dish. Sprinkle with cheese and dot with butter or margarine. Bake about 5 minutes or until cheese is melted. Makes 8 servings.

Herb Crepes au Gratin

16 cooked crepes
4 tomatoes, peeled, chopped

1-1/3 cups freshly shredded
  Parmesan cheese (4 oz.)

Filling:

About 1/2 lb. lean cooked ham
8 oz. cottage cheese (1 cup)
2 egg whites
4 fresh basil leaves, chopped

1 tablespoon chopped parsley
1/2 teaspoon dried leaf thyme
Salt and freshly ground white
  pepper to taste

To make filling, trim any excess fat from ham, then dice ham and place in a bowl. Add cottage cheese, egg whites, basil, parsley and thyme. Mix well, then season with salt and white pepper.

To complete, preheat oven to 425F (220C). Grease a baking dish. Spread cottage-cheese mixture evenly over crepes, then roll up and arrange in greased baking dish. Sprinkle tomatoes evenly over crepes. Sprinkle with Parmesan cheese. Bake about 5 minutes or until Parmesan cheese is lightly browned. Makes 8 servings.

Foil-Baked Potatoes with Tasty Toppings

8 small (about 4-oz.) russet
   potatoes
1 tablespoon vegetable oil
About 1/8 teaspoon salt
2 tablespoons caraway seeds

Dip a la Russe:
2/3 cup dairy sour cream
6 tablespoons finely diced
   canned beets, drained
1/4 cup finely diced dill
   pickle, drained
1 small onion, grated
1 small garlic clove,
   finely minced
1 to 2 tablespoons prepared
   horseradish

Herb Cream:
1/2 lb. lean cooked ham
2/3 cup dairy sour cream
1 tablespoon prepared mustard
1 teaspoon lemon juice
Dash of Worcestershire sauce
3 to 4 tablespoons chopped mixed
   fresh herbs, such as parsley,
   and chives

Anchovy Topping:
8 oz. cottage cheese (1 cup)
Dry white wine
10 anchovy fillets, chopped
About 2 tablespoons
   chopped capers
1 small onion, finely chopped
1 dill pickle, finely chopped
2 tablespoons chopped chives
Salt and freshly ground pepper

Preheat oven to 425F (220C). Cut a cross in top of each potato. Brush 8 sheets of foil with oil; sprinkle salt and caraway seeds evenly over foil. Place each potato on 1 sheet of foil; wrap tightly. Bake 50 to 60 minutes or until potatoes feel soft when squeezed. While potatoes are baking, prepare your choice of toppings.

To make Dip a la Russe, in a small bowl, combine all ingredients.

To make Herb Cream, finely dice ham; place in a bowl. Add remaining ingredients. Mix well.

To make Anchovy Topping, in a bowl, beat cottage cheese and a little wine until smooth. Stir in remaining ingredients.

To serve, unwrap baked potatoes; squeeze gently to open. Pass toppings at the table. Makes 4 to 8 servings.

Stuffed Potatoes

8 medium russet potatoes,
  scrubbed
2 tablespoons vegetable oil
1 onion, very finely chopped
1 garlic clove, very
  finely chopped
1/4 lb. pork liver, finely
  chopped

1/4 cup chopped chives
1/2 lb. lean ground pork
Salt and white pepper
1 cup shredded Cheddar cheese
  (4 oz.)
2 tablespoons butter or
  margarine

Preheat oven to 425F (220C). Brush 8 sheets of foil with oil. Prick each potato with a fork; wrap each potato tightly in 1 sheet of oiled foil. Bake 50 to 60 minutes or until potatoes feel soft when squeezed. Remove from oven (do not turn off oven) and cool about 10 minutes. While potatoes are cooling, heat oil in a large skillet. Add onion and garlic; cook, stirring, until onion is soft. Stir in liver and chives; crumble in pork. Cook, stirring frequently, until meat is no longer pink. Spoon off and discard fat. Slice off top 1/3 of each baked potato. Using a spoon, scoop out inside of each potato and cut-off slice, leaving a 1/2-inch-thick shell. Place scooped-out potato in a large bowl; mash coarsely. Mix in pork mixture. Season with salt and white pepper. Grease a baking sheet. Fill potatoes with potato mixture; arrange potatoes on greased baking sheet. Sprinkle with cheese; dot with butter or margarine. Bake 10 minutes or until cheese is melted and filling is hot. Makes 8 servings.

Potatoes with Roquefort Cheese

8 medium potatoes, scrubbed
8 oz. cottage cheese (1 cup)
1-3/4 cups crumbled Roquefort
  cheese (about 7 oz.)
2 tablespoons chopped chives
2 tablespoons butter or
  margarine, room temperature

Salt and freshly ground white
  pepper to taste
2 teaspoons coarse salt
1 teaspoon paprika

Cook unpeeled potatoes in boiling salted water until tender throughout. Grease a baking sheet. Preheat oven to 400F (205C). Drain cooked potatoes well; slice off top 1/3 of each potato. Set cut-off "lids" aside. Using a spoon, scoop out inside of each potato, leaving a 1/2-inch-thick shell. Place scooped-out potato in a bowl; add cottage cheese, Roquefort cheese, chives and butter or margarine. Mash ingredients together thoroughly. Season with salt and white pepper.

To complete, fill hollowed potatoes with cheese mixture; replace "lids" atop potatoes and press gently. Place filled potatoes, "lid"-side down, on greased baking sheet. Sprinkle with coarse salt and paprika. Bake about 10 minutes or until heated through. Makes 8 servings.

Dutch Cheese Fondue

12 cups coarsely shredded Gouda cheese (3 lbs.)	1 qt. Traminer or Gewúztraminer wine (4 cups)
1/2 teaspoon freshly ground white pepper	1 teaspoon sugar
Pinch of ground nutmeg	Juice of 1 lemon
1 garlic clove	1 tablespoon cornstarch
3 tablespoons gin	1/2 pint half and half (1 cup)
	6 tablespoons water
	1 (1-1/2-lb.) loaf French bread, cut in cubes

Place cheese in a large bowl. Sprinkle with white pepper and nutmeg; press garlic through a garlic press into cheese. Toss lightly to mix. Sprinkle gin over cheese, cover and let stand at room temperature 2 hours. In a fondue pot, combine wine, sugar and lemon juice. Heat over low heat until steaming. Sprinkle in cheese mixture, a handful at a time, stirring with a wooden spoon after each addition until cheese is melted and mixture is smooth. Stir together cornstarch, half and half and water; stir into fondue. Heat through, stirring constantly. Do not allow fondue to boil.
To serve, bring fondue to the table and place over heat source. Adjust heat so fondue bubbles slowly. Let guests spear bread chunks on fondue forks and swirl in fondue to coat. Makes 12 servings.

Camembert Fondue

7 oz. ripe Camembert	1/4 cup finely chopped onion
1/4 cup butter or margarine	5 cups coarsely shredded Emmentaler cheese (1-1/4 lbs.)
1-1/2 cups plus 2 tablespoons milk	1 tablespoon cornstarch
2/3 cup dry white wine	1-1/2 tablespoons kirsch
1/2 teaspoon freshly ground white pepper	1 (1-1/2-lb.) loaf French bread, cut in cubes
1 teaspoon paprika	

Several hours in advance, remove Camembert from refrigerator and bring to room temperature. Cheese should be ripe enough to be runny at room temperature. Melt butter or margarine in a fondue pot, then stir in milk, wine, white pepper, paprika and onion. Heat over low heat until steaming. Add Camembert; stir with a wooden spoon until melted. Sprinkle in Emmentaler cheese, a handful at a time, stirring after each addition until melted and smooth. In a small bowl, stir together cornstarch and kirsch; stir into fondue. Heat through, stirring constantly. Do not allow fondue to boil.
To serve, bring fondue to the table and place over heat source. Adjust heat so fondue bubbles slowly. Let guests spear bread chunks on fondue forks and swirl in fondue to coat. Makes 8 servings.

Italian Fondue

3 cups shredded Provolone
  cheese (12 oz.)
11 oz. Gorgonzola cheese,
  cut in small pieces
1 cup milk
4 eggs
1/4 cup firm butter or
  margarine, cut in
  small pieces

1/2 teaspoon freshly ground
  white pepper
2/3 cup Asti Spumante or Italian
  white wine
1/4 lb. mushrooms, thinly sliced
1 (1-1/2-lb.) loaf French bread,
  cut in cubes

In a fondue pot, melt Provolone cheese over very low heat, stirring constantly. Gradually add Gorgonzola cheese, stirring constantly, until mixture is melted and smooth. In a bowl, beat milk and eggs until blended. Gradually stir into warm cheese mixture. Do not allow fondue to become too hot—over 140F (60C), eggs will curdle. Stir in butter or margarine, a few pieces at a time. Stir in white pepper, wine and mushrooms. Heat through.

To serve, bring fondue to the table and place over heat source to keep warm. Let guests spear bread chunks on fondue forks and swirl in fondue to coat. Makes 8 servings.

Swiss Cheese Fondue

3-1/2 cups finely shredded
  Gruyère cheese (14 oz.)
3 cups finely shredded
  Emmentaler cheese (12 oz.)
1/8 teaspoon ground nutmeg
1/8 teaspoon freshly ground
  white pepper

1 garlic clove
1-1/2 cups dry white wine
1 teaspoon lemon juice
4 teaspoons cornstarch
1-1/2 tablespoons kirsch
1 (1-1/2 lb.) loaf French bread,
  cut in cubes

In a large bowl, combine Gruyère and Emmentaler cheeses. Sprinkle with nutmeg and white pepper; toss lightly to mix. Set aside. Cut garlic clove in half and rub cut sides over inside of a fondue pot. Pour wine and lemon juice into pot; heat over low heat until steaming. Gradually sprinkle in cheese, a handful at a time, stirring with a wooden spoon after each addition until cheese is melted. In a small bowl, stir together cornstarch and kirsch; stir into fondue. Heat through, stirring constantly. Do not allow fondue to boil. Fondue should be completely smooth, with a slightly wrinkled surface.

To serve, bring fondue to the table and place over heat source. Adjust heat so fondue bubbles slowly. Let guests spear bread chunks on fondue forks and swirl in fondue to coat. Makes 8 servings.

Index